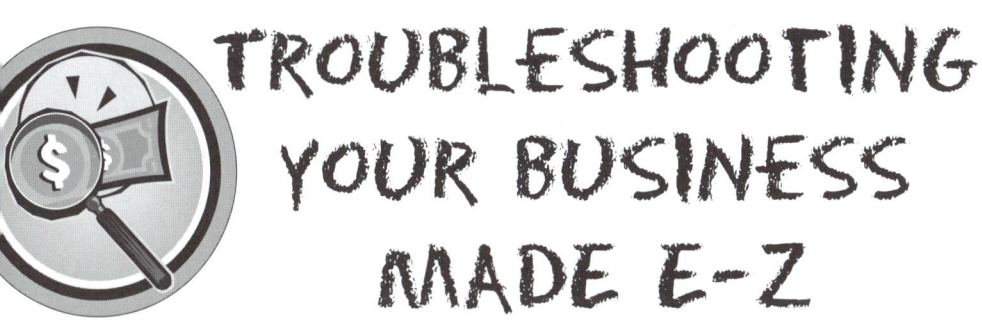

TROUBLESHOOTING YOUR BUSINESS MADE E-Z

Arnold S. Goldstein, Ph.D.

MADE E-Z PRODUCTS, Inc.
Deerfield Beach, Florida / www.MadeE-Z.com

NOTICE:

THIS PRODUCT IS NOT INTENDED TO PROVIDE LEGAL ADVICE. IT CONTAINS GENERAL INFORMATION FOR EDUCATIONAL PURPOSES ONLY. PLEASE CONSULT AN ATTORNEY IN ALL LEGAL MATTERS. THIS PRODUCT WAS NOT PREPARED BY A PERSON LICENSED TO PRACTICE LAW IN THIS STATE.

Troubleshooting Your Business Made E-Z™
© 2000 Made E-Z Products, Inc.
Printed in the United States of America

384 South Military Trail
Deerfield Beach, FL 33442
Tel. 954-480-8933
Fax 954-480-8906
http://www.MadeE-Z.com
All rights reserved.

1 2 3 4 5 6 7 8 9 10   CPC   R   10 9 8 7 6 5 4 3 2

This publication is designed to provide accurate and authoritative information in regard to subject matter covered. It is sold with the understanding that neither the publisher nor author is engaged in rendering legal, accounting, or other professional services. If legal advice or other expert assistance is required, the services of a competent professional should be sought. From: *A Declaration of Principles jointly adopted by a Committee of the American Bar Association and a Committee of Publishers.*

Troubleshooting Your Business Made E-Z™
Arnold S. Goldstein, Ph.D.

Important Notice

This product is intended for informational use only and is not a substitute for legal advice. State laws vary and change and the information or forms do not necessarily conform to the laws or requirements of your state. While you always have the right to prepare your own documents and to act as your own attorney, do consult an attorney on all important legal matters. You will find a listing of state bar referral services in the Resources section of this product. This product was not prepared by a person licensed to practice law in this state.

Limited warranty and disclaimer

This self-help product is intended to be used by the consumer for his/her own benefit. It may not be reproduced in whole or in part, resold or used for commercial purposes without written permission from the publisher. In addition to copyright violations, the unauthorized reproduction and use of this product to benefit a second party may be considered the unauthorized practice of law.

This product is designed to provide authoritative and accurate information in regard to the subject matter covered. However, the accuracy of the information is not guaranteed, as laws and regulations may change or be subject to differing interpretations. Consequently, you may be responsible for following alternative procedures, or using material or forms different from those supplied with this product. It is strongly advised that you examine the laws of your state before acting upon any of the material contained in this product.

As with any matter, common sense should determine whether you need the assistance of an attorney. We urge you to consult with an attorney, qualified estate planner, or tax professional, or to seek any other relevant expert advice whenever substantial sums of money are involved, you doubt the suitability of the product you have purchased, or if there is anything about the product that you do not understand including its adequacy to protect you. Even if you are completely satisfied with this product, we encourage you to have your attorney review it.

Neither the author, publisher, distributor nor retailer are engaged in rendering legal, accounting or other professional services. Accordingly, the publisher, author, distributor and retailer shall have neither liability nor responsibility to any party for any loss or damage caused or alleged to be caused by the use of this product.

Copyright Notice

The purchaser of this guide is hereby authorized to reproduce in any form or by any means, electronic or mechanical, including photocopying, all forms and documents contained in this guide, provided it is for non-profit, educational or private use. Such reproduction requires no further permission from the publisher and/or payment of any permission fee.

The reproduction of any form or document in any other publication intended for sale is prohibited without the written permission of the publisher. Publication for nonprofit use should provide proper attribution to Made E-Z Products.

Table of contents

	Introduction	6
1	Making that big decision	11
2	Why good companies go bad	28
3	Who's in trouble	48
4	Wake up the survivor in you	64
5	White knights and the turnaround team	79
6	Designing your turnaround	104
7	Cat-scanning your business	122
8	26 ways to find quick cash	139
9	How to jumpstart your employees and customers	159
10	How to turn your business into a creditor-proof fortress	176
11	Workouts and cramdowns: tackling your problem loans	198
12	How to settle with creditors for pennies on the dollar	216
13	Bewitched, bothered and bewildered about bankruptcy	233
14	Dump-buybacks: the fast track to a debt-free business	246
15	Making your money machine	256
16	Secrets of second-hand financing	270
17	How to bail out for a super-soft landing	284
	Glossary of useful terms	293
	Resources	296
	Index	307

Introduction to Troubleshooting Your Business Made E-Z™

How this book will help you

Is your business . . .
- losing money?
- up to its neck in bills?
- giving you headaches?

If you found yourself nodding yes, then like millions of other business owners you are finally discovering that staying in business is far tougher than getting into business.

The signs of quiet desperation are everywhere. While many struggling entrepreneurs overcome their problems, survive and eventually prosper, too many others fail. In their wake, they leave vanished hopes, lost investments, destroyed aspirations and a heap of unpaid creditors.

Perhaps the real tragedy is that so many of these failed companies could have been saved had their owners applied even a few of the many survival secrets I reveal in this book.

Unless you know these survival strategies, you too may fail. That's why I wrote *Troubleshooting Your Business Made E-Z*.

Introduction

If your business is on the fast track to failure, this book is for you! Don't fail because you don't know essential success strategies. You'll find here the precise, proven and practical ways to rescue your company from the clutches of bankruptcy, the very same survival strategies I have successfully used to help rescue more than 1,000 financially troubled companies during my 30 years as an insolvency lawyer and turnaround consultant. So this book is not based on theory. It is based on proven business-saving strategies that can work for any kind of enterprise, regardless of the situation.

Can these survival strategies work for you? Absolutely. But you must keep three points in mind!

First, salvaging your business will take plenty of hard work, luck, pluck and a bushel basket of determination. There's no quick fix. I don't insult your intelligence by offering quick, easy and simplistic solutions.

Second, no business is beyond redemption. You may believe your business can no longer be saved, but don't give up! I've saved more than my share of businesses about to be auctioned by the bankruptcy court. Your business isn't dead until you bury it. Even then, *Troubleshooting Your Business Made E-Z* can show you many ways to capitalize on a dead business.

Third, keep an open mind. You'll see unorthodox strategies not found in other books. I know. I have read every pablum-filled book on the subject of turnarounds. What you need now are real-world tactics. And that's what I intend to give you—brass knuckles and all!

Buckle up your seat belt

What you are now reading will give you all the tools you will need to:

- Decide where you want to go with your business—and your life!
- Uncover whether your business is in trouble—and how much.

- Overcome your cash crunch—quickly and forever!
- Design a surefire blueprint for building big profits.
- End creditor problems for pennies on the dollar, without bankruptcy or borrowing.
- Avoid Chapter 11 and survive if you must file for reorganization.
- Sell your sick business for top dollar.
- Protect yourself and your personal assets from business liabilities

    . . . and much more!

Together, we'll tear your business apart and put it back together again.

I'll guide you through each critical step for fixing your broken business: Cash management, internal controls, personnel, marketing, pricing and selling. We'll even play some head games. Head games? Absolutely. There's an emotional side to business trouble. If you can't think straight, you can't make those all-important decisions or fight as hard as you must to save your business.

Right now you may be consumed with stress, fear and even panic. You may question your ability to save your business. You're afraid of defeat, afraid to lose your paycheck, and afraid you'll lose the family home and your personal assets.

You also are tired from too many lawsuits, too many unpaid suppliers and too many bounced payroll checks. You're frustrated by endlessly operating in a twilight world of no cash, no credit, dwindling sales and mounting bills. You don't know where to go, where you want to go or how to get there. Plain and simple, you hurt. Sure, you hate to go to work in the morning. I know the feeling. I've been there with my own entrepreneurial misadventures. When things go really wrong, it makes you numb, even unwilling to continue the fight.

My goal is not simply to give you business strategies, but to help you through this nerve-wracking maze. Once you see your problems more clearly, with a fresh, positive outlook, you'll bail

Introduction

out your business with new determination and purpose. Make a game of it, and you'll even have some fun doing it!

Troubleshooting Your Business Made E-Z won't merely explain turnaround strategies—it will show you these strategies in action. Example after example will illustrate how others, with problems very much like your own, reversed course and turned their headache business into a debt-free money machine.

Now here's what you must do to get maximum value from *Troubleshooting Your Business Made E-Z*. As you relive the experiences cited in this book, keep your own business in mind. Imagine yourself in the middle of each situation. Anticipate each action, each development, each outcome. Ask yourself whether some or all of these strategies can work for you, or what modified approaches or alternatives would be better.

By discovering possible solutions to individual problems, you will begin to see the big picture and how to piece together a total turnaround plan. You'll see how to tackle difficult problems and convert those problems into your own unique business-building opportunities. You'll discover how to uncover and exploit your untapped resources and achieve your own peak performance.

You will learn all this and more. But I repeat, it will be no easy task. At best, *Troubleshooting Your Business Made E-Z* can do only half the job. While I prescribe to the ailing firm the strategies and every trick of the trade I have learned from three decades as a "Business Doctor," you must take the medicine and apply the therapy.

Flip through the book and you'll see that much of what you're about to learn is truly common sense. They're the ideas that, once pointed out, cause you to slap yourself on the head and say, "Of course," or, "I should have known that." In fact, many of these ideas are so simple and obvious that you'll snicker, "I know that. Everyone knows that!"

But they don't.

And even if some of these strategies seem basic, don't underestimate their worth. They have helped save thousands of failing companies. What I provide in this book is the essence of what works when you're in trouble.

The book every business owner must read

No matter what size or type business you own or operate, whether you are a struggling retailer, wholesaler, manufacturer, service business operator or restaurateur, this book is for you.

It's for you whether your business is big or small, old and tired or young with growing pains.

You'll want to read *Troubleshooting Your Business Made E-Z* whether your business has just begun its downturn or is now deep in the throes of bankruptcy.

You'll want to read it if you are just starting out in business—or even planning a business—because I give you the smart ways to fortify yourself against future problems.

Whoever you are, whatever the nature of your business, regardless of your troubles, the first thing you must understand is that survival principles are universal to every business!

Remember this always, because the moment you lose sight of it, you'll think your business and its troubles are different, and that the advice I give you doesn't apply.

Rest assured. It does.

So sit back, relax, keep an open mind and discover the simple yet powerful and proven ways to turn your headache business into a debt-free money machine.

Arnold S. Goldstein, Ph.D.

Making that big decision

1

Chapter 1
Making that big decision

During the past 30 years, over 1,000 owners of failing businesses have sat across the desk from me. They ran small retail shops and mid-sized manufacturing plants, gas stations and bowling alleys, software firms and employment agencies. One owned a zoo, another a small commuter airline and another a string of massage parlors.

All told essentially the same story: Too many bills, too little cash, too heavy losses and too few ideas on how to straighten out their mess. As an insolvency lawyer and turnaround consultant I understood my role was not to rescue the sick business, but to rescue the owner caught up in a financially troubled business. Corporations don't walk into my office; people do. People and their businesses are two very different things.

> **note** What is best for you is what is important, whether or not this means saving your business.

Don't assume you should save your business, nor hastily decide to sell or close it. So let's begin with your objectives, your desires, your capacities.

Find your true goals

What do you want to do with your problem business? Most owners tell me they want it to be a debt-free profit-maker. Is that an honest answer? Are these your true goals and objectives? Think carefully and objectively. Your true objectives may be quite unlike what you first thought.

Chapter 1

> **HOT spot** Your objectives might be best achieved by not saving your business.

Ask Mike, a spunky young guy who hired me to save his small electrical contracting firm, barely surviving in the hills of North Carolina. Mike had a healthy income, but if you listened to Mike carefully, he only wanted to save his business to protect his income. That was a darn good reason until a California electronics firm offered Mike twice the salary he could earn from his own struggling company. Suddenly, Mike no longer needed the business for a paycheck. Is your business only a paycheck?

I asked the Claflin brothers why they wanted to save their retail hardware chain, they sputtered, "Because we're stuck on a $200,000 bank note. And they'll sue us if our business goes bust." Finally, we were getting somewhere. What did their business mean to them aside from a troublesome bank note? I saw their one big concern and threw every last dollar of cash flow to the bank to pay their worrisome note. The Claflins happily abandoned their business. Is avoiding personal liability for business debts your reason for staying with it?

Ann, a novice entrepreneur, sobbed, "I can't afford to lose the $50,000 I invested in my sinking cosmetic distributorship." Ann didn't care a hoot about her business; only about the $50,000 she invested. I finally found a competitor anxious to buy Ann's valuable retail accounts and Ann's inventory at a bargain price. They paid Ann $75,000 for an agreement not to compete with their business. Ann had her investment back, and $25,000 profit to boot.

Why save Ann's business—to recover her investment?

Greg figured he was over the hill at 52. Desperately, he tried to save his failing soft-drink bottling plant in New Jersey, but I knew the business was Greg's security blanket; it had always supported him, and it was the only business Greg knew. I could have saved Greg's business, but instead urged him to sell to a conglomerate who gave Greg a five-year employment contract at twice his salary.

Security can handcuff you to your business.

> **note:** Money is a poor reason for saving a business. Maybe you can't admit defeat, because saving your business saves your ego.

Paul couldn't easily accept failure. How could he hold his head high at the Rotary Club or Knights of Columbus and symbolize success as president of the local Chamber of Commerce, with his debt-ridden appliance store mired in bankruptcy? Disgrace, Outcast, Failure, Bankrupt! These words haunted Paul. He could never allow his appliance store to fail.

So Paul arranged for Mort's Appliance Store to fail. Mort? Yes, good old Mort, conveniently plucked from the local unemployment office and overjoyed to pocket $2,000 to "buy" Paul's appliance store. Two months after Mort hung a bright, new sign announcing his proud ownership of Paul's Appliances, the business went bust. Paul still cackles to his never-the-wiser friends, "I built a healthy, thriving business, and this jerk Mort ruins it. Some people just don't belong in business."

How true! So what are your true goals and priorities?

- Income?

- Security?

- Saving your investment?

- Avoiding personal liability?

- Ego?

So you really want to save your business? Why? Which goals are truly important to you? Can you otherwise satisfy those goals? Begin by knowing what you really want. You may have conflicting goals, so you must prioritize.

Chapter 1

For example, if you want to save and rebuild your business, you will reinvest every penny the business earns. If you want to pay personally guaranteed debts, your cash must go to creditors with your guarantee. Do you want to recover your investment? You must legally pluck from the business whatever you can.

To get there, you must know where you want to go.

Keep your business or let go

Is your business really for you? You do yourself no favor by walking away from your business because you let your problems beat you. On the other hand, you do yourself a greater disservice by staying with a business you should abandon. Why waste your most precious resources, time and talent? Of course, you must decide whether a business is right for you. Your business is not for you unless you can:

- Enjoy the business.

- Manage the business.

- Earn what you are worth from the business.

> **CAUTION** Many businesses fail, not from managerial incompetence, but managerial disinterest. Owners can't develop the enthusiasm their business needs.

Dennis and his near-defunct drycleaning plant is such a case. His dry-cleaning plant had the same old problems: Too many creditors and too little cash. Dennis turned his business problems over to me, but I soon knew his business wasn't the real problem. It was Dennis' love of computers, not drycleaning. I'd talk creditors, and Dennis would talk microchips.

15

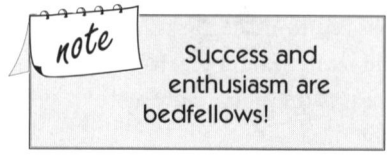

note Success and enthusiasm are bedfellows!

Dennis didn't belong in a drycleaning plant. So we sold his business, paid his creditors, and gave Dennis the few extra dollars needed to start a software development firm. He still struggles, but he'll eventually make it. Smiling entrepreneurs always do.

Never try to save a business you'll never enjoy. People choose wrong careers, and equally choose the wrong business. When they perform poorly on their job they get fired. When they perform poorly in business, they fail.

It's so easy to end up in the wrong business. Dennis found himself in the dry-cleaning business because it was his father's business, and Dennis had worked there as a kid. But Dennis isn't his father. What was right for the father wasn't necessarily right for Dennis. Yet, parents force their kids into the family business, and kids without strong career goals go along. Too few ask whether it is their right career.

Seductive, high-glamour businesses attract novice entrepreneurs like honey attracts bees. Pat, my mechanic, sold his garage to buy a business-brokerage franchise. He couldn't wait to get back to his first love, fixing cars. Why then did he give it up to sell businesses?

"Because I was tired of dirty hands and greasy clothes. I wanted a more professional career, where I could wear a nice suit and sit behind a big desk," Pat confessed. Today, Pat's back in his garage, with dirty hands, greasy clothes, and a very big smile!

Every aspect of a business adds or detracts from your enjoyment. If you are inflexible, even a slight variation from what you enjoy can throw you off balance.

CAUTION Mismatches between entrepreneurs and business doom many a company.

Chapter 1

A manager of a high-class steak house won't necessarily enjoy operating a pizza parlor. On the other extreme, some entrepreneurs can adapt to a variety of opportunities. You must discover this about yourself.

Countless people hunt for a franchise. A franchise can make a free-wheeling entrepreneur's life miserable; or a less-secure entrepreneur welcome the opportunity to leave decision-making to the franchiser. The same can be said about partnerships.

Then there are business hours or travel demands. Travel can be an attraction, but the novelty soon wears off.

How about you? Do you really enjoy your business? Overlook your problems. Pretend your business is healthy and stable. Would it give you full enjoyment, or would you be more fulfilled in a different business or career?

Can you manage your business?

I know there's no such thing as a bad business or bad management. There is only management that's wrong for the business. These owners simply failed to measure their own management mentality. Their businesses demanded management skills they couldn't or didn't provide. Not all owners see it that way. In the large corporation, management becomes the sacrificial lamb when trouble arises. The small-enterprise owner is a fixed, unmovable object. The small business must accommodate the owner's limitations.

If your poor management caused your present business problems, why would you think you can run your business better in the future?

Bill, a young Connecticut entrepreneur, had considerable managerial talent, but still couldn't measure up to the demands of his fast-growing candy business. He started the business in the basement of his home. At first, he sold

17

Troubleshooting Your Business Made E-Z

only to local gift shops. The following year, Bill opened a retail store and two more within the next two years. Soon he had eight stores and 15 franchise stores featuring his delicious candy. Bill could see his business grow, but not that it was out of control because of faulty internal systems.

Bill, a terrific candy maker and promoter, was in over his head operating his shaky empire. I could either bring in people with the right management skills or shrink the business to what Bill could manage. The fast growth justified finding a talented business partner. Today, Bill owns 60 percent of a business that will gross over $25 million this year!

Good management can be stifled management. That was Al, a bright young pharmacist who took over his father's humdrum corner drugstore. But without the challenge Al's interest quickly withered. Nursing homes sparked Al's interest. Why not provide pharmaceuticals to nursing homes? Day and night, Al worked to build his nursing-home business. Al's corner drugstore is long gone. In its place, Al has nursing home dispensaries throughout the country, grossing more than $120 million. With a slight twist, his business became exciting.

> **HOT spot** Entrepreneurs don't always use the right yardstick to measure their management mentality.

Or the solution may be to reduce the oversized operation to the owner's limited managerial ability. At what point will he grow beyond his capabilities? Al, like most potential achievers, finds himself landlocked in a business with limited potential. But, any business can become more exciting with imagination.

It's not really about what the entrepreneur can manage, but about when he or she is ready to manage. Timing and experience, not capability, are usually decisive factors. I've seen

> **CAUTION** While you're learning, you can be nickeled and dimed to death with 101 small, but nevertheless fatal mistakes.

Chapter 1

enough slip-ups in my embryonic ventures to teach a course in mismanagement at the Harvard Business School.

A business can look as if it's fun and easy to operate. Few businesses are as easy to operate as they seem. Naive optimists ask, "What do you have to know to run a pinball arcade, shoe store or coffee shop?" I don't know. I have never operated them. But why don't you ask someone who has? Be prepared for a long and hard education. Every business has its tricks.

Many people who have never worked in a business and know nothing about it, through sheer optimism, throw their life's savings into the venture. More amazing, some people actually make it. They're the fast learners. Slow learners come to my office.

That brings us back to you. Can you do a better job, with another chance in your business? Can you reshape your business to manage it more effectively? Can you gain skills? Can a partner or key employee help?

Can you make money from your business?

Having fun operating your business is one consideration. Money is another. If the business can't give you the financial rewards you need, then why stick with it?

> **E-Z TIP**
> Who knows how wealthy your business will make you years from now? That depends on you and the business. It's now that counts.

Entrepreneurs may leave a $100,000-a-year job to start a bootstrap business, producing only $15,000 a year for the first year or two. For some people, it's not a problem. For the people who need $100,000 a year to support a family, it's an $85,000 problem.

Put away your rose-colored glasses. With a jaundiced eye, underestimate income 20 percent and overestimate expenses 10 percent to get closer to reality.

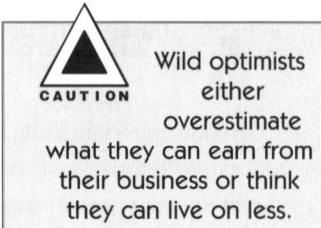 Wild optimists either overestimate what they can earn from their business or think they can live on less.

You won't defy the odds. Don't work backwards to conveniently pump up sales to produce the bottom line and salaries you're looking for. It's an idiot's game.

Partnerships produce more strain. A single-owner business may juggle personal finances to subsidize the business. Two partners can seldom perform the same juggling act. Ultimately, the creditors pay. Don't repeat the story. Make your business make more money, take home less money, or get rid of the business and get into something that will give you the income you want. There are other reasons why your business may not be for you. My neighbor realized that the stress from his plumbing business would endanger his weak heart. So Mark closed his shop.

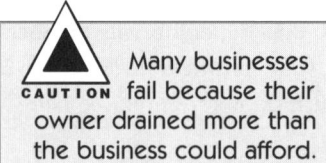 Many businesses fail because their owner drained more than the business could afford.

 Who can argue with wanting to live? Is your business ruining your marriage? Divorce and business failure often go hand in hand. Do marital problems interfere with managing a business, or does the tension, stress and lack of money from a failing business destroy the marriage? If you have problems both at home and at work, try to separate the two and assess each situation on its own.

Letting go may simply come from being honest with yourself about where your future will be happiest. Some people desperately want their business to survive; others are thrilled to walk away. There's no right or wrong answer. Decide for yourself. It will always be the right decision, if you have the right reasons.

Chapter 1

Clear the cobwebs

Panic and confusion are normal when your business goes bad, but clear your head so you can think straight. First, avoid negative thoughts which defeat your ability to think clearly. Negative thinking spawns only emotional, usually irrational decisions. Unless you can clear the cobwebs, you'll only have muddled thoughts about your business and your future.

1) **Step back from your problems**—Take a short vacation to clear your head. Granted, life's important decisions are not always made under the best circumstances. Still, you are now trying to make an objective, critical career decision while neck-high in alligators and shell-shocked from fighting everything and everyone. The army calls it combat fatigue. Rest and recreation is Uncle Sam's remedy. Make it yours.

Get away from your business for awhile. Take a vacation from your problems. Your business will still be standing when you return.

2) **Bandage your battered ego**—Many people see their business problems as a personal defeat. Whether your problems were caused by managerial blunders or factors beyond your control, what difference does it make?

If factors beyond your control torpedoed your business, why should it shake your self-confidence? And if you blundered, so what? Mistakes aren't defeats. They're only learning experiences. That's what managerial growing pains are all about. Besides, who doesn't make mistakes?

An inspirational pep talk? Sure! But it's therapeutic. Why wallow in self-doubt and slam the door on your entrepreneurial spirit, as almost happened to me once?

I don't forget the days when I was fresh out of college, when a buddy and I sought our fortune by starting a discount chain. Foolishly, we expanded much too quickly. Failure? Well, I know our creditors never called us a stunning success. My chain went down the drain, and with it went my self-confidence, entrepreneurial spirit and more money than I can bear to think about. Even today I cringe.

What restored my self-confidence? A candid self-assessment. Grabbing a piece of paper, I commanded myself, "What did you do right and where did you mess up? No cheating!" My scorecard wasn't bad when I saw my many accomplishments along with my few fatal missteps. It's important to see your failures. After all, you do want to learn. But it's equally important to see your strengths. You'll then see yourself in a different light. I have owned many other businesses since; some were a huge success, others were not. I seldom make the same mistakes—only new ones. We all do. It's part of the game.

> **3) Look for the light at the end of the tunnel**—You can't think objectively, or positively, when you see only problems—not solutions. When you don't know how your business can be saved, you doubt that it can be saved, and then feel frustrated and powerless.

You no longer feel rudderless. I know clients usually spring to life once I map an action plan and roadmap to go forward. They now have positive, specific steps to take. We may change our game plan, but there is still forward movement, rather than the helplessness that comes from standing still.

> *A game plan can do wonders for your outlook.*

> **4) Probe the bottom of the pit**—The world is a big, dark, scary place. Can you get a job? Who would hire you? Can you start over in another business? Where will you go? Where will you get your next paycheck? Measure what you will lose by giving up your business. Stand back and objectively explore opportunities elsewhere.

Security is important for people who have owned their own business for many years. They don't see how they can function as employees. A few good job offers will give you an enormous sense of security. You may

"Job shop" even while trying to turn around your businesses.

be worth considerably more to another employer than you ever thought. After all, you have acquired years of experience running your own show.

Adopt a positive attitude

Dr. Erwin H. Schell, a highly respected lecturer on leadership, claims, "There is something more than abilities and competence that makes for accomplishment. This linkage factor catalyst is found in one word—attitude. When our attitude is right, our abilities reach a maximum effectiveness and good results inevitably follow."

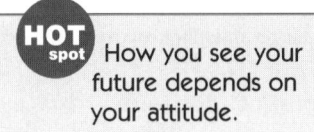

How you see your future depends on your attitude.

Nowhere is Dr. Schell's theory clearer than in a turnaround. Attitude does make a difference. With the right attitude you get good results because you expect good results. The positive attitude lets you see your problems and win cooperation from people. Check your own attitude. Compare your attitude with some common "types" I see in my business.

A common creature is the "Ostrich," who believes his business is on the fast track to failure and keeps his head buried in the sand until he loses it. More frustrating is the Ostrich who knows he's in trouble but won't admit it. "Ignore it and it will go away!" he chants. Yes, the Ostrich is a mighty tough bird to save. Most only lay more eggs. Ostriches need a special diet of reality, but seldom swallow it. If you think you're in trouble, get help! Don't put it off. Don't be an Ostrich.

Close cousin to the Ostrich is the "Confirmed Optimist" who knows he's in big trouble, but hopes things will magically improve. "Wait until tomorrow which will bring a big sale, a great invention, or the demise of that nasty competitor." For the Confirmed Optimist, success is always a day away. Optimism is a priceless commodity when your boat is sinking, but temper optimism with reality. With healthy optimism you control events, confident you can succeed.

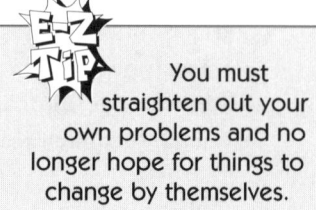

You must straighten out your own problems and no longer hope for things to change by themselves.

The trademark of the "Perennial Pessimist" is gloom and doom. In his world, everything goes downhill—never uphill. The pessimist probably started his business expecting the worst. And if his business can be saved, which he doubts, it will become worse. Pessimists lack everything needed for success: Enthusiasm, imagination and hope!

Sure your problem business will get you down. Nor does it mean you shouldn't be a hard-nosed pragmatist. But if you naturally see the clouds and never the lining, then you must remove the dark glasses.

Other characters who populate the business world:

The "Nervous Nellie" can't handle stress. With emotions in high gear, they panic and run from their problems, or suffer a nervous breakdown. I don't ridicule the Nervous Nellie. We each have our own stress threshold. Sometimes the toughest people can least cope with their financial pressures. Sometimes their frail spouses successfully battle the business back to health. You never know who is bravest in the trenches.

I often choose one spouse, partner or key employee to spearhead the turnaround. The individual may not have the best management skills, but the ability to cope with pressure is the essential qualification.

Chapter 1

The "Dreamer" hides in the clouds. He can't be bothered with mundane business problems. And losing somebody else's money is not a big concern. The Dreamer sits busily inventing a better mousetrap, and pondering grandiose schemes, while the business flounders.

Every business needs a Dreamer—also a doer who can handle the checkbook. If you're that Dreamer, find yourself a bottom-line manager for those important details that make your business tick.

> **note** Some eventually accept their fallibility, but most Buck Passers are happier pointing their finger.

The "Buck Passer" never asks the tough questions. He doesn't have to. Nothing is the Buck Passer's fault. He is victimized by everyone else. He is always right. I walk away from these creatures, because it will be my fault if their business goes down the drain.

The "Absolute Moralist" wants to save his business and save his creditors. Tell him its not in the financial cards to do both, and he'll quote you the Ten Commandments and Boy Scout Oath. Predictably, most Absolute Moralists lose both their business and even more money for their creditors!

One holier-than-thou couple consulted me about their failing San Bernardino food distributorship. I estimated it would be necessary to cut their debts from $2 million to about $600,000. "What?" they screamed, "And not pay our creditors the other $1.4 million we owe them?' Suddenly I was a leper. Rather than accept my advice, they blundered along with their business until they went bankrupt. Their creditors, now owed $2.6 million, received a grand total of $150,000. What price virtue!

That brings me to the "Pirate," who is anything but honest. He rapes, pillages and plunders the business and to heck with everyone he hurts. Some pirates don't know the rules, so I closely guide them to stay legal. Others knowingly break the law to line their pockets. If that's you, then why not rob a few banks instead? You'll make more money with less work. People are people, warts and all. What's important is that you spot yourself in the crowd, so you can change your attitude!

Possibility thinking

Above all, you must brew decision making with optimism. About 600,000 new businesses will be born this year. Three years from now, relatively few will still be around. The failures will have excuses (the economy, the competition, the government, etc.). The truth is, the rocky road of entrepreneurship frequently breeds defeatism. When you think you are beaten, you are. But not until then.

You must believe you can save your business. Don't believe your business can't be saved. Businesses collapse every day because of owners who can't see a future. A business neck-high in trouble never seems to have a future. The transformation a business can undergo is amazing. Some examples from my own files:

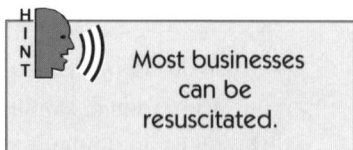
Most businesses can be resuscitated.

- A faltering $2-million-a-year Ohio lumberyard grew in eight years to gross $90 million-a-year, with lumberyards in five states. Its profits this year? $4.5 million.

- A San Francisco ambulance service, pushed into bankruptcy in 1991, now has 24 ambulances profitably zooming the streets of Frisco. A $600,000 loss in 1991 became a $2 million profit this year!

- An Atlanta restaurant that came out of Chapter 11 in 1997, and quickly branched out with 85 canteen trucks, producing a hefty $3-million-a-year profit.

Chapter 1

Could these owners have possibly envisioned their ultimate success from their depths of despair? But each had somehow seen their businesses' future, when it apparently had no future.

Never give up hope for your business if it can give you enjoyment and the income you need—and you can give the business the management it needs. Owners who think they can save their businesses usually succeed. Those who predict failure usually fail. It's not so much what your business is. It's what you think it can be.

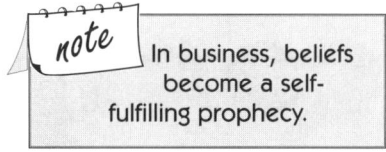

In business, beliefs become a self-fulfilling prophecy.

Also, remember you have a limited perception. You may have not been in a turnaround before, and have not seen the startling revivals which I frequently see.

So my friend, if you think you have a business worth fighting for, roll up your sleeves. You'll only lose the fight when you give up hope and believe your business can't be saved!

Checkpoint

1) Do you really want to save your business? Why? Why not? Are you thinking objectively or are your decisions based on fear and worry?

2) Do you enjoy your business ? Would you enjoy it if it were problem-free?

3) Can your business foreseeably give you the income you need?

4) Can you effectively manage the business? What can you do so it is properly managed?

5) Can you save your business? If not, how do you know?

Why good companies go bad

Chapter 2
Why good companies go bad

To quote Aristotle: "It is possible to fail in many ways . . . while to succeed is possible in only one way." Aristotle is half right! Many once-proud organizations are either adrift in red ink or have vanished. Why do so many businesses manage to plummet from heady success to spectacular failure?

> **HOT spot** — Every business carries within itself the seeds of failure. Your company also bears its seeds for self-destruction. You must find and uproot them before you fail!

You may see failure as a lurking demon, ready to grab others, but not you. Beware! The grim reaper is alive, and works overtime as business failures peak higher each year. Companies seemingly indestructible only a few short years ago now fail with alarming regularity.

> **note** — Only two of the top 25 American industrial corporations operating in 1900 still operate today.

It is not whether a business will fail, but when. Eighty percent of all start-ups succumb within their first five years. Few survive a few decades, and those that do are significantly changed.

Corporate casualties abound in stunning numbers in every industry. Most professional basketball leagues have gone belly-up, with others now being formed. More than 90 auto manufacturers shrunk to three major automakers. We see a shakeout in the computer field. Only a handful from the hundreds of computer companies still survive.

29

No industry is safe. Franchised businesses, once the safest entrepreneurial path, have suffered—as many franchise companies vanished. Surprising, too, is how swiftly healthy businesses are transformed into debt-ridden cripples. That one big disaster is becoming more commonplace. A.H. Robins, once a top ten pharmaceutical firm, stumbled when its Dalkon-Shield intrauterine contraceptive device spawned thousands of product liability claims. Manville Corporation fell to asbestos claims.

> **note**
> One faulty product can quickly and unexpectedly fell even the strongest companies.

Texaco also demonstrates the thin veneer between corporate success and failure; when, in moments, a Texas jury handed Pennzoil a $10.5-billion victory over Texaco. Robins, Manville and Texaco shatter the myth of the indestructible large corporation. The biggies, also, have glass jaws. Every company has a glass jaw.

Failure is only another dirty word

"Failure" defies definition—your firm can be a managerial failure, a financial failure or a legal failure. These terms have distinctively different meanings. Your company may be a managerial failure long before a financial failure, and linger as a financial failure—without becoming a legal failure.

Managerial failures do not meet their potential. We condemn unprofitable managers when they lose money, even when they side-step far greater losses due to skilled management. But is the true managerial failure the manager who earns a $1-million profit for a company that should have earned $5 million? Or the manager who loses $1 million for a company ordained to lose $5 million? It is not enough for your business to be

> **note**
> The great myth is: Management is successful when it turns a profit. How much profit seems unimportant.

profitable, it must be the profit-maker it can be. Anything less *is* managerial failure.

Many companies, large and small, are managerial failures long before they become financial failures. They lose money or earn so little that their stockholders would do no worse with their investment under the mattress. Stockholders who want their money to earn more have an objective too few managers achieve. Will Rogers had a quip for this: "Executives who do not produce successful results hold on to their jobs only about five years. Those who produce results hang on about half a decade."

Study a business' earnings to spot managerial failures that will become financial failures. For every firm that drowns in a sea of red ink, hundreds more are doomed. About half of the nation's businesses lost money. These firms are striving to be average. Two-thirds of the profit makers earned less than a savings account could earn. Only one corporation in seven performed better.

Family businesses frequently shuffle along, giving their owners less than a week's pay. But, we can't accurately measure profitability of the smaller business. Their owners can hide profits, and only they know whether they are making or losing money.

Managerial failure becomes financial failure when your business has chronic and serious losses, or becomes insolvent with more liabilities than assets. Financial failure

> *note* Troubled companies are usually unprofitable, and continuing losses will weaken their organization.

may overlap managerial and legal failure. Financial failure bridges the company that is sub-performing (managerial failure), and the company formally declared a legal failure through bankruptcy.

DEFINITION

Legal failure, according to the Bankruptcy Code, occurs when a company's liabilities exceed its assets. Yet some companies operate for years with more debts than assets. They survive through creditor leniency and patience. Many "upside-down" companies eventually turn the corner, produce a profit, and brighten their balance sheets. However, few debt-ridden firms survive without creditor patience and rapidly improved profits.

A legal failure can't punctually pay its debts. Under this rule, most American companies are bankrupt. This standard is undoubtedly a throwback to a time when business people actually paid their bills on time.

A business that closes its doors isn't necessarily a legal failure. Illness, retirement and other personal reasons force closings. When a losing business is closed, it is not a legal failure if it fully pays its debts. And companies that are financial failures may endlessly linger without becoming legal failures. Others file Chapter 11 bankruptcy—an admission of legal failure—but emerge with a new balance sheet and lease on life. No longer legal failures, they stay financial failures until they become profitable, or finally disappear. Failure, also, is a relative term. Your company's performance can be measured against all other businesses, comparable companies within your industry, and its own potential and prior performance.

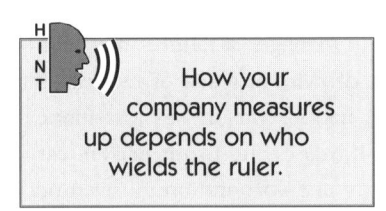

> **HINT:** How your company measures up depends on who wields the ruler.

Unraveling the big mystery

Why do some companies succeed while others, with more resources or opportunities, fail? The right answer is elusive:

> **HOT spot:** You can't oversimplify causes of failure or narrowly pinpoint the problems. Nor is there a simple solution or a quick fix.

1) Business failure usually has several causes.

Generally, no single problem is the sole culprit. Suffering companies frequently have many roots to their problem and need multi-pronged solutions to resolve them.

Chapter 2

2) Symptoms of failure cannot be distinguished from the causes.

DEFINITION

Organizational failure, like organic illness, has symptoms not always easily distinguished from the disease. Tactical or managerial errors may be confused with fundamental weaknesses that precipitate them. Failure is categorized as a cluster of symptoms, when there are a number of underlying causes.

3) The causes of failure relate to the nature of the firm.

Conglomerates seldom share the problems of simple, small companies. Hi-tech firms seldom face the same threats as stable industries. For example, hi-tech firms fail through ill-conceived products or faulty market innovations. Those in stable industries suffer hardening of the arteries. Larger, highly diversified firms lose control of their sprawling divisions.

4) The causes of failure can relate to corporate maturity.

Startup firms face different problems than mature organizations. Companies cannot easily move from one stage to another. The startup company may fail because of a poor business concept, poor financial planning, undercapitalization or poor management. The mature organization has perhaps too much corporate flab and archaic management policies, leaving the company vulnerable to changes in the marketplace and more progressive and nimble competitors. So there are no simplistic causes of corporate failure, as there are no simplistic formulas for success.

Organizations, however small, are complex. And what is a weakness for one company may be another's strength. Tom Peters admitted in *In Search of Excellence,* "Managers in every field are re-thinking the tried and, as it turns out, not-so-true management principles that have so often served their institutions poorly."

> **HOT spot** Perhaps the one unshakable principle for avoiding failure is to be true to those few strategies that work best for your organization.

33

Beware the nine deadly business killers

Companies share common risks. They also share a common managerial snafu: Errors of omission (the failure to act when action is needed) and errors of commission (incorrect actions).

Even well-run companies can make staggering mistakes. Superbly managed companies may make fewer mistakes, but may fail because they lack the resources or abilities to correct or overcome their mistakes. These companies fail not because of their problems, but because they can't afford to solve their problems. Well-heeled companies can overcome considerably more serious situations than weak companies.

But, with few exceptions, the failure of the company is the failure of management; a point with which most turnaround consultants agree. You may not see your troubles that way. Most struggling business owners blame external factors to deflect

> *note* The Small Business Administration estimates nine out of ten business bankruptcies result from poor management.

blame away from their own bad management, comfortable with the illusion they have fallen victim to circumstances beyond their control.

While potential pitfalls are endless, "Nine Deadly Business Killers" are the death blow to most failed enterprises:

Business Killer #1: Failure to change

With today's fast-changing world, companies, and entire industries, quickly become vulnerable. These changes are not the minor shifts in everyday business life, but dramatic and often unexpected events that strike at the core of a business. Unadaptive businesses fail.

Chapter 2

Government regulations, court decisions, trade tariffs, raw material shortages and changes in technology are some devastating changes that tumble the strongest company. Events occur with such suddenness and severity that they are neither predicted nor can be protected against. Still, the inability to foresee events is its own form of mismanagement. Those who stagnate fall victim to competitive, technological, market or economic changes.

> **HOT spot** The adaptive organization turns change into opportunity.

What competitive changes does your organization face right now? Competition is in constant flux, whether from a low-cost foreign producer, a new competitor on the next block, or a new spark of an idea from a present competitor.

Many troubled firms have stagnated while young upstart companies swept away their markets with new, innovative products, attractive services, or perhaps, just a fresh and more aggressive way of doing business. These troubled firms never had their ear to the ground, and took their customers for granted. No longer leaders, they became followers—companies forced to react. Companies on the cutting edge of their field may have problems, but seldom feel the sting of a competitor puncturing their soft underbelly. Retail-giant Sears watched its retail leadership slip away to more aggressive, dynamic, and innovative retailers—the deep discounters, specialty stores and warehouse clubs that nibbled at Sears' broad customer base.

Alvin Toffler's best-selling book *Future Shock* warned of technological change. The world, as Toffler suggests, is indeed changing at a breakneck pace; too many companies simply cannot keep in step. Consider software companies: This fast-moving industry loses 20,000 shakeouts a year. "New companies fasten their signs with Velcro," is now the standing joke in Silicon Valley.

> **HOT spot** Fast-paced technologies spawn hundreds of new industries, and derail others unable to adapt to turbulent change.

35

But traditionally stable industries also fall victim to new-age technologies. The printing industry, squeezed by desktop publishing and larger plants with more efficient, technologically advanced equipment, is an example. American auto-makers, painfully pinched by foreign competition, fall further behind their overseas competitors, who are a decade ahead in robotic automation. Smoke-stack industries futilely strain to compete in the 2000s with the techniques of the 1950s. Companies victimized by technological change are victims of their own myopia. They see change, but neglect to reinvest in their own future, losing to cutting-edge companies by default. Companies lose touch with their changing markets. The garment industry dooms firms lacking a strong market sense. Each year, hundreds of Seventh-Avenue fashion houses bet their bankroll on America's ever-changing perception of style. Many lose the bet!

note Other industries serve a less-fickle consumer, but must still adapt to subtle market changes. The marketplace changes for every company as lifestyle, demographics, social attitudes and consumer preferences change. Survivors change with it, but the largest and most sophisticated companies ignore this lesson. American automakers, slow to spot changing preferences in autos, lost much of their domestic market to more responsive importers. Fast-growth companies, such as Reebok, achieved phenomenal success because they had an exquisite market sense.

note A turbulent economy and other economic woes are commonly reported reasons for failure, but the excuse invariably covers up for other management sins. A poorly run company can get away with a great deal when times are good and sales strong, but a tight economy magnifies corporate weakness. Marginal companies then vanish.

Economics can play havoc with your company. In the early 1980s, inflationary interest rates of nearly 20 percent devastated companies programmed to pay 10 percent. They folded by the thousands.

> **CAUTION:** Tighter credit is another hidden cause for business collapse.

A credit squeeze is common during inflation, when

suppliers restrict credit to avoid high-interest borrowing. Credit also tightens when sales are strong and suppliers are more willing to forfeit marginal-credit customers.

Economic conditions can't be easily predicted, and management has no crystal ball. Truly clairvoyant managers would be playing the stock market, not running companies; but survivors instinctively position themselves for the bad times as well as the good. They plan for the worst, confident they can sustain the worst should it come. In today's fast-changing world, every business is vulnerable to the dramatic and often unexpected events that rapidly strike at its core. Change creates opportunity for some, failure for others. The lesson? Adapt to survive. To spearhead change is to excel.

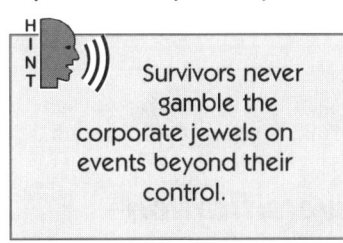

> **HINT:** Survivors never gamble the corporate jewels on events beyond their control.

Business Killer #2: Undercapitalization

Did you start your business with too little capital? Some shoestring start-ups soar to exceptional success. However, there would be fewer failures if entrepreneurs started with the capital to match their enthusiasm.

Undercapitalization results from over-optimism. But throwing too much money into a business can be an even greater mistake. It invites slipshod spending and risking more than necessary. Well-planned, well-managed companies carefully balance invested equity, borrowed funds and trade credit.

The undercapitalized firm, with decent management and a sound business concept, usually can survive if it knows how to raise cash quickly to overcome the humps. We find financing for poor but promising startups. It may be an investor, a timely loan or simply coaxing more credit from suppliers and landlords. Overexpansion also spells trouble if you borrow heavily to finance growth and your overly rosy projections wilt. Many businesses grow helter-skelter and outstrip their capital and management. New acquisitions or startups also bleed companies dry.

You can also outgrow your management. You need different skills to run a large operation than those of a small one. Entrepreneurs must suddenly build complex organizations and delegate. Few grow into that job gracefully. Companies must grow or shrink. Nothing stays constant.

> **CAUTION:** Try baby steps, not giant leaps. Grow too fast and you can become too big for your own britches!

Business Killer #3: Diversification

Many companies, lost in familiar territory, journey into unfamiliar territory. Diversification has become a corporate buzzword, with companies of all sizes and types roaming in unrelated areas—whether through expansion or acquisition. Conglomerates discovered pyramiding companies was the quick way to a fortune. The conglomerate, never fashioned to make money, could only manipulate stock prices. But diversification is not only for the big boys:

- A Boston textbook publisher bought a boating magazine and lost $800,000 in six months.

- A successful Texas radio station operator bought a Southern California movie chain and failed after losing $1.3 million.

- A 20-year-old Florida eyeglass manufacturer took control of a large Miami hotel that went bust with $3 million in unpaid bills.

What sound relationship or synergy existed between the present and new business? Why should success in the present business promise success in the new business? You know the answer. In overdiversification cases, the owner must go back to the business he knows and limit growth to ventures that "fit."

> **HOT spot** Businesses diversify to reduce risk.

The vagaries of any one industry encourage companies to put their eggs in several baskets. Yet management guru Peter Drucker disagrees with diversification, and suggests, "Complex businesses (conglomerates) have repeatedly evidenced their vulnerability to small, but highly concentrated, single-market or single-technology businesses. If anything goes wrong, there is a premium for knowing your business."

Owners justify diversification. The three most common reasons are:

1) inability to expand within existing industries

2) synergy between the existing and expanded operation

3) highly advantageous acquisition opportunities

Each seems logical for diversification—if you have the managerial and financial resources for your diversified empire.

> **HINT** Out-of-control growth and diversification stem from "sales worship," or the blind pursuit of sales for the sake of sales. Sales worship spawns failure, because you focus on sales not your bottom line. Sales are important—if they add profits. The sales chase may be an ego trip, an attempt to increase cash flow, or the simplistic hope more sales will inevitably produce more profits. Even smart managers get into big trouble with this faulty thinking.

> **E-Z TIP** Profits, not sales, must control your planning. The smaller company may lose sales, but gain profits!

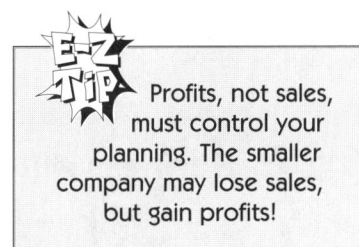

Business Killer #4: Poor controls

Without good controls you don't know where you've been, where you're going, or how you're getting there. Good controls reach into the heart of your

> **HOT spot** Good controls expose discrepancies between plan and performance. Without controls, you never know when you're off course.

business. Yet financial control can't guarantee operational control. Many multi-million-dollar companies can't control orders, product costs, customer sales or operational break-even. Without such basic information at their fingertips they get into trouble.

Business experts frequently pinpoint poor financial controls as the major cause of business failure. I disagree. Poor controls are only another symptom of bad management. An owner who avoids solid financial and operational controls will be just as inept in other management areas. Poor buying, excess overhead, inadequate inventory controls and faulty pricing are inevitable problems. You can't run your business by the seat of your pants. Too much information is nearly as dangerous.

> **E-Z TIP** In today's computer age, managers are swamped with too much worthless data. This obscures the few important numbers buried in the pile.

You need a management-information system that quickly, accurately and consistently feeds vital facts. Your accountant or MIS people can't tell you what information you need to take the corporate pulse. You must tell them.

Business Killer #5: Overdependence

If you depend on one key product, customer or supplier, your future is no better than that one product, customer or supplier. Relationships don't last forever, and you may be out of business tomorrow.

Companies can downplay their dependencies, or think their business relationships are permanent. Once-successful companies are out of business because they relied on too few customers. Your customer may go out of business, a long-loyal buyer may be replaced by one less friendly, your customer may decide to drop your product, or switch to a competitor with a better deal.

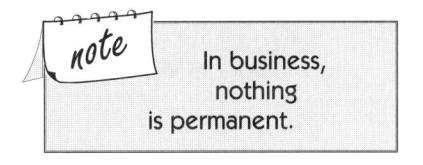

> **note** In business, nothing is permanent.

A fabric-treatment plant client counted on one of America's leading dress manufacturers for most of its $10 million-a-year volume. Jack never dreamed his 7-year relationship could end, but it did. A new assistant manager decided the manufacturer should split the work among several processors, Jack's volume plummeted 80 percent. Unable to cover his fixed costs, Jack failed.

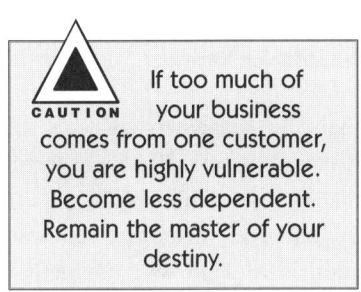

> **CAUTION** If too much of your business comes from one customer, you are highly vulnerable. Become less dependent. Remain the master of your destiny.

Equally vulnerable is the company with one source of supply. Without a backup supplier you quickly find yourself out of business. The United States discovered this during the Middle-East oil embargo. So do hundreds of franchisees whenever a franchiser closes its doors. No company can afford to be dependent. You need many customers. You need many suppliers.

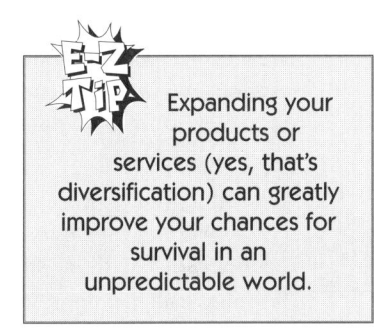

> **E-Z TIP** Expanding your products or services (yes, that's diversification) can greatly improve your chances for survival in an unpredictable world.

Business Killer #6: Poor location

Retail businesses frequently wither because of poor location. Urban decline and population shifts slowly kill locations and destroy businesses. Every retailer's fortunes are directly tied to high-traffic, high-volume, high-profit locations. Shopping is increasingly concentrated in chain-dominated malls and shopping centers. Independent retailers who remain shackled to poorer locations eventually perish.

My retail clients usually say poor locations are their primary problem. They must choose: Aggressively compete for more desirable locations, stagnate in their marginal locations or close. As locations change, retailers must change, sometimes radically, to thrive in their new environment and meet the needs of the changing market. An upscale clothing store can no longer survive in a decayed location with a low-income population. The owner must merchandise to his market or abandon the location.

Constant adaptation to the changing market is difficult for long-entrenched retailers who want a status-quo business. A retailer's fortunes are almost always directly tied to the ability to capture high-traffic sites. The old Liggett drugstore chain, once the nation's largest drugstore retailer, proved how vulnerable a retailing organization is to aggressive competitors who know how to grab the best locations. Liggett clung to dying downtown locations, while young start-up chains like Rite-Aid, Revco, and CVS, nimbly monopolized newer suburban shopping centers. Liggett now has a handful of tired outlets.

Times are changing. Retailing is returning to the specialty shops. Independents with a strong specialty focus are again winning choice shopping mall locations. Walk through your local mall. You'll see what I mean.

Business Killer #7: Unprofitable pricing

"When was the last time you compared your current costs of doing business to last year's operating costs? When did you last calculate your break-even point?" I asked this to 300 furniture manufacturers at a management seminar I was invited to give at a furniture-manufacturers convention. Only one in ten had gone through this basic exercise within the past three years. Nine out of ten had no answer. Little wonder the room was loaded with manufacturers in big trouble! Many companies don't know their costs, and price unprofitably. Northfield Brick sold its decorative brick artificial wallcovering for 65 cents when competitive bricks were about 75 cents. But each brick cost Northfield 74 cents to produce, so Northfield was losing its shirt.

Remember the businessman who, when asked how he could afford to sell for 10 percent below his cost, innocently replied, "Simple, I make it up in volume." For Northfield this was no joke. Inefficient productivity or poor buying strangles profits unless these inefficiencies can be passed on to the customer through higher prices—seldom possible in today's competitive world. Yet many companies sell too cheaply when they can easily get a higher price; too many small operators choose to compete on price—instead of service and quality.

> **E-Z TIP:** Identifying increased expenses or pinpointing labor and material costs is easier than controlling them.

I can't give you the magical pricing formula for your business, but the difference between a healthy profit and whopping loss may be nothing more than a few pennies more per widget.

Business Killer #8: Government red tape

Big Brother strangles every industry and causes serious business problems. Locally, politicians may change zoning or traffic flows, but Washington regulations can wipe out entire markets overnight. More often than not, it means no business, less business or business done less efficiently. Insidious encroachment by government festers in every aspect of corporate life: Taxation, employment, pollution control, product safety and consumer rights—to name but a few. We are well beyond George Orwell's *1984*.

> **note:** Hundreds of new laws and regulations are passed each day, each indelibly leaving its mark on how business is to be done.

I recently represented a bankruptcy trustee who liquidated a nursing home unable to wait nine months for long-overdue Medicaid payments. I also bailed out a construction firm with projects delayed 14 months by environmentalists. Wherever I travel, I find a government imposing its stifling bureaucracy on companies that can neither function nor flourish in a strangling climate of regulation. Whether you believe that governmental constraints are necessary or a needless obstruction is, of course, secondary. You must deal with the world as it is. But companies long frustrated by governmental red tape increasingly throw in the sponge, if they are not forced out of business.

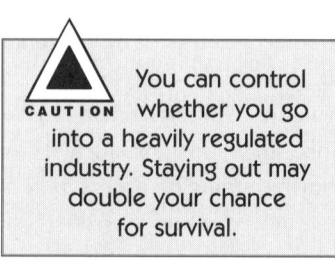

> **CAUTION** You can control whether you go into a heavily regulated industry. Staying out may double your chance for survival.

Business Killer #9: Excess overhead

The big killer, in about half of my cases, are extraordinarily high expenses, which even strong sales can't overcome.

Several years ago, I turned around a magazine publisher perched in one of Boston's choice office building penthouses. The publication reeked of success, while the financials revealed massive losses. You'll now find that same publisher in the basement of a suburban supermarket. It's not plush, but they are still in business.

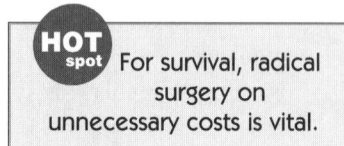

> **HOT spot** For survival, radical surgery on unnecessary costs is vital.

Survivors cut, cut and cut. Nothing escapes their scalpel. Your own bloated salary is a good place to start.

# Chapter 2

Management and other great myths

These and other managerial blunders illustrate most companies do not die natural deaths. They are murdered through managerial incompetence. Running a business is never easy. Still, entrepreneurs bravely venture forth without appreciating how complicated and challenging it is. Or they fail because they were unwilling, unable, or too undisciplined to put in the long hours, cope with the pressures, or keep their hands out of the till, particularly in smaller companies, where the business is the owner and the owner the business. Such businesses also are frequently destroyed through death, sickness or other personal problems.

It may be a mismatch between owner and business. People choose a business for all the wrong reasons. They don't ask whether they would really enjoy the business and can effectively manage it. They seek profits or prestige. So we have entrepreneurial misfits who gave less thought to selecting a business than to the car they drive. Eventually, they must reassess.

A plumber may think he can operate a plumbing-supply firm, but will managing the supply firm require more than the plumber's skills? We see a company out of balance. The owner may have strong sales skills, but weak financial know-how. Or the owner may be creative, but a weak implementer.

> **HOT spot** Owners with an interest in their business may lack essential skills.

Larger companies create larger problems. The larger organization, no longer the sum and substance of its owner, becomes what the owner creates or fails to create—usually a strong foundation. The management team may be unbalanced, uncoordinated, improperly staffed or poorly structured, all producing basic problems.

Conflicts within the management team abound, particularly when the company has partners constantly in squabbles or power battles. Partnerships

45

are a leading cause of business failure. Partnerships face the same hazards as other companies, and partners often cannot blend their differences, objectives and styles cohesively. Whether it's the owner of a mom-and-pop enterprise or the leader of a major corporation, the top dog must live with the words of Harry Truman, "The buck stops here."

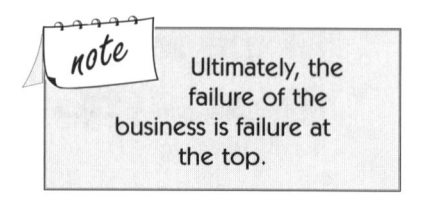

> **note** Ultimately, the failure of the business is failure at the top.

You can't personify the ideal manager. We may catch a glimpse of successful managerial personalities and styles, but there is no one ideal manager or management style. We are warned against one-man rule, yet McDonald's flourished under the autocratic Ray Kroc. Conversely, ITT's Harold Geneen performed superbly by delegating authority to divisional managers. Observe managers and you'll see no correlation between style and results. And when you are in business, results are what count.

Style is not substance. Still, even sophisticated companies suffer from managerial deficiencies. They perform poorly because management is inbred, secure and complacent after many years on the job. Or they flounder from corporate rigidity, unwilling to try new ideas, resistant to change, and with low tolerance for independent action within the ranks. They may waddle along under their own momentum. However, they will eventually learn the difference between success and mere survival—and later between mere survival and failure.

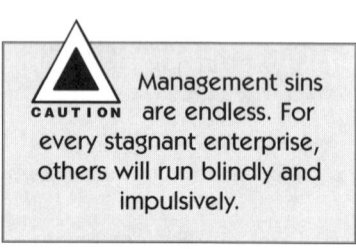

> **CAUTION** Management sins are endless. For every stagnant enterprise, others will run blindly and impulsively.

The headless firm has neither leadership nor a profit strategy. It runs on automatic pilot, with no direction from the top, and soon grinds to a stop.

Chapter 2

So managerial failure frequently comes from extremes: Too much ambition or too little, too much centralized control or too little, an overly powerful CEO or one who is benign.

No business or manager is blemish-free. Some weaknesses are trifling, easily offset by important strengths.

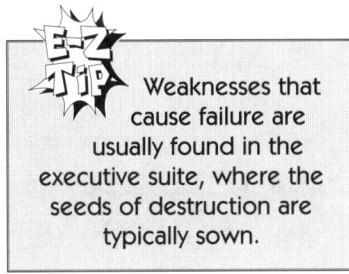

> **E-Z TIP:** Weaknesses that cause failure are usually found in the executive suite, where the seeds of destruction are typically sown.

Checkpoint

1. Is your business a managerial failure, a financial failure or a legal failure?

2. Businesses fail for several reasons. Why is yours in trouble?

3. Which of the nine deadly business killers are destroying your company?

4. Your own bad management may be the number-one culprit. Are you objective enough to see it?

Who's in trouble

3

Chapter 3
Who's in trouble

Who's in trouble? Not me! That's what they all say two weeks before they flop. Or is it you? Perhaps you need some help evaluating your situation objectively.

Beyond your blinders

Businesses fail not because they can't solve their problems but because they won't see their problems. Even the seasoned business owners prefer blinders to reality when their business begins to slide.

When the signals clearly point to future disaster, like most owners you may not accept the facts for what they are. A troubled company first needs a crisis, and until that crisis, they tolerate trouble. Other turnaround consultants share my frustration with stubborn business owners who refuse to believe their businesses are going broke. It's more pleasant to cling to the illusion that your company is simply encountering a nasty bump in the road that all companies periodically experience.

Owners of troubled businesses only call me when their situation becomes too uncomfortable. Hopefully the assets and resources needed to revitalize their company are still intact. But many still don't get serious about a turnaround and disappear for months, until they can no longer ignore their expanding problems. Usually it's after their bank has

> **CAUTION** Delay destroys businesses!

foreclosed, the IRS padlocked their doors, or another catastrophe struck. By then, there may be too little left to rehabilitate. Inventory, cash and credit are gone, as are essential employees and customers.

As with any progressive illness, if you stay alert and respond quickly to a serious and worsening problem, you greatly improve your odds for recovery. The critical point is when your company starts downward. You either act decisively, or play ostrich and squander your assets and your future. Survivors feverishly conserve their cash and assets for a turnaround.

⚠ **CAUTION**

A delayed turnaround delays acknowledging defeat. Big executives, from big corporations, keep their paychecks coming, and hide dismal facts from their corporate boards, lenders, creditors and stockholders. They drain the balance sheet until the losses can no longer be absorbed.

Optimism is another factor, and is what fuels all startups and propels their growth. But optimism can blind you to the early warning signals. You may see your answer as one business-saving customer, a new product breakthrough, or another miracle that never happens. Ironically, the same optimism that fueled your startup may cause its failure. You also may be too close to your problems. Your business may deteriorate too gradually to see the changing picture. Problems become accepted rather than warnings.

> ⚠ **CAUTION** Inexperienced or oblivious owners never see the gathering storm because they look for the wrong signs in the wrong place at the wrong time, if they look at all!

The ability to detect and act quickly on problems is the essence of good management. The cardinal management sin is not the error made, but the error you neither see nor cure. Small problems are far simpler to solve than big ones. Poor managers avoid problems. Good managers stand up to trouble whenever they run into it. Great managers prowl for trouble.

Chapter 3

> **HOT spot** Tinkering with a business that needs tackling is self-delusion. Don't kid yourself.

Ignoring problems is only one potential evil. Thinking you are solving your difficulties when you only tinker and twiddle is another. Aspirin won't cure a brain tumor. It is a considerably more dangerous medicine when you believe aspirin is your cancer cure—and you don't get the treatment you really need. The medicine you need may be unpleasant. If you even suspect you may be in trouble, remove your blinders to see what's really going on. Learn how to fix the problems.

The gathering storm

Companies seldom fail without clear warning. A troubled company's operational and financial signals are weak at first and grow more frequent and powerful with the downturn.

Of course, no two companies generate precisely the same early warnings, because businesses, like ships, never sink precisely the same way. Some go down at the bow, others stern first. For every company that suddenly vanishes, others endlessly linger before rolling over. Some giants,

> **E-Z TIP** Most companies produce a wide window of opportunity to see trouble brewing and have ample opportunity to avert disaster.

such as Rolls Royce and Penn Central, succumbed with little warning.

Warning signals largely mirror the company. Some are plodders; the garden-variety, run-of-the-mill enterprises that are the backbone of American business. Others are high-rollers that suddenly reach spectacular heights, and as quickly plummet and crash. The dinosaurs are large, outdated, ponderous corporation—sluggishly out of touch with their markets and dying from hardening of the arteries.

Plodders are led by storekeepers, welders, machinists, printers and other steady-but-less-visible people with personalities in rhythm with their businesses. Characters heading high-roller companies are usually as colorful as their companies—flamboyant, restless dreamers whose ambitions reach the sky. They build firms on blind ambition—if not absurd concepts. These enterprises capture the imagination of the investing public, fueling them to fantastic heights where they attract even more money.

High-roller companies are the most interesting casualties because we have a curious fascination with any company that can appear and disappear in a flash. Headed by luminaries who become household names, the intrigue deepens. High-rollers have obvious warning signals—sharply declining sales as fickle customers lose interest in their fad and switch to more intriguing fads. High-rollers live and die by their ability to hold a fickle public.

Dinosaurs, in contrast, see slow sales erosion and profitability. It can take years to kill a well-heeled dinosaur. The high-roller is the rose that quickly blossoms and fades, the dinosaur wilts slowly.

But I'm most interested in the plodders who fail for so many different reasons. You cannot predict their early warning signals, which explains why you can never rely on certain signals and ignore others.

Scan the far horizon

Look beyond the horizon to see the first clouds of trouble sweeping in.

note As the causes of failure depend largely on the size, age, and type business—the symptoms of failure also depend on these factors.

Early failure signs may not show up in your financial statements. The first and clearest signs are frequently managerial, not financial, and appear long before your financials reflect problems.

Hi-tech firms, victimized by competition, will see new orders drop long before the financials reflect their decreased sales. Distant problems may be seen far earlier. For hi-tech firms it is too late to spot oncoming problems by watching sales. They must see what's going on in their labs, what they're spending on R&D, and decide whether it's ahead or behind competitors in product development. Today's sales reflect yesterday's research; tomorrow's income reflects today's inventiveness.

Causes and symptoms of failure can be too intertwined to distinguish. Lee Iacocca predicted Chrysler's downfall years before its sales dropped 50 percent. The earliest warning, Iacocca reasoned, was the oil embargo, producing long lines at the gas pumps, with Chrysler still stubbornly producing only lumbering gas-guzzlers.

If the gathering storm has its origins in the causes of failure, your earliest warnings can be new and more formidable competitors, a shrinking market or decreased market share, new legislation that could hurt profits, technological lag or less-competitive products.

What do *you* see when you scan the far horizon?

Four stages to failure

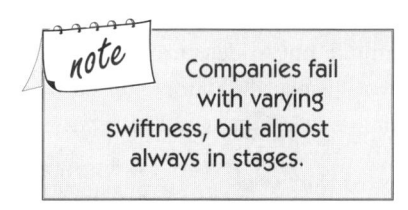

note: Companies fail with varying swiftness, but almost always in stages.

In the first stage, faulty management decisions or failure to respond to change weakens the company's competitive position. The company loses market share and plateaus or grows more slowly as it lags technologically or slips competitively. You sense loss of momentum or less firepower. Somehow, its future is not as bright as it once was.

The second stage brings clearer operational and financial symptoms. Sales slip further as more customers are lost. Advertising, promotion and new-product development are cut. Morale dips. Money troubles become chronic. This second stage shifts from positive, long-term planning to focus on short-term financial and operational problems.

> ⚠ **CAUTION** Once your company reaches the second stage, it is unlikely to correct on its own. You need more than cosmetic improvement.

The third stage creates total defensiveness. There are greater losses, less inventories, no credit and insufficient cash flow. You enter the "bankruptcy spin," where fewer assets generate fewer sales, and greater losses, producing still fewer assets, to continue the cycle.

Once in the fourth and final stage, few businesses recover. You are sued by creditors and lenders, pressed for long-overdue taxes, operate with too little cash and inventory, and lose employees and customers. In the third or fourth stage, you accept the reality that your company won't turn itself around with reorganization. But how do you determine when your company has passed its point of no return—a point beyond which it won't recover without a full-scale turnaround?

An ear to the washroom wall

Your ear may be close to the ground, but to detect problems listen to your employees, customers and suppliers—especially your employees. Hear all that can possibly be wrong with your business. You will hear about problems as they develop and hear about them loud and clear.

> **HOT spot** Your employees must know that bad news is as welcome as good news—even more valued!

Your employees are on the firing line, and may best know what is going on. They will tell you if you communicate with them. Good employee communication doesn't just happen. You must cultivate communication.

Chapter 3

Employees know problems must be corrected at the top and that his/her message will quickly reach the top. Adopt an open-door policy which rarely works in practice because many bosses build barriers between themselves and their front-line troops. These are the middle managers, who cannot or will not resolve the problems, nor relay bad news to a boss who only wants good news!

In my turnarounds, I interview employees from various departments for a good cross-sample of the corporate condition. I encounter frustrated employees delighted they finally have someone to talk to. I am their sounding board for pent-up frustrations, with many a tale of unhappy customers who complain about inventory shortages, poor delivery or shoddy product quality. I also find unhappy suppliers who won't ship because of overdue bills, or unhappy and demoralized employees whose salary cutbacks or job insecurities prevent them from performing well.

HINT: Let your employees tell you about shoddy products, inventory shortages, lost accounts, low morale and countless other ills of the stricken company. You may find your employees know more than you do about what is happening with your company!

The small, informally organized company won't have an easier time with employee communication. You can be as distant from one or two employees as the CEO in a penthouse office, with thousands of employees working his factory or retail chain. However, you can turn your employees into an early warning system with a three-step policy:

1) Let your employees know that you know the company has problems. If you don't acknowledge and communicate this, your employees will think you're either oblivious or are purposely being secretive. Neither conclusion makes you stand tall with your employees.

2) Set up a system for communicating. Tell your employees what information you want reported, when and how.

3) Encourage all the direct communication you can handle. Hear the problems directly from the up-front and front-line employees— oftentimes, intermediaries may attempt to discourage bad news.

> **HOT spot** When your people don't come to you with problems, that doesn't mean you don't have problems. This may be your biggest problem!

Creditors through the looking glass

Alice in Wonderland had her looking glass. Your suppliers, creditors, customers, and others outside your company have theirs.

HINT A distressed company has no secrets. Your creditors, suppliers and customers may be the first to detect impending problems on the horizon. Turn this to your advantage. Learn to look at things as they do. From the outside, matters are appreciably clearer. Creditors are trouble-sensitive because they have a stake in your business. They ultimately foot the bills you cannot pay.

You may instinctively conceal troubles from your creditors. You need credit from unsuspecting suppliers, and want to subdue their scramble to collect overdue bills. Creditors kept in the dark will temporarily help your cash flow, but it never solves underlying problems.

Buying time from unaware creditors is counterproductive. You simultaneously fool yourself, and may throw in more of your own money before you and your creditors realize a workout is your only possible solution.

On the other hand, early detection of your problems by alert creditors can force you to face your problems, because creditors can push you into a badly needed turnaround. They will more likely give you vital support and assistance, if you react quickly to your problems and ally them to your cause.

Creditors can detect problems in many ways, but creditors are hardly foolproof. Countless billions of dollars are lost each year in the bankruptcy courts. Alert creditors visit their customer's premises, and are open to rumors within the trade. They closely review financial statements. Each creditor has its own distinct opportunity to spot early signs of financial duress.

> **HOT spot** Creditors are more cooperative in a workout if they don't feel abused by someone who carelessly played with their money.

Trade creditors notice changes in your payment or buying patterns. A company that normally discounts its bills, but now pays in 30 days, may be in as much financial difficulty as the debtor who consistently pays late. Similarly, customers who buy illogically or in abnormally large quantities may anticipate their supplier closing their credit. Alert credit managers have their information network of customers and other suppliers within the trade—all anxious to spread the bad news of a sick account. Banks and other secured lenders can't easily tap trade sources and depend mostly on financial, not operational signals. Troubled companies usually pay their secured loans long after they become delinquent to trade suppliers. Therefore, lenders cannot rely on payments alone as a good indicator of advancing problems. Secured lenders will review their collateral together with shipments, purchase orders, accounts receivable collections and inventory changes.

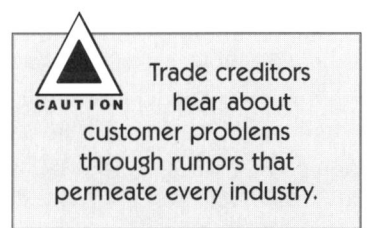

> **CAUTION** Trade creditors hear about customer problems through rumors that permeate every industry.

Tell-tale signs creditors look for:

- personnel changes, with your best people leaving

- changes in accounting or other reporting methods

- payments later or less consistent

- erratic buying

- shrinking inventories

- overdrafts and returned checks

- unusual returns for credit, or demands for other trade concessions which indicate financial problems

- buying from new suppliers on new credit

- credit reports that show more collection claims and lawsuits

- security interests to new lenders, tax liens or other creditor attachments

- loss of key customers

- deteriorating physical plant

- less advertising and promotion

HINT Creditors who spot these danger signals become defensive. They want to secure past-due payments and protect themselves on future shipments. Such creditor actions can be valuable signals.

The view from the opposite side of the counter

note Customers have a sixth sense. Most customers will simply abandon a crippled supplier who can no longer give them what they want. A defensive position can benefit customers who will take advantage of your weak bargaining power and desperation. They may withhold payment or demand lower prices or other unreasonable concessions, because you desperately need their business. Stronger suppliers can hold firm. Major customers cannibalize faltering suppliers.

Predatory customers with that predatory instinct will look for:

- unusually low prices or "fire" sales to raise cash
- factored receivables or big discounts for cash payments
- chronic inventory shortages
- erratic delivery and reduced service
- rapid personnel turnover

What things you suddenly find yourself doing to stay alive also are clues. We each have to "stretch" our capacity to do things in desperate times that we would never normally do.

> **E-Z TIP**
> Honest, ethical business owners can become crooks when pressured.

CAUTION Beleaguered business owners sometimes steal from their family, rob banks or even commit murder. To stay afloat you may predictably ship defective or substandard products, short-change your customers, pad your invoices, con vendors to ship goods you will never pay for, fall behind on payroll taxes—you see the point. Perhaps you are too honest, or are not that desperate to catch yourself doing these things. When you do, you are in big trouble!

Watch the scorecard

Only your financials can tell you whether you are really in a downturn. Other signals are intuitive. When your financials bleed, you have serious problems.

- failure to issue credits, extend customary trade concessions or pay earned rebates

- tightened credit

- poorer product quality

Game playing

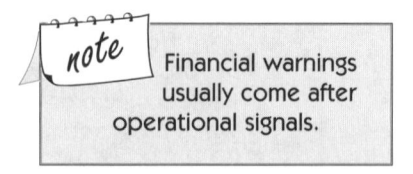

note: Financial warnings usually come after operational signals.

Even when aware of developing problems, you may not have the financial controls to signal approaching danger.

Failed companies frequently have non-existent or poor financial reporting systems. Good accounting information is not just physical data, such as units sold, items in stock, production per hour, or mounds of operational data most managers rely upon. You may lack accurate and critical information in three areas: profits, costs and cash.

Without a good budget, you don't know how profitable you are or even if you are operating below your break-even point. Without costing, you won't understand how key activities relate to bottom-line profits. And without good cash-flow projections, you can't anticipate the next peak demand for cash or how you will meet it.

Financials will worsen with approaching insolvency. You won't see the deterioration by casually inspecting your statements. And creative accounting

Chapter 3

can disguise poor performance. For many years, Rolls Royce deferred millions of dollars in losses by capitalizing its enormous research costs to mislead even the most sophisticated London analysts who believed the badly bleeding Rolls Royce was healthy. You're not Rolls Royce, but your financials may also be distorted.

Small losses may be whoppers. Losses may, in fact, be profits. Allow a margin of error if you have a small business with non-certified financial statements. You may have mistakenly overestimated inventories, overvalued receivables, capitalized items to be expensed, or other accounting distortions which can navigate you off course.

> **CAUTION:** Small businesses without audited statements are far more prone to financial distortions, whether or not intentional.

Financials can't be built on faulty data. An overestimated inventory will disguise losses, yet many businesses ignore physical inventories and estimate the inventories at last year's amount. Reduced inventory is easily overlooked when it gradually drops. An experienced manager may not realize inventory dropped $700,000 to $600,000; however, this $100,000 loss must be reported, if the financials are to have any value.

You may accurately report assets but not liabilities. Good managers watch liabilities closely. Through payment schedules, they instantly detect bills remaining unpaid longer. Small-business owners often have no idea what they owe. An owner who guesses $500,000, may owe $900,000. How accurate are your financials?

> **note:** Financials are worthless unless you know what they say.

You may ignore your financials because you don't understand them as management tools. Small business owners can seldom interpret financials and cannot tell you whether they are making money.

61

HINT: If you don't understand your financials, have your accountant toll the warning bell. Many accountants are only tax preparers and don't offer their clients close financial guidance. Companies frequently come to me deeply in debt after years of huge losses. Never was there a warning from their accountants. But, I don't indict the accounting profession. Many accountants yell loudly at the first sign of trouble. Others drag their confused, sometimes screaming, clients to professionals like myself. Still others defend their lack of navigational involvement by reporting, "The client didn't want my help. He paid me only to do the taxes, nothing more." But you need more than a tax preparer. Make your accountant your financial navigator!

Checking accuracy in the company's financial reporting system is oftentimes my first role in a case. I reconstruct financials when I doubt reliability. I want to know:

- How much money is the company losing, and for how long?

- What are the debts compared to the assets?

Answers to these two questions give me a good idea of "who's in trouble!" You may discover that you're not in big trouble after all. Your financials may show you are making money and have a good balance sheet but a tight cash-flow because you manage your assets poorly. Businesses can make loads of money, but strangle to death on negative cash flow. They may build inventory or receivables too rapidly or assume more financing than they can service.

Heed your gut feeling

Mountains of financial reports may not tell you what is instinctively in your gut. If you have been in business for a while, you know intuitively when things are abnormally bad. Sometimes your intuition helps you figure out how to correct your problem. Precise formulas or rigid rules are seldom as reliable as what your gut tells you.

Checkpoint

1) Are you problem oriented or do you still wear blinders?

2) Do you think your business is in serious trouble? Why? How much trouble?

3) Do you encourage your employees to come to you with problems?

4) How would your creditors and customers view your business? What symptoms of serious problems do they see?

5) What do your financial statements tell you about your business? Are your statements reliable? Do you know how to use them to navigate?

6) What's your gut feeling about your business?

Wake up the survivor in you

Chapter 4
Wake up the survivor in you

Good things don't just happen. You must make them happen. Turning around a failing business is more than balance sheets or business plans. Whoever they are, whatever their business, no matter how desperate their circumstances, these stalwart souls stand ready to do what they must to take their businesses from where they are to where they must go, overcoming nasty obstacles along the way. Successful workouts have more than good managers. They have survivors.

> **note** A successful workout happens when a helmsman with special qualities knows how to salvage a sinking ship.

Sharpen your survival instinct

What makes a survivor? First, think like a survivor. Break away from textbook management practices which work for healthy enterprises. Failing companies need unconventional strategies, often contrary to Management 101 principles. You can no longer operate for profits alone, as do well-heeled managers. Cash flow is your game. You hire and fire not by the "safe" rules, but by what leaves you with the people you most need to survive. You have different priorities when in trouble, and you achieve objectives differently. You can't think long-term. Your goal is to make it to next week.

Running a crisis company goes contrary to guiding the stable enterprise. Unless you have been there, de-program yourself from how you have done things in the past. Beyond a survival instinct, you need that survivor mentality!

Stripes for a survivor are earned with managerial qualities that custodial managers seldom have. Custodial managers are content to keep their companies on a straight line, buoyed by occasional small gains. They can run their businesses by the book because they have the resources for a conventional game. They stay safe as long as they avoid serious blunders. Good custodial managers are adequate caretakers of the corporate fortunes in good times, but rarely in bad times.

Who are these survivors I speak about? "Blood-and-guts" managers who take big risks because they are unavoidable. They kick butts, snub their noses, and fight everyone, both inside and outside the company, who blocks their way. They know exactly what their businesses need. A survivor necessarily becomes an S.O.B., because a survivor understands popular decisions are seldom correct decisions. Survivors are General George Pattons in business— unlovable but effective.

Custodial managers can't easily be converted. It's part personality and part style. Prior training and experience shape how they handle things. While a survivor must manage, a manager doesn't need sharp survival instinct; and surviving is your one goal in a workout. Unfortunately, survival skills aren't taught in college.

America's 600 business schools churn out 150,000 budding executives annually. One innovative institution now presents its MBA program on New York's commuter trains. The program might more usefully be taught on the subway leading to the bankruptcy court. Yet business schools continue to turn out textbook managers, who quickly become disoriented when things go wrong, because business schools ignore such nasty subjects as turnarounds and bankruptcy.

Chapter 4

In my business school days, our cases always presented lofty problems of plush Fortune 500 corporations. I never knew companies could lose so much money until I graduated from "B" school and went into business, where my education really started!

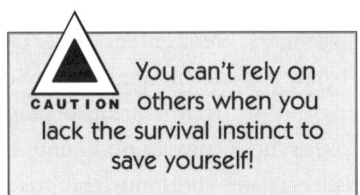

> ⚠ **CAUTION** You can't rely on others when you lack the survival instinct to save yourself!

Professionals can support you, and good employees may bolster your managerial deficiencies, but when your survival instincts fail, your business fails.

If you aren't that survivor, you have options. A partner? Sell the business? Liquidate? Hire a workout consultant? They are all possibilities. The "rent-a-boss" idea may be smart if you think an outsider can run your business more efficiently. You may consider your presence doubly important in troubled times, but your involvement can destroy whatever your company's chances for survival, if you are not that survivor and stand in the way of someone who is!

Small- to mid-sized businesses must center their workouts around their owners. Then, workout strategies must be what their owners can tolerate and achieve, even if it is not the best possible strategy. If you lack the stamina for a grueling, prolonged Chapter 11 reorganization, then you need a simpler solution. Each survivor has tolerance parameters. You alone must decide how badly you want to survive and what you will endure to survive. Most importantly, you alone must decide what survival capabilities you can bring to the workout.

A survivor is an architect for change

Survivors reshape their businesses from what they are to what they must become. They are architects of change. You, too, must quickly, clearly and objectively assess your company's present condition, realistically visualize its

> **note** Even when you have entrepreneurial talent and broad business experience, you need a certain creativity and ability to see things as they can be, not as they are.

future, and develop and implement a workable game plan to get it there. Creativity is more important in a workout than is business know-how. Experience may entrench your way of thinking so that you lose creativity. You ignore or reject new ideas or concepts. Highly creative people can tire in a turnaround, and become uncreative and unadaptive. It's hard to be creative when you're hit on the head a thousand times a day by angry creditors while you are coping with bushels of problems.

Survivors remember the long-enduring tale of the two market researchers independently dispatched by a shoe manufacturer to an undeveloped country. Two telegrams soon arrived at corporate headquarters. One dismally read, "No market here. Nobody wears shoes." The other happily promised, "Great market here, nobody has shoes." Survivors are opportunity-oriented, not problem-focused. Opportunity-oriented will make you an effective architect for change.

> **HOT spot** Fortunately, there are opportunists willing, even eager, to breathe fresh ideas into tired companies. Sometimes a more objective outsider can spot opportunity where none was found before.

How do you change your business into a money machine? No serious book can tell you. I have no magic formula for making money. You must decide whether to upscale or downsize, to add or drop a product, to raise or lower prices, or whether new marketing can turn the tide.

Radical change, not minor alterations, is needed to turn losers into winners. Visualize that radical transformation, or you may forfeit your fortunes while you tinker.

Chapter 4

See your business through new eyes. Abandon old business ways. But be guided by the numbers. Where are you making or losing money? How can you make money? How can you turn losses into profits? Talk to people: employees, suppliers, customers. Their ideas may be right on target. Be inquisitive. What new and exciting things are happening in your industry? What can you copy from your more successful competitors? Why do prospective customers shop your competitors, not you?

Basic? Of course. But architects of change answer basic questions. Vision is not enough. You also must implement change, which is tougher than the dreaming! For every ten managers who can foresee their company's future, only three can make it happen. These are the survivors.

Survivors create a climate for success

Survivors expect success! Survivors demand success! Survivors let everyone know their loser is about to become a winner, and they unshakably believe it. You hear it in their voices when they sell the proposition. Expecting success becomes a self-fulfilling prophecy. The same with failure.

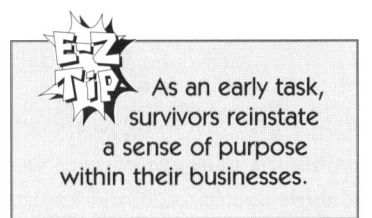

> **E-Z TIP:** As an early task, survivors reinstate a sense of purpose within their businesses.

Your employees, customers, suppliers, stockholders and creditors may be disenchanted with you and your company. When you're in trouble, you have few believers.

Somehow you must change how people think about you and your business. They must no longer see failure on the horizon, but success. Everyone involved in your business must be your partner in this self-fulfilling prophecy. When they truly believe you will come out of your tailspin, they will help make it happen—but only then. People won't perform futile gestures.

69

Your people must believe. Make them believe! When you do, you can slink home, down a stiff drink, and privately drown in your own doubts. Old-timers, like myself, remember President Franklin Roosevelt navigating the country through the Great Depression, history's largest workout. Long after his social and economic programs have blurred in history, Roosevelt is still best remembered for his inspiring "fireside chats." Americans knew things would indeed change for the better once they heard Roosevelt's sincere, convincing words.

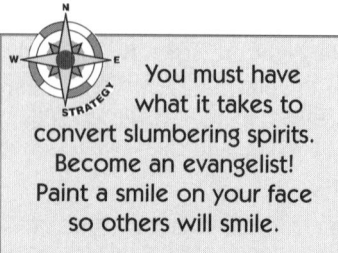

> **You must have what it takes to convert slumbering spirits. Become an evangelist! Paint a smile on your face so others will smile.**

Demoralized employees and financially troubled companies go hand in hand. Why shouldn't employees be down? They may soon be fired, or their pay cut. Your people work in the same bad conditions and nagging pressures as you do. You can't erase employee worries when you mope around with your own unhappy face.

So smile and throw back your shoulders. Make a game of it. Convince your people you will succeed. Convince your employees you need their help to succeed. Motivate everyone connected with your business with special incentives and rewards as a special thanks for their support through the hard times.

Yes, all this is easy to say and difficult to do when you're weary, depressed and overloaded with business problems. But you must inspire, even when you don't feel inspired. Either develop that spirit or step aside, and let that spirit flow from somebody else.

If your people are scared, show them self-confidence. Roosevelt had his fireside chats; Churchill his famous victory sign—even when London smoldered in ruins. What did these two great leaders really think? Who knows? The world only knew they would succeed.

Chapter 4

Survivors activate and energize

Survivors give their organization a strong kick because it's the quickest way to shake the doldrums. The complacent business needs a good jolt to pay attention. Your people must see that things are finally happening. You will make wrong moves, but at least you're moving, and that's what counts. Even small actions show forward movement.

Get the adrenaline pumping. Fire long-entrenched laggards. Scrap favorite but costly projects. Dump big but unprofitable customers. Unwrap a new marketing campaign, an exciting product, a new and better way to do an important job, or a new and profitable customer! Get your troops to think about things beyond problems. The kick-in-the-pants carries a vital message: You intend to stay in business, and have what it takes to stay there.

Symbolic and substantive shock can shake your company. Circulate bulletins. Call your employees together. What a swift kick announces to your troops is that a survivor has finally arrived.

> **E-Z TIP**
> Action alone is not enough. Spread the word that you are moving again.

Survivors communicate

Survivors communicate, communicate and communicate—with everyone connected with the business—inside and outside the organization. Through effective communication you win support, while keeping people in the dark builds resentment.

> **E-Z TIP**
> Sincere two-way communication is as vital to a workout as is selling.

Communication also helps you motivate. Workouts suffer when poor communication exists between management and employees, creditors, lenders and customers. When they hear nothing, they assume the worst.

Communicate meaningful, accurate information. Demand in return a constant flow of information, to help monitor performance during the workout. Communication is more than a device to send or receive information. It mends relationships easily strained during a workout. Don't hide. Take a major customer or supplier to lunch to build confidence. Without confidence you won't see your next order or shipment. Good communicators are goodwill ambassadors.

Start with monthly progress reports to your suppliers, creditors, lenders and employees. Newsletters or bulletins to your customers may instill the positive tone needed for them to stand by you. However you do it, communicate sincerely and frequently to the people whose help you need.

Good, strong communication is the glue that holds the various groups together. But honest, open communication during a workout is never easy, even for good communicators. If you are a poor communicator in the good times, then you will be reluctant to communicate bad news that risks losing support.

Managing a troubled company usually means dodging those who are hostile, which is, of course, virtually everyone involved with your company. But true survivors take the heat in face-to-face confrontations with angry employees, hostile creditors and skeptical stockholders. Survivors understand that when you need people to rebuild, you win their support by communicating—even when the message is painful!

Survivors are S.O.B.s

Survivors don't win popularity contests, nor try to. You can't be a sheep in sheep's clothing. They roll up their sleeves and fire long-loyal workers, cut

Chapter 4

salaries, scrap pet projects, withhold payments to desperate suppliers and say no to a hundred people who beg for a yes. Saying no is a very unpleasant, but essential, part of saving a business. Survivors become tough-minded and thick-skinned because their decisions are usually painful. They must be, to fire loyal employees of 25 years who can no longer pull their weight. Or withhold payment to a small, struggling supplier who needs that check. Every day, survivors make hard, but very necessary decisions. Survivors spread blood and guts because sacrifice is necessary for survival.

> **note:** Survivors become S.O.B.s because unpopular, tough decisions keep their businesses going.

Can you orchestrate a massacre? Most people can't. My clients are typically kind, sensitive people who desperately want to succeed while "doing right by everyone." But that's not how you survive. Choose between being a nice guy and giving away the shop, or becoming a grizzled S.O.B. and staying in business. There's no middle ground.

That hardly makes survivors insensitive. Hard-nosed survivors are as sensitive as benevolent failures. Survivors simply make decisions—painfully aware they are necessary decisions. Look at it from this perspective. Fire a long-standing, but incompetent, employee and you are kind to other employees, who now have a better chance of holding onto their own jobs. An unpopular decision benefits everyone if it helps the business survive. Tough decisions are usually the fairest, and S.O.B.s are usually the fairest turnaround leaders.

Yes, I feel like Attila the Hun when I commit mayhem to rescue a business. But when I must save a business, I know nice guys don't finish first. Nice guys don't finish. Okay, Mr. Nice Guy, how do you become that S.O.B.? You can train yourself for many things, but becoming an S.O.B. is not for everybody. More sensitive souls hire me to be their resident S.O.B. It's a role I accept. The meek may inherit the earth, but the S.O.B.s keep it in business! Become an S.O.B. or hire one for those dirty but necessary deeds.

73

Survivors give and take

A workout is negotiation. Yin and yang. Give and take. You divide a few corporate resources among players who each want more. Survivors negotiate deals so everyone wins—or think they won. But without deal-making there's no business.

Lenders, suppliers, creditors, employees, prospective partners, investors and financiers all test your negotiating skills. You're on the defensive, so they assume you have no negotiating power. You want your business alive and need them to do it. That's how they think. You must level the playing field to negotiate the deals that spell survival.

Lee Iacocca's great negotiating ability saved Chrysler. He masterfully negotiated essential loan guarantees from the government, major wage concessions from the United Auto Workers, and significant profit cuts from his own dealers. Iacocca's "equality of sacrifice" pitch didn't save Chrysler. His ability to sell the pitch saved it.

Your business is not Chrysler, but your role as masterful negotiator is no less important. Consider the very different interests and objectives of each group involved with your company and how you need their support. As a veteran negotiator I can tell you that it's like magic to pull a deal together. You need Henry Kissinger's tact and Will Rogers' wit to get a creditor to accept ten cents on the dollar, and shake your hand. Your ability to persuade is even more keenly tested with employees who are asked to produce more and get paid.

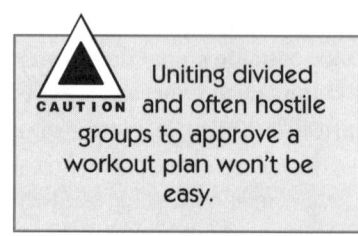

> ⚠ **CAUTION** Uniting divided and often hostile groups to approve a workout plan won't be easy.

Through negotiating you pull together the people, resources and money needed to reshape your troubled company into a winner. If negotiating isn't your strong suit, it's one more skill you can hire. Your consultant and lawyer may have plenty of experience in the yin and yang of business workouts. However, unless you enjoy a good game of poker, let them cut your deals.

Survivors innovate

Merchandise on the shelf and cash in the till spell successful companies. Survivors innovate. Survivors have the consistent ability to make something from nothing which is perhaps their most intriguing quality. To survive they must innovate, because nothing is usually all they have.

DEFINITION

Innovation creates new policies and procedures, produces new ways of doing business, and teaches people new jobs. Innovation is much more than change. Even healthy companies change. Innovation is the art of improvising and juggling to compensate for shortages everywhere. Survivors innovate because innovation is borne of desperation.

Survivors unshackle themselves from traditional procedures when traditional procedures no longer work. Innovation makes your business work with the resources you have today. Companies fail when they can't adapt to poverty. Those too accustomed to fixed ways of conducting business don't easily replace cash with creativity.

Talk to Chuck Collins about innovation. When the electric company cut power to his floundering Toledo meat-processing plant, he hooked up a rented generator to keep it operating. Genius? No. But it is innovation, and this one innovative maneuver, along with 1,001 other small tricks, helped save Chuck's business. The Chucks of this world survive because they innovate!

Innovation is critical in a turnaround because no workout goes according to plan; they zig, zag and bump against unexpected obstacles. The smallest obstacle can stop the largest corporation unless it's an organization blessed with an innovative leader who knows how to navigate.

Survivors bust butts

Survivors bring that critical ingredient to their sick company: Plenty of hard work. Trying to survive is never glamorous. You must possess endless problem-solving techniques, the ability to work against intense pressures from every direction, and a willingness to slave 16 hours a day, seven days a week. This "sweat-on-the-brow" commitment to your survival is often the difference between failure and success.

> **E-Z TIP:** Survivors start by busting their own butts.

A workout can consume twice the effort needed to maintain a stable enterprise. Without enthusiasm, after endless hours in a pressure-cooker world, you'll inevitably quit. Scores of clients say essentially the same thing: "It's not so much the long hours, but what you have to put up with that gets to you." And they're right! Ten hours on the job feels like 30 when you spend all your time dodging bullets. So how do you cope and bust your butt when things are at their darkest? Believe things will soon improve, and that your business will be worth the effort you gave it.

A stint with a troubled business is like a stint in Marine boot camp. You not only work harder than ever before but you reach an endurance level never before reached. As so many survivors report, once they've reached this peak performance, they never again want to slide back to mediocrity.

Survivors persevere

Survivors don't quit

Perseverance is essential. All other talents and strengths are meaningless if you quit or throw in the towel when things go wrong—as they invariably

Chapter 4

> **HOT spot** — Survivors are optimists and perpetual believers because they often have nothing to trade on but their hopes and expectations.

will. When optimism gives out, there's nothing left to the word "survivor." There's only a quitter.

A dramatic lesson on the value of perseverance came my way about five years ago when I started to work with a brilliant, young Chicago semiconductor engineer. Carl, a frustrated engineer, developed a series of microchips that represented a substantial technological advance, but because of serious production problems his young company was soon floundering in Chapter 11. His company languished in bankruptcy court for nearly three years while Carl ran into virtually every obstacle imaginable. I can't recall another case when so many things went wrong, and so few things went right. Sure, Carl was down in the dumps.

But there's a difference between disappointment and quitting. Survivors know how to get through their disappointments. Carl, after endless efforts, worked out his problems, and his company, now publicly traded, grosses about $150 million a year. Most people I know would have quit years earlier. Perseverance is a remarkable strength, but one that must be tempered with reality. After all, there can be a time to call it quits. So balance perseverance and objectivity. Knowing when to give up can be as virtuous as perseverance, if you surrender for all the right reasons, at the right time and in the right way.

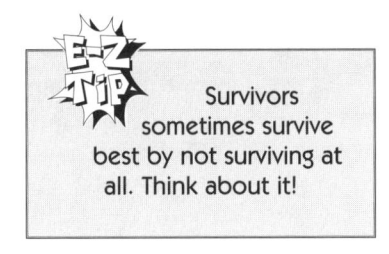

> **E-Z TIP** — Survivors sometimes survive best by not surviving at all. Think about it!

Checkpoint

1) Can you create the change your company needs to survive?

2) Can you build a climate of success for your organization?

3) Can you shake your organization out of its doldrums?

4) Can you talk about your problems and your progress with employees, suppliers, customers, lenders and creditors?

5) Can you make those tough decisions?

6) Can you negotiate effectively?

7) Can you innovate and make something from nothing?

8) Can you work your tail off to survive?

9) Can you persevere and stick it out . . . and can you call it quits when that's the right decision?

White knights and the turnaround team 5

Chapter 5
White knights and the turnaround team

Turnarounds are seldom one-person shows. Most well-orchestrated corporate comebacks team skilled workout and insolvency professionals with the best talent from within the company. This blend achieves optimum results.

Misery loves company! And company can be a mighty valuable commodity when your business hits the skids, particularly if you pick the right company to help piece your broken business together again. Ask Ted Kaplan, whose Seventh Avenue Kaplan's Fashions sales plunged deeper than the daring necklines on its dresses. Its beleaguered owner had no answers and knew it was time to call in someone who did. Nor was Ted ashamed to admit it. "We walked around in circles," he says. "Our stockroom bulged with unsold inventory. Our desks were buried under an avalanche of unpaid bills, and our competitors were hustling our best accounts. Disaster! My wisest investment was a 25-cent phone call to our attorney."

Kaplan's attorney quickly called in a top insolvency lawyer, who threw Kaplan's into a Chapter 11 reorganization to freeze creditor lawsuits, and buy time to regroup and reshape the troubled manufacturer. Next, a sharp accountant came on board to control Kaplan's finances with a strict, no-nonsense budget. To raise fast cash, they hired a liquidation consultant. Kaplan's excess inventory was soon unloaded to several discount outlets. A more aggressive advertising campaign breathed new life into Kaplan's tired image. Soon Kaplan's showroom bustled with buyers from Macy's, Filene's, Bloomingdale's, and Neiman-Marcus. Kaplan couldn't produce his stylish dresses fast enough to fill the orders. You should have seen the smile on his boyish face.

If you ask him what magic saved his business, Ted laughs. "No magic. We were just a little too close to our business to see our problems—much less find the solutions. You sometimes need more objective and hard-nosed professionals to see what you can't see!"

Call now, call collect

You can't be too proud to accept your own limitations and call for help from the growing cadre of consultants, lawyers, accountants and other workout specialists who each offer essential skills and resources you need to save your business. When you finally seek help, your business may be beyond the point of no return.

> **CAUTION** Timing is critical. When you ignore your problems, you also prolong seeking professional help.

Why won't you call for professional help? You may see it as admitting failure or inability to solve your own problems. We turnaround consultants often play psychiatrists to convince struggling business owners there is no shame when you lean on stronger shoulders. You are not infallible, nor are your business problems a loathsome disease. Every business eventually gets into trouble; the smartest business people use every resource at their disposal to survive and build a better business. Money is always a factor when you can't even meet your payroll—you hardly welcome a $200-an-hour consultant or lawyer.

> **E-Z TIP** A few dollars in professional fees can save you more money and save your business.

At that point, professionals are seen not as a vital investment but as an unaffordable cost. One reluctant client once told me, "I don't need a high-priced consultant to tell me I'm running out of money." But he did! More importantly, he needed someone objective, forceful and skilled to show him how to not run out of money. Reverse your thinking. Think about investment, not costs.

If you own a small- to mid-size business, you are probably less familiar and hence less comfortable with outside professionals than are corporate executives. You may not fully understand the many ways professionals can help you. The idea of a consultant can be scary. Perhaps you envision a mystery man in a three-piece suit drowning you in complicated reports, charts, and hieroglyphic graphs. It happens—but not if you choose the right professionals. Success or failure often depends on you finding the right professional talent—but you must find them! Keep one point in mind: You got your business into trouble. Why would you think you can get out of trouble on your own?

> **HINT** Technical skill is only part of what a consultant, attorney or accountant can offer. More important is how these professionals think.

As difficult as it is to navigate the thriving business, a complex turnaround demands unique skills and strange techniques that defy conventional management practices. Pros who understand how to put together broken companies play by rules only others within the insolvency field understand.

Like Ted Kaplan, you may get too close to your problems to see them clearly. Your situation blurs when you are deeply involved emotionally and financially. Independent professionals are not tainted by existing biases. They enter the picture with the fresh ability to look at things as they are, not as how you see them or want them to be. You can have the right answers and correct solutions to your problems and still need outside professionals as a sounding board to confirm that your

> **HOT spot** While managerial and professional skills are invaluable, professional objectivity is critical.

solutions are right. Your intuition about what must be done will usually be correct, but unless you have been through a turnaround or two, you may lack confidence in your own game plan.

Chapter 5

> **E-Z TIP**
> When a pro ratifies your decision, you can more confidently follow through and more forcefully press your decisions into action.

Outside professionals do for you what you cannot do for yourself. They tackle the dirty work of firing people or standing up to creditors, jobs you have no stomach for. Dirty work becomes my job when my client's company doesn't have a bastard on board.

Then there are the resources your advisors can provide. Insolvency consultants, attorneys and accountants form a small, closely knit professional network and can help you locate other star players for your team. I have a nationwide roster of hundreds of other consulting firms and law firms, each outstanding in its specialty. We routinely match difficult-to-find professionals with financially troubled business owners.

> **E-Z TIP**
> Most professional advisors similarly maintain close affiliations with banks, lenders, liquidators, business brokers and the many other specialists who serve troubled firms.

Of course, no two troubled companies need precisely the same professional aid. If you are unprofitable but still solvent, you need a consultant who can help you regain profitability. An insolvency attorney is of no value at this point. If you suffer from poor financial controls or a weak marketing strategy, your professionals must have those specialized operational skills; broad turnaround experience may not be enough. So your one most important decision is determining precisely the assistance you need from:

- turnaround consultants

- business or operations consultants

- insolvency attorneys

83

- auditors and accountants

- key personnel

White knights to the rescue

Turnaround consultants, or "white knights," ride to the rescue of the company in distress. For a fee, of course!

There are still relatively few good turnaround consultants, for the many distressed companies that need their help. Only a handful of America's management consultants (fewer than one percent) do turnarounds. Despite skyrocketing business bankruptcies, "corporate fixer-uppers" are so rare a breed that their craft lacks a universal name. I call myself an R&R expert in the "repair-and-rebuild" business.

> **note** — Turnaround consulting is one of the fastest-growing specialties within the broader field of management consulting.

Turnaround consulting is highly segmented; you won't easily find the right consultant. They excel in different situations, seldom work the same territory and operate in narrow niches. Some turnaround consultants, for example, handle only certain types of businesses like manufacturing, wholesaling or retailing. Others work specific industries such as textiles, real estate or nursing homes. Consultants also can characterize their practice by the size of their clients' businesses. Few consultants handle small businesses because small businesses can least afford their fees. More skilled consultants seek the challenging and financially rewarding opportunities only a big company with big problems, and a still bigger bankroll can provide.

> **E-Z TIP** — Turnaround consultants offer very different skills, but no one consultant is an expert in every phase of the workout. Don't let one who claims to be fool you.

Chapter 5

Despite the turnaround consultant's aura of mystique, they still put their pants on one leg at a time. And a consultant waving impeccable credentials can easily con the unwary. Plenty of guys and gals run around with degrees from Harvard and Stanford, but they have never talked to a creditor or may not know what to do when the checks start bouncing. Nor does a stint at Booz-Hamilton or Arthur Anderson necessarily produce a pro who knows the 101 dirty little tricks you must resort to when the going gets rough.

The turnaround consultant's strengths and weaknesses are based on his or her own training, experience, aptitudes and interests. A consultant who can brilliantly stem losses may be helpless with your creditors. I have a nationwide reputation for restructuring corporate debt; but I don't become deeply involved in operational problems. Many turnaround consultants handle only one or two stages of the turnaround. I frequently work with one busy Chicago consultant who stabilizes cash flow for companies in deep financial crisis. Once stabilized, the business is turned over to other consultants, who tackle the debts and make the company profitable.

Some prefer companies in the early stages of the downturn, rather than the challenge of a company on the edge. Yet others thrive in the pressure-cooker climate of "one step away from bankruptcy." The stress-induced exhilaration is, for many in my kind of work, its own reward. Turnaround consultants also work in different ways. Some rescue floundering companies by completely taking over their management until it is fully revitalized. Such "fixer-uppers" rely heavily on teamwork and bring in their own turnaround people to chart the course and implement the plan. They bet on themselves. When they win, as they nearly always do, they rake in big fees. In contrast, small-firm consultants are usually part-time advisors who simultaneously service many clients on a per-diem or hourly basis. Most turnaround consultants don't work for the troubled company.

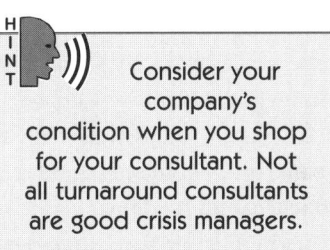

> **HINT:** Consider your company's condition when you shop for your consultant. Not all turnaround consultants are good crisis managers.

85

They represent banks, other lenders and creditor groups. Their job then is to recoup what they can from the stricken debtor. Commercial lenders routinely employ workout consultants, to breathe new life into a dying borrower with hopes that prolonged life can produce prolonged payments.

The chicken should never look to the fox for comfort. In a workout, you and your creditors have adversarial interests. You need an independent consultant with no allegiance to creditors. Turnaround consultants, whatever their differences, usually share an accidental career born when their own company fell onto hard times.

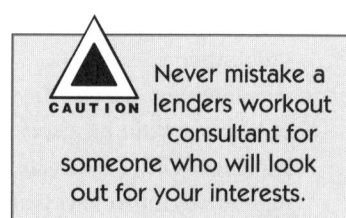

> **CAUTION:** Never mistake a lenders workout consultant for someone who will look out for your interests.

Virtually all turnaround consultants I know, including myself, can recollect the days when they wrestled the very same problems they now wrestle for clients. From this experience, they discovered that the challenge becomes even more enjoyable when they save someone else's sick company!

How do you find a capable turnaround specialist? The Turnaround Management Association, Society for the Advancement of Management, and the American Society of Consulting Engineers are three national organizations with turnaround consultants as members, although consultants in these organizations usually handle only larger companies. Court-appointed bankruptcy trustees are frequently skilled at rehabilitating financially troubled companies. Ask the clerk at your local bankruptcy court for some references. Trustees appointed by the court to operate Chapter 11 companies are who you want, not trustees who oversee Chapter 7 (liquidating bankruptcy) cases.

HOT spot: Credit associations, banks and lenders are other good sources if they can recommend conflict-free consultants. This is an important point. Your consultant must be doggedly on your side as a debtor, and consultants who consistently represent creditors don't always switch gears easily.

Chapter 5

The Small Business Administration's SCORE (Service Corps of Retired Executives) program also can provide workout consultants. You need not be an SBA borrower to qualify for this valuable free aid. One drawback is that SCORE consultants are part-time volunteers, so you may not get the firepower you need. Look around. If you still can't find a good consultant, give me a call. I work with consultants throughout the country; I can probably recommend a good consultant in your area. Talk to several consultants before you hire one. Probe their ideas. Beware consultants who paint too optimistic a picture or guarantee results. The field is full of phonies who trade on false hopes. Listen carefully to your prospective consultant's ideas and how thoroughly he or she approaches your situation. Fast answers and glib solutions are not what you need. The consultant's questions will reveal more about the consultant than will his answers.

Scrutinize references! A good consultant will gladly refer you to former clients. While professional skills are important, you also must develop a comfortable and compatible relationship with your consultant, so personalities are equally important. Selecting the right consultant is only half the battle. Unless you effectively use your consultant, you will accomplish nothing worthwhile. A poor working relationship between you and your consultant can do more harm than no relationship.

> **HOT spot** Investigate your prospect's track record in similar situations and for comparable companies.

Having run your own business, you may find it difficult to suddenly accept direction from a newcomer, even one with impeccable credentials. We all naturally resent outsiders, and you will certainly resist a consultant who is forced on you by lenders or creditor groups who have lost confidence in your ability to rescue your business.

CAUTION Even if you welcome your consultant, your employees may not. Employees typically view consultants with disdain, because they see the consultant as a threat to their jobs and authority.

87

On the other extreme, you may be only too glad to abdicate complete managerial responsibility and decision-making to your consultant. You may be too weary to continue the battle, or foolishly believe your consultant has magical managerial powers. Turnaround consultants may better understand the turnaround process, but you are best qualified to coordinate turnaround decisions with everyday business operations. After all, you best know your own business! Consultants who control decision-making make serious mistakes. If you relinquish total control to a consultant, you may harbor unrealistic expectations about what your consultant can accomplish, and be disappointed if those results are not achieved.

For an effective working relationship, you and your consultant must each understand your respective roles in the workout. You must then clearly communicate the consultant's authority and functions to the key people within your company. Establish a clear chain of command. Start by deciding whether your consultant will have direct decision-making authority or will only serve as an advisor and report to you.

Your consultant's role must not only be clearly defined within your company, but also within the turnaround team. Only then can the consultant develop a good working relationship with your attorneys, accountants and other advisors. Consultants can overstep their managerial roles just as lawyers offer business advice and accountants practice law. Good professional teamwork starts with mutual respect for the respective professional roles.

Conflict between turnaround consultant and attorney is common, as each sees themselves as captain of the team. Lawyers have traditionally headed the team, but this is only because they can so easily intimidate. Then too, turnarounds usually are steeped in legal proceedings. A

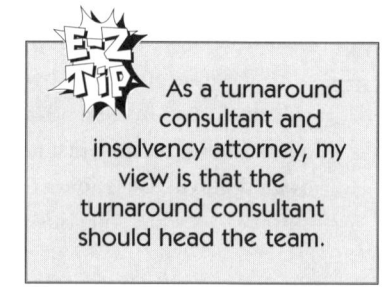

> As a turnaround consultant and insolvency attorney, my view is that the turnaround consultant should head the team.

turnaround consultant has a better grasp of the overall situation and can emphasize practical business solutions rather than legal solutions. Lawyers are usually too pigeon-holed in the law to be good turnaround leaders.

Chapter 5

Your consultant can only be fully accepted if presented correctly. Employees who might view your consultant as a sign of your managerial inadequacy must instead see the consultant as bolstering your capabilities. Creditors who believe the consultant's fees may drain cash best used to pay their bills must instead see

> **HOT spot** An effective consultant knows that to repair a faltering business, he or she must communicate credibly to employees, suppliers, lenders, creditors and stockholders.

the consultant as their best hope for recovering even more of their money. Everyone concerned with the company's future must see the consultant as a source of credibility—a voice to say exactly what is—when you can no longer be taken at your word. That means an ability to anticipate and satisfy their respective concerns.

What about fees? Good consultants are worth whatever their price, because they alone spell the difference between success and failure. Because you will find plenty of incompetents and frauds who will hit you for a big retainer and never give you the help you need, pay your consultant as your case proceeds. Refuse big retainers. Let the consultant generate his or her own fees by producing more cash flow. Nor should you dig into your personal pocket to pay the consultant. If the consultant isn't clever enough to figure out how to extract fees from your business, he shouldn't be your consultant.

All in all, the turnaround consultant's life is far from easy. You may unrealistically expect too rapid or smooth a turnaround, and others involved with your company also may expect miracles. You may see a consultant as a substitute for bad management. But that's wrong! A consultant can only help a good manager straighten out a bad business.

Business consultants

Back to Basics

Business consultants, a breed apart from turnaround consultants, are equally critical for most turnarounds. While the turnaround consultant cures the effects of corporate ills, business consultants attack their root causes. One example: The six-month turnaround of a near-bankrupt Texas kitchen cabinet manufacturer. I successfully stabilized their cash flow and restructured over $1,200,000 in liabilities. But why did the company get into trouble originally? Inefficient production and poor marketing were the two big reasons. The company is rapidly becoming a big profit-maker because I found a production engineer who improved productivity 200 percent; and a top-notch Fort Worth advertising agency soon will roll out a hard-hitting marketing program. I know this will dramatically boost their sales and profits. Troubled companies are sometimes victimized by very basic production, merchandising, marketing, distribution or similar operational problems that are best solved by consultants with specialized operational skills or industry experience.

Turnaround consultants may see obvious problems within a troubled company, yet not know the tricks of that particular trade. But those tricks can make the difference between a failed, mediocre, or highly successful turnaround. That's why we summoned a five-star Boston restaurateur to help a struggling Cape Cod restaurant break away from three years of big losses. Profits came with a new menu, stricter portion control, smarter buying and a vastly improved waste-prevention program. Only a hands-on restaurant pro could deliver this valuable know-how. A turnaround may only involve correcting one or two very basic problems, solved by someone with good industry experience.

To find your business consultant, look for someone with a track record from within your industry. You don't need inexperienced business consultants in the operational areas where you need help. Seek practical, nuts-and-bolts answers. Identify your operational weaknesses. Who in your field excels in merchandising, promotion, inventory control and buying? Your industry has its heavy hitters who don't compete with you. Do you need a restaurant consultant? Why not approach a highly successful restaurant owner outside your trading area?

Ask prospective consultants what they can do for you and how long it will take. Remember, few consultants can take much time from their own businesses, but they may improve your business significantly with only a few hours of valuable tips.

Most of the best "consultants" never consulted before, but work full-time in their own businesses. I look for retired business people who were highly successful in their industries. They offer more time and more experience. I find these people are flattered when you ask for their help because you are acknowledging their business skills and success. Give your consultant a free hand to thoroughly review your entire operation. If you define the problem, you lose the opportunity to have your consultant detect other problems. This can be his or her most important function.

Set guidelines

Ask your consultant to outline your major problems. Rank each by priority and decide how each may be best solved. You may need more than one consultant if your business needs help in different operational areas. But too much reliance on outside consultants can be overkill for the smaller business.

Still, no business is too small to seek outside help. And the smaller the business, the more help it may need. When Zisson's Bakery began to lose customers, I called on Harry Winston, Boston's bakery king. Harry gladly appeared in his colored apron, which served as his trademark, sampled a few cookies and, within two minutes, rendered his diagnosis: "Too much salt." Harry's prescription? A new recipe, an advertising campaign and higher prices. Harry even threw in recipes for a few of his famous ethnic delicacies guaranteed to attract every sweet tooth within ten miles. Zisson's sales climbed steadily from $350,000 to more than $1 million a year. Harry, always delighted to help a fellow baker, boasts, "Why not? I'm still king! Why not kiss a few toads if I can turn them into princes." The Harry Winstons of your field mean business! Plenty of business!

And I have had plenty of similar cases. Higgins Motors couldn't sell enough new cars to stay afloat until a high-powered dealer from a nearby state showed the Higgins brothers all the proven tricks to sell more cars. All it took was a small fee. Higgins Motors now ranks first in Mercury dealership regional sales.

Save-On Foods was victimized by its own poor merchandising until a retired buyer from a large supermarket chain loaded Save-On's shelves with precisely the right merchandise—at the right price. Sales doubled. Salvatori's Italian Foods, a neighborhood pizza and beer favorite with the college crowd, never made any money. Mary Salvatori couldn't see her problem, but a more successful Italian restaurateur did. Following her consultant's advice, Mary upgraded her restaurant and dropped the pizza and beer from the menu. Higher-priced Italian cuisine boosted sales and profits dramatically, as the big spenders replaced the college kids on tiny budgets.

> **note** Your business has only your talent, experience and capabilities to rely upon.

When you lack certain know-how on these countless decisions that affect your bottom line, you often guess wrong (it is invariably a guess). If you stumble on a few big decisions, or too many small ones, your profits quickly become losses. To correct the situation, detach yourself from your business long enough to stick your head out the front door and yell for help.

> **CAUTION** Without a consultant's help, your turnaround will suffer from the same day-to-day errors that originally caused your losses.

Chapter 5

Too few troubled firms follow my advice. Perhaps you never thought about a consultant to show you how to run a better business. So give top priority to a consultant who can give you objective, expert advice on how to make your business a money-maker. It's smart business. The winners within your industry will put you on the fast track to profitability if you ask for their help!

Lawyers riding shotgun

Good legal advice is vital. As much as we all want to avoid lawyers and big legal fees, a turnaround always involves legal issues and problems, even when bankruptcy is unnecessary. You too will invariably need an attorney, even if it's to forestall and defend creditor suits and to threaten your creditors with bankruptcy if a more pleasant and cooperative workout is unsuccessful. Yet after nearly 30 years as a bankruptcy attorney, I confess that too many troubled small- to mid-sized businesses are lost each year because of poor legal advice.

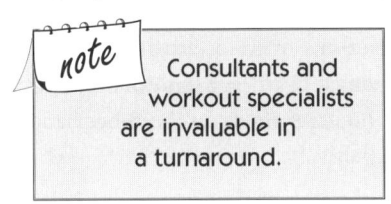

> **note** Consultants and workout specialists are invaluable in a turnaround.

Real estate, criminal and probate lawyers, who wouldn't know a balance sheet from a cash-flow statement, too frequently get involved in complex business and insolvency cases. Since law is as specialized as medicine, forget Uncle Joe the lawyer. He drafted your superb will, but what does he really know about business insolvency, bankruptcy and turnarounds?

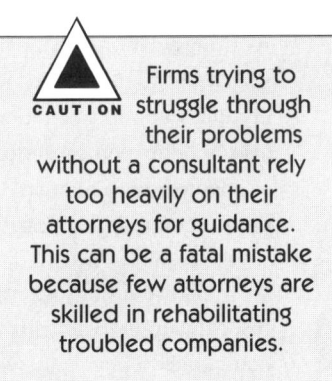

> **CAUTION** Firms trying to struggle through their problems without a consultant rely too heavily on their attorneys for guidance. This can be a fatal mistake because few attorneys are skilled in rehabilitating troubled companies.

Hire an attorney well-experienced in saving troubled companies. You need a legal gunslinger who knows every trick and strategy to defend you and

93

Troubleshooting Your Business Made E-Z

your beleaguered company from your numerous foes. A rare breed? There are fewer attorneys who can legitimately claim competence in this field than there are bona fide turnaround consultants. Many lawyers routinely handle Chapter 7 business and personal bankruptcy cases, but these liquidating bankruptcies are relatively simple and require far less skill than complex corporate turnarounds and reorganizations.

> **CAUTION**: Salvageable businesses are liquidated every day because their attorneys didn't know how to save them.

If your attorney can't recommend a workable rescue strategy, find one who can. Whatever you do, do not liquidate or throw your business into bankruptcy without a second opinion from a seasoned turnaround consultant, because too many lawyers don't see solutions other than liquidation or bankruptcy. A turnaround consultant, on the other hand, seeks ways to avoid liquidation and bankruptcy.

The right lawyer knows not only the right legal strategies, but how to maneuver within the insolvency system. She or he has battled creditors' lawyers many times before and knows what to expect. Creditors' and debtors' counsels meet on many cases and necessarily forge a smooth, if adversarial, working relationship. Having handled scores of Chapter 11 cases, I can tell you it's easier to negotiate a plan of reorganization with an attorney for the creditors' committee when you are on a first-name basis. This same familiarity also benefits you in the courtroom. A bankruptcy judge may give the benefit to a lawyer who regularly appears before him. This judicial leeway can decide the outcome of your case.

> **HINT**: Insolvency attorneys, like turnaround consultants, have a network of resources to help a business survive. They know which banks lend to troubled companies. They deal with accountants who can untangle your numbers. Consultants? Your insolvency attorney is probably your best referral source.

Your regular lawyer probably can refer you to a good bankruptcy lawyer. Don't be reluctant to ask for a reference. Few lawyers resent referring a client to a specialist in another area of practice. Or ask the clerk of the bankruptcy court for the names of local practitioners. State and local bar associations also list qualified bankruptcy attorneys, and some states even provide certification to bankruptcy specialists who have passed rigid competency exams. In these states, this probably is the best place to start. Stay away from large, silk-stocking, law firms unless yours is a larger company. Blue-chip law firms are too expensive for the smaller business. I also don't recommend them because they are too conservative and stick to traditional textbook remedies, such as Chapter 11, when a more creative zig-and-zag strategy may be your answer. Nor do larger firms guarantee you better service for their bigger fees. Small, less important clients end up with overpriced junior associates, not the more seasoned partners. The best bet in almost any city are the small, aggressive law firms, or even sole practitioners.

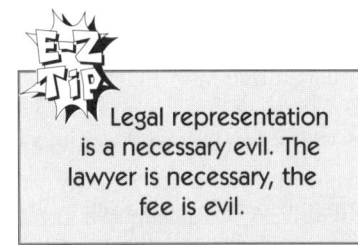

> **E-Z TIP:** Legal representation is a necessary evil. The lawyer is necessary, the fee is evil.

Here are four money-saving tips:

Tip #1) Don't avoid legal help because you don't have the money.

A good insolvency lawyer, like a seasoned turnaround pro, knows how to squeeze fees from the business. No small-business owner ever walked into my office with a large retainer. Few insolvency lawyers expect it. If you had plenty of money, you wouldn't be there.

Tip #2) You and your counsel should plan what your business can afford to pay and when.

Your attorney will, of course, want reasonable progress payments, while you instinctively will fight for every dime to help keep your business afloat.

But you can't expect lawyers or consultants to bill you at the end of your case any more than they should insist upon a large, unaffordable retainer.

Tip #3)   Don't negotiate a fixed fee arrangement.

It's impossible to predict how many hours will be required to properly handle your case, as unexpected problems may arise. But do ask for a fee range.

Tip #4)   Your workout options will depend on what you can afford.

Attorneys, for example, cannot profitably handle even a small Chapter 11 reorganization for less than $15,000, a fee well beyond the reach of a tiny corner store whose solution must fit its pocketbook.

Remember, when you retain an attorney (or other professional) you do not spend your money. You spend your creditors' money. Creditors, for all practical purposes, own the insolvent company, and it is they who eventually and indirectly pay your bill for professional services.

Plenty of my colleagues agree with me when I say that lawyers are counterproductive to a turnaround because they think narrowly in terms of legal solutions. They don't understand business, which must, after all, be the foundation of the turnaround. But the lawyer does have a role in a turnaround. Lawyers shouldn't drive the stagecoach, but they are great for riding shotgun.

The number crunchers

I fire accountants who don't help our mutual clients to financially manage their business. We regain credibility and creditor confidence only when new accountants take the financial controls. Replacing accountants is absolutely essential when your accountants helped conceal your poor corporate condition through manipulative accounting. Fire your accountants if they were too slow to alert you to your declining financial condition.

Chapter 5

Accountants who only prepare neat balance sheets, but won't tell you how untidy those numbers really are, do not belong on your turnaround team. Every company needs basic financial controls to stay on course, but accurate, detailed and timely financial data is absolutely critical for the crisis company. One highly successful certified public accountant in my area specializes in workouts for financially troubled nonprofit schools. To bolster his effectiveness, he designed a remarkably efficient financial-information system that has proven invaluable in navigating troubled schools back to health. This level of specialized expertise is uncommon, yet it shows that accounting nurtures its own brand of specialists. Even the once-stodgy Big Seven accounting firms are now organizing boutique-turnaround consulting divisions.

> **E-Z TIP**
> Your accountants must understand your business, if they are to know how to plug in the important controls quickly.

For those important numbers, your accountant must thrive in a world of cash flows, cost analysis, break-even projections, forecasting and budgeting. Your accountant must answer critical questions: Where are you making or losing money? What is your new break-even point if you drop a product or shut a plant? What is your forecasted cash position in the next 60 days? Bring on board a first-rate financial navigator!

The right financial navigator will skillfully analyze your operation. He or she is a rare breed; a blend of comptroller, visionary, and magician who coordinates the numbers to guide you toward a positive cash flow and ultimate profitability.

I consider the financial function so important to a successful workout that I frequently hire a comptroller for even small firms that ordinarily would operate without this level of financial support. Larger firms may have number crunchers, but not necessarily the right ones. So we then search for new financial talent.

Larger firms usually have their financials audited by the creditors' accountants. Auditors for lenders and trade creditors also may check for fraud, embezzlement, creditor preferences as well as monitor the company's financial controls. This includes the cash flow and profit projections creditors must rely upon for credit and settlement decisions. Most accounting firms are eager for turnaround work. However, not all accounting firms can commit the time and personnel. Complex workouts demand considerable accounting work, particularly in the early stages. A major bankruptcy reorganization can consume thousands of accounting hours.

The financial function is considered so important to a turnaround that some turnaround consultants employ their own accountants to ensure they get the support they need. Even a company with good accounting systems may have its consultant's accounting staff monitor accuracy. Because turnaround companies can over optimistically forecast, I continuously challenge the assumptions upon which they base their rosy future. Only then do I see things as they really are. Your accountant's most important function is to see things as they really are, not as you would like them to be! What type of accounting firm should you look for? A new professional designation, CMA (Certified Management Accountant), is now awarded to accountants expert in managerial accounting (as opposed to auditing, taxation and statement compilation, the CPA's bread and butter). CMA's are ideal to navigate your turnaround. But titles are unimportant. Bookkeepers guided some of my most successful cases, and they performed exceptionally once we told them the numbers we wanted.

Bankruptcy courts frequently appoint accountants as trustees for Chapter 11 re-organizations. These accountants are usually in private practices and can be an excellent addition to your team. They possess the right financial skills because they have handled many other financially distressed businesses. Considering the importance of accountants' reports to both the courts and creditors, employing an accountant they know and trust can be a very smart move.

Chapter 5

Talent from within

Your turnaround also will need all the help it can get from key employees who can work closely with your outside advisors as valuable members of your turnaround team. The employees you select will, of course, depend on the size and nature of your company, its organization and the quality and capabilities of your staff. Include no more than four insiders, as larger groups become too unmanageable.

Select employees with the broadest operational responsibilities. This will give you a more balanced input and a more accurate assessment of how the turnaround decisions will affect general business operations. Line managers best understand the practicalities of turnaround decisions, and since they must implement those decisions, it is best to have them participate in their formulation.

Encourage employees on your turnaround committee to express their own views and to freely disagree with you and your professional advisors. Also choose key managers ready to initiate and carry out the changes. In fact, populate your team with employees most anxious for change. Avoid long-entrenched employees who will resist change when it discredits their prior actions or threatens their authority. Otherwise-excellent employees impede progress when they fight change. They seldom work well on a turnaround committee whose goal is to bring change. Look deep within your organization for those mavericks. Pick people who can enthusiastically put your company on a more profitable path.

> **CAUTION:** You don't need followers or "yes men."

To pick the right people for your turnaround team you must know your people. And you only know your people when you plan with them, work with them and encourage them to communicate openly with you. Are they results-oriented? Can they work well in a crisis? Can they carry out difficult orders?

99

Can they implement and improvise without essential resources? Can they motivate their subordinates? Do they possess the unique skills and strengths your turnaround needs? A rising star glows most in a moment of need.

> **note** Many of today's corporate leaders won their stripes in the combat of a turnaround. Few return to the boring luxury of working in normal companies that simply make money.

I always invest time talking to the key employees of a troubled business. It's a good investment, because they usually see the problems and solutions most clearly. They offer objective and sensible advice, because they have watched the company deteriorate daily. I test their interest and measure the added responsibilities they can assume. I ignore complex organizational charts. I simply assign individual tasks to those who can best handle them.

When it comes to getting your business out of trouble, you must accept the reality that you cannot do everything yourself. And you must know which of your employees can perform various functions better than you can. That's why I routinely delegate creditor problems to a tough-skinned employee. I know employees usually can run interference and field the time-consuming creditor threats more easily than the owner. Tough-skinned employees make invaluable turnaround-team players.

A key and trusted employee also can be a godsend when you're tired and beaten. A key employee may be your perfect takeover candidate. Dyson Lumber's owner, Dick Dyson, will tell you he was only hours away from a nervous breakdown when his assistant manager grabbed the reigns. He had sound ideas for curing the ailing multi-million dollar lumberyard, and he had the energy and ability to convert those ideas into reality. Dick's up-and-coming assistant was quickly appointed captain of the turnaround team and worked with me night and day to save the business. Thanks to his help, today it operates six highly successful lumberyards in eastern Pennsylvania. The turnaround process also includes detecting and curing staff deficiencies. If your people won't support you, change your people, not your game plan. If

Chapter 5

Dick Dyson's aggressive assistant manager hadn't been around to spearhead the turnaround, I would have found that person. I knew Dick Dyson couldn't handle it, but the job had to be done. Surviving means plugging the holes in your team. Key employees adequate for the solvent enterprise are not always the answer for the troubled company.

To motivate employees on your turnaround team, you must effectively use their talent. They then feel involved because they are making good things happen. Sometimes you need a crisis to get the best from your employees.

> **note:** These key employees can create an infectious enthusiasm that inspires other employees.

When Star Electronics, a $6-million-a-year St. Louis transistor firm, overexpanded, our turnaround team included the sales manager and production manager. These two employees had a bushel of terrific ideas for expanding sales and production. Why didn't these ideas surface before? The owner never asked them for their opinions, and seemed uninterested in their views. The turnaround team was their open forum.

We encouraged Star's sales manager to pursue institutional accounts. The production manager was invited to act on his recommendation to dump their old and inefficient typesetting equipment for a leased state-of-the-art computerized printer. The turnaround team carefully analyzed their ideas before flashing the green light. The sales manager and his staff of twelve salespeople became balls of fire. The production department also came alive. Positive things were happening, and these two employees kept it no secret. Your key people may not be of this caliber. Your support may be from someone outside your company. Is a partner your answer? Conglomerates merge for managerial synergy. It can make even more sense for the small business owner with neither the inclination nor the talent to whip a company back into shape.

101

It was the answer for Carlos, the once-proud owner of New York's Skyway Stereo Centers, whose $3.2 million-a-year business was mired in bankruptcy. Poor Carlos just couldn't cope; and Carlos had no employees capable of taking control. I developed the turnaround strategies, and Carlos' accountant ran the numbers. But who would implement our plans? We were convinced the business could succeed, but who could turn it into a reality? Certainly not Carlos, busily putting away his sorrows on the golf course. With Carlos no longer on the turnaround team, we searched for a designated hitter. To the rescue came Barbara, who had masterfully converted a nearby Radio Shack store into the pride of the Tandy chain. Barbara soon became Carlos' partner, acquiring her share in the business from her share of future profits. Carlos and his golf course are now inseparable. That's OK. Carlos can afford 18 holes every day because his business now earns him over $600,000 a year!

> **HOT spot** Leadership, for what it's worth, is most prized when it comes from the top.

Your starting lineup may or may not be your best team, but without a good captain there's no team! The owner still is the best leader for any turnaround team. An owner can delegate substantial responsibility to employees, but turnaround success usually needs an owner who cares—as only an owner can.

Checkpoint

1) Do you need professional help? Why?

2) What type of professional assistance do you need?

3) Have you considered hiring a turnaround consultant?

4) What operational problems do you need assistance with?

5) Is your lawyer qualified to handle your financially troubled business?

6) Has your accountant financially navigated your business well in the past? Can he effectively guide you throughout the workout?

7) What key employees would be valuable members of the turnaround team?

8) Are you ready to assume your role as leader of the turnaround team?

Designing your turnaround

6

Chapter 6
Designing your turnaround

Any troubled business can find success with that one correct strategy to improve profits: Change products or services, undertake new marketing, improve efficiency and productivity, make organizational changes and reduce costs.

Consider these same options with large losses to combine strategies. Turnaround strategies are basic management manipulations. Some correct fundamental operational weaknesses, such as introducing stricter financial controls, while others exploit new markets, products or services.

> **note:** A turnaround must reshape your organization on a faster speed and greater scale than the stable, well-performing firm.

Turnaround companies usually downsize, but others may grow rapidly through acquisition. Nearly all turnarounds restructure their debt. All share one goal: creating a financially stable, profitable and solvent company.

Key recovery strategies

From working with hundreds of troubled firms, I have found successful recoveries nearly always improve their financial controls. Failed businesses usually don't use their financial data intelligently. Successful recoveries prioritize cash-generation.

105

Both successful and unsuccessful companies try to improve marketing, but successful firms make fundamental product changes in services and prices. Failures are status-quo marketers.

> **note** Cost reduction is attempted by nearly all troubled firms. While always important, it is only one of many strategies for survivors.

Selling profitable parts of the business to raise cash is also common, as is improved communication and decentralization. Failing firms remain autocratic, uncommunicative and centralized.

Larger firms typically bring in new management to spearhead their turnarounds. Most importantly, survivors use many turnaround strategies. Failed firms rely upon too few.

> **E-Z TIP** Strategy is important, but so is how you implement your strategies.

One or two well-implemented strategies beats dabbling with a dozen. Yet all successful turnarounds must do enough important things well!

Five keys to successful turnaround strategy

Which turnaround strategies are right for you? The answer is partly intuitive, but guided by five factors:

1) the severity of your problems

2) your resources

3) the reasons for your troubles

4) your type of business

5) the attitude of those involved with your company

1) Severity of the problem

note: If your business is steadily losing money, it needs a turnaround. A crisis (whether you are making or losing money) is when you run out of money, or creditors threaten to close you down.

Serious cash crisis requires cash-raising strategies with priority over everything. Stability, not long-term profitability or solvency, is essential for your turnaround. Do whatever you must to produce cash.

Non-crisis firms may be unprofitable and insolvent, have less need for fast cash, and can more leisurely assess their problems, options and opportunities. They can delay organizational and operational change more than crisis firms.

2) Available resources

What you can and will invest to pull your business out of trouble depends on resources; within the business, your own, and what you can borrow. You may have enough strength to withstand an always-draining Chapter 11, but more anemic firms need faster, less costly solutions.

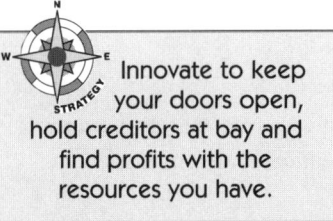

> **E-Z TIP:** Any business can be saved if you throw enough money at it. But you don't necessarily want to throw money at your problems.

> **Strategy:** Innovate to keep your doors open, hold creditors at bay and find profits with the resources you have.

Apply common sense. Resource-rich is not always good. Companies losing money with a healthy balance sheet may not develop a survival instinct. Firms without two pennies to rub together must learn how to do without.

3) Why you're in trouble

To discover how to get out of trouble, discover how you got into trouble. An oversimplification? A good starting place nevertheless. Poor financial controls demand good financial controls on excessive cost and cost reductions. Your overall strategy includes sub-strategies. A non-competitive firm plagued by price predators may try cost reductions, product changes or new marketing tactics. Turnarounds tackle the root causes of their problem and other problems.

4) The type of business

The industry influences the turnaround. For instance, undifferentiated products are overly price sensitive. This eliminates price increases as a feasible strategy, while product-focusing will work on highly segmented markets with identifiable customer preferences.

Rapidly changing high-growth industries encourage turnarounds for several reasons: First, they can more readily regain the competitive edge through new technology. Second, their companies more easily attract capital. Third, mergers and takeovers create more opportunities.

> **HOT spot** Firms in fragmented industries will more likely survive than those in monopolistic industries, because the troubled firm too easily falls victim to its customers' stronger bargaining position.

5) Attitude

How a company wiggles out of trouble rests chiefly on the attitude of its managers, employees, shareholders, creditors and customers.

In a downturn, problems at first are internalized. Outsiders remain unaffected. Decision-making is left to managers. As corporate fortune erodes,

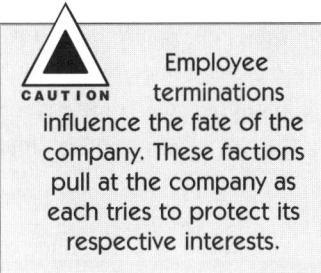

> ⚠️ **CAUTION** Employee terminations influence the fate of the company. These factions pull at the company as each tries to protect its respective interests.

shareholders become more vocal. Non-performing loans bring lender pressure.

Lenders and creditors may see liquidation as their best way to recover. Managers or labor unions may want the business and the paychecks to continue. Shareholders may want liquidation or continuation, depending on how they view the business' future. Even shared, broad objectives can create conflict. One group may prefer Chapter 11, others an informal workout. To improve profits, one group supports downsizing, another supports acquisitions.

The family-owned business is less political. "Mom and Pop" decide what happens. Attitude is still important because their turnaround must match what they can comfortably handle. Your attitude, skills and how you react to your situation are important when selecting your right remedy.

> 💡 **E-Z TIP** A winning strategy fits the business and its people.

My most successful turnaround plans are those the owner could handle. Failures were mismatches. I may have correctly analyzed the business, but not the owner.

Types of turnarounds

Every turnaround company faces a variety of possible outcomes—from complete and immediate failure, to short-term survival, to a sustained but unexciting future, to phenomenal success. Unsuccessful turnarounds are either "no-hopers" or temporary survivors.

Troubleshooting Your Business Made E-Z

DEFINITION — *No-hopers* can't even survive short term. They usually are insolvent and slowly bleed cash without prospect of ever making money. No-hopers have no *raison d'etre* and cannot justify the time, money or effort for a turnaround. No-hopers, whether a tired, beaten corner store or a Fortune 500 company, are dinosaurs or companies without futures.

DEFINITION — *Temporary survivors* may linger for years, and to the untrained eye, may appear to have achieved a successful turnaround. One reason these firms ultimately go bust is that they may have artificially survived, buoyed by cash or credit transfusions. Their short-term profits never lasted.

DEFINITION — *Long-term survivors* first are the drifters, who endlessly cling to life without the resources, skills or opportunities to become formidable companies. Still, drifters may produce enough to keep their owners happy. And, as long as they do, they continue their unremarkable existence.

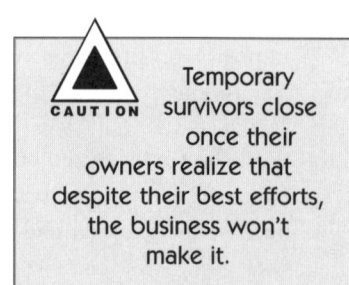

> **CAUTION**: Temporary survivors close once their owners realize that despite their best efforts, the business won't make it.

Achievers are true turnaround successes who emerge from their workouts to consistently earn above-average profits, or become industry superstars. Few survivors become achievers because most turnarounds continue with serious weaknesses. But any firm stands more chance of becoming an achiever if it tackles its problems sooner, not later.

No company is static. Today's drifter may sparkle tomorrow, and today's achievers may go bankrupt.

Stages of recovery

Businesses fail in stages, and recover in phases:

- the evaluation phase
- the stabilization phase
- the reorganization phase
- the growth phase

The evaluation phase:

In the evaluation stage you identify the causes of your problems, detect immediate threats and select short-term survival strategies. You start a long-term strategic plan to restructure your company's debts and become profitable.

The stabilization phase:

This phase may begin with the evaluation stage, but last longer. The stabilization stage centers on staying afloat through cost-cutting, cash-raising and revenue-generating. Cash flow and tightened financial controls become priorities: terminating excess employees, closing plants, selling idle assets and reducing surplus inventories. Stabilization usually lasts three months to a year or more, depending upon the size and complexity of your company.

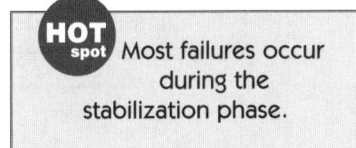

> **HOT spot** Most failures occur during the stabilization phase.

The reorganization phase:

There are two important events in the reorganization phase. First, through strategic repositioning, your business should begin to make money.

You still cannot ignore cash flow, improved controls and operational efficiency. These become necessary for continued stability and you also begin to restructure your debts.

Companies that are both unprofitable and insolvent must become both solvent and profitable. But even consistent profitmakers can become insolvent. Once financially stable they must contend with their creditors. Unprofitable companies with a strong balance sheet must become profitable. Yet, few businesses get serious about their problems until either they run out of money or creditors seriously threaten.

> **note** Whether regaining profitability or restructuring debt, the primary objective depends on the company.

Companies that remain financially stable have excellent survival odds. They may never earn big profits, but can squeak by.

The growth phase:

A company's problems are largely solved in the growth phase. The business is financially stable, the balance sheet clean—you're making money. You are ready to grow, whether through new products, improved marketing or acquisitions. Growth may be modest, but the business is no longer heading downhill.

> **E-Z TIP** For turnaround firms, staying level can be its own form of growth.

Implementing your turnaround

You can't precisely chart a turnaround, because what you must do and in what order will depend on the factors discussed. Speed is the one common denominator.

Chapter 6

Your initial plan may lack detail, but nevertheless needs a framework and action steps to:

- visualize where your company should be
- develop strategies to get there
- implement change
- measure progress

Action Step #1: Set turnaround objectives

note

Clear and achievable objectives are to a business what a rudder is to a ship. Companies flounder without clear objectives and achievable goals.

To create and communicate a new direction, begin with a mission statement of what you expect your business to become within a set time. Turnaround leaders who mastermind brilliant comebacks for failing companies are captains who knew exactly where they wanted their ships to go.

General Electric, a once-stodgy smoke-stack company, with old-fashioned products and ways of doing business, became an industry pacemaker and trend-setter for numerous consumer products. Jack Welch, GE's leader, had a precise vision for GE.

RCA, unlike GE (which later acquired RCA), envisioned a different future and downsized to more familiar consumer electronics, while shedding unrelated companies that dragged it down. RCA also knew exactly where it wanted to go.

General Electric and RCA are different companies with different problems, that turned around in different ways. They still shared a vision of what they must become. Companies seldom stumble into a better future.

113

note: Corporate transformations aren't always radical. Minor modifications may do. Good turnaround objectives are often mundane. For example, a stagnant New Hampshire wood-burning stove manufacturer carefully grouped five objectives into a clear, three-year mission:

- Double sales in the midwestern states from $2 million to $4 million a year.

- Finance growth only from profits.

- Increase plant utilization from 70 to 90 percent.

- Reduce payroll from 12 to 9 percent of sales.

- Go from break-even this year to 6 percent profit next year and 8 percent in year three.

This entrepreneur knew exactly where he wanted to take his company.

E-Z TIP Notice how marketing, financial, operational and cost-reduction objectives are neatly rolled into one coordinated blueprint.

STRATEGY Your corporate objectives must be a target that you and your employees can shoot for. Turnaround targets must be singular and specific, not platitudes or generalizations. Specific results must be achieved—so make your objectives measurable. Set deadlines for achievement.

Good turnaround objectives are also simple. Complex, ponderous objectives don't work. MBAs may author 300-page strategic plans that few understand and fewer can implement. If your turnaround objectives are too complicated your employees won't understand them.

Unrealistic turnaround objectives also are worthless. Keep your objectives financially and operationally achievable, considering its rocky track record and limited resources. Overly ambitious turnaround objectives fail. Prioritize objectives. An insolvent company losing money must improve

Chapter 6

profitability and become solvent. But which is most important? Which problem should you tackle first?

With changing circumstances, reshape your objectives. Those involved in your business will have competing objectives, so your nervous system will go through the wringer as

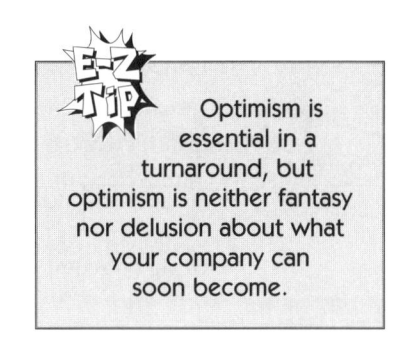

> **E-Z TIP**
> Optimism is essential in a turnaround, but optimism is neither fantasy nor delusion about what your company can soon become.

you try to mesh these varied objectives. So don't define your objectives in a vacuum. Diplomacy may force you to publicize one agenda and secretly work another. Reduce conflict. Set long-term objectives first. You can work back to short-term objectives. Interchange, feedback and fine-tuning will keep your objectives on target and in-sync with those involved in your workout.

> **note:** Owners are visionaries, employees pragmatists. Good objectives need both.

Top managers, who don't easily see the forest for the trees, are more likely to set unworkable, ill-conceived objectives. Employees may more accurately assess the corporate condition and its future.

Your objectives must be your own, but you must sell your plan to lenders and creditors with different objectives. Weak managers have turnaround objectives set by their lenders, creditors, suppliers, distributors and customers. Each adds a piece to the jigsaw puzzle, but you must piece together a total picture.

Action Step #2: Plan the right strategies

How will you turn your business into a debt-free money machine?

- Shutter losing activities?
- Cut costly programs?

115

- Undertake new marketing?

- Develop new procedures?

- Merge with another company?

- Grow by acquiring new companies?

- Shrink operations?

During the emergency stage, you improve cash flow and cut costs. Once stabilized, you plan for profits and restructured debts. You consider new acquisitions and new products or more aggressively market. These are strategies of opportunity, not the strategies for survival.

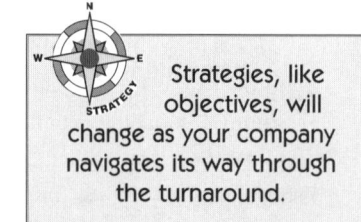

> Strategies, like objectives, will change as your company navigates its way through the turnaround.

You must overcome three obstacles to good strategic planning: **First,** sound strategies demand accurate short- and long-term financial forecasts. Without dependable financials, strategic plans can't be monitored. Incorrect strategies usually the come from faulty financial assumptions.

Second, your strategies may be too rigid. Quickly adapt to the rapidly changing corporate condition. Sound turnaround strategies are flexible, adaptive and reactive. Stay loose. You can't anticipate every unexpected bend in the road.

Third, strategies, like objectives, may be unrealistic. While objectives tell you where you want to go, strategies suggest how to get there. Coordinate the two. For instance, a goal to double the company's size is useless without a strategy to raise the necessary funds.

Objectives and strategies must match what you can afford. Distressed companies don't generate cash more quickly. A strategic plan that depends on

Chapter 6

serious cash carries a presumption of faulty thinking. Strategies also mirror personalities. Some troubled companies are run by dare-devils anxious to risk the corporate jewels on one bold turnaround gamble. These adventurers "atomize and synthesize." Others are "fix-'em, close-'em or sell-'em" strategists. The turnaround style becomes the style of its leader. You have your own style and risk level. You must be comfortable with your strategic moves. Stay loyal to your inner feelings.

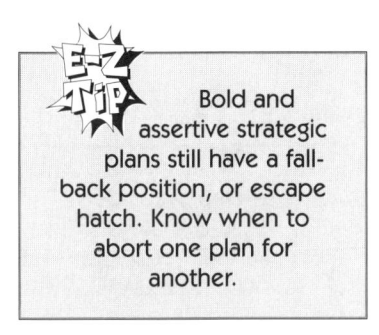

> **E-Z TIP:** Bold and assertive strategic plans still have a fall-back position, or escape hatch. Know when to abort one plan for another.

Don't expect to achieve every goal or to accomplish them on schedule. Turnarounds never travel straight lines without pauses and spurts. Prepare for what is, not for what was supposed to be.

Planning becomes bedraggled when you believe in the infallibility of planning for its own sake. Business problems cannot be completely and objectively recognized, defined, analyzed and solved. Human brains don't function neatly.

HINT: Still, you must somehow define and arrange strategies. Keep it simple. Those around you will make decisions at different levels, at different times and from different perspectives.

Napoleon said, "Unhappy is the general who comes on the field of battle with a system." Napoleon knew its importance.

Action Step #3: Implement change correctly

To implement your turnaround plan, watch four points:

1) What will be done?

2) Who will do what?

117

3) How will it be accomplished?

4) When will it be completed?

Organize your company for the task. Large corporations appoint squads to orchestrate different aspects of their turnarounds, which need close coordination if turnaround decisions are to mesh well with everyday operations. Everybody must know his job.

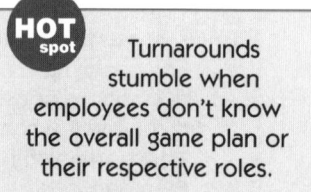

> **HOT spot** Turnarounds stumble when employees don't know the overall game plan or their respective roles.

Implementation requires strong management control. Employees won't always know how to transform broad goals into practice which goes against routine procedures. The old ways may have been the wrong ways. New procedures may be necessary to overcome obstacles and limited resources.

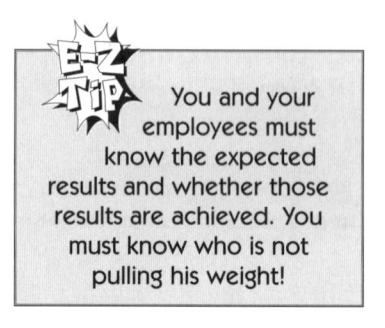

> **E-Z TIP** You and your employees must know the expected results and whether those results are achieved. You must know who is not pulling his weight!

Good communication makes your implementation program understandable, credible and appealing to your employees. Their commitment to achieve corporate objectives builds when you clearly explain the process and the purpose behind each action. Pinpoint responsibility. Who is responsible for each turnaround activity?

Set quantifiable standards to measure employee performance and your own. Delegating is vital in a turnaround, where responsibilities shift and authorities blur. Without strict accountability, planning and implementation become only gestures in the right direction.

Avoid sweeping changes your company is not prepared for. Move slowly but deliberately with small steps, not quantum leaps.

Employees won't understand what you expect unless you communicate. You will then see any potential problems they may foresee and possible alternatives. Building a house needs an architect, a builder and a carpenter working from the same blueprint.

Your employees also need the resources for the job. But, passive or hostile employees sabotage turnarounds by demanding unessential or unobtainable resources. Discuss needs and what you can and cannot deliver. Enthusiastic, motivated employees innovate—particularly if you innovate! Apathetic employees find excuses and reasons for poor performance. Change these employees. But you still must control this change if your firm is to go from here to there. "Here" is one set of operating circumstances. "There" is another set. This is how you make good things happen to a bad company.

> **EZ TIP:** The resources you need depend on your employees' attitudes.

Implementation takes commitment

Don't get sidetracked, which happens when:

- You don't have enough time to do everything and ignore the critical tasks.

- You get buried in day-to-day problems and lose sight of your overall agenda.

- Your priorities and problems constantly change and your plan loses substance.

Focus first on cash flow

1) Identify every turnaround task.

2) Determine the importance of each.

3) Develop workable action plans for each.

4) Commit everyone to completion dates.

Action Step #4: Monitor the plan

Workouts are change-sensitive. Constant, detailed feedback alerts you to new threats and opportunities. Swiftly and decisively modify plans when you are steered in the wrong direction.

Quantify turnaround objectives. A turnaround plan is useless if you can't accurately track performance and recovery.

> **E-Z TIP:** Numbers provide greater control, because you can objectively compare performance against results.

Start with weekly sales reports, cash flow, major controllable expenses and purchases. Obtain daily reports if you are in deep crisis. Don't get too much information—only the few essential indicators. For instance, a manufacturing firm knows its situation if it knows its break-even point and the orders shipped and in-process.

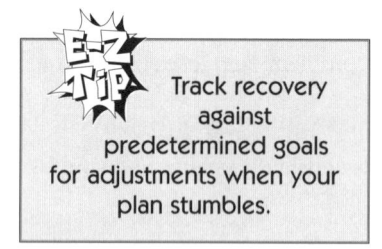

> **E-Z TIP:** Track recovery against predetermined goals for adjustments when your plan stumbles.

Successful turnaround pros can track corporate progress on the back of an envelope. They find simplicity a virtue.

Don't measure performance and progress by your financials alone. Physical measures, such as units of sale, orders received and units produced, may be quicker, and more accurate. Set realistic benchmarks. You must know what you expect from your business next week, next month and next year.

Chapter 6

Checkpoint

1) What factors will most influence your turnaround strategy?

2) Do you have the resources needed to get your business out of trouble?

3) What are your turnaround objectives?

4) How can you best implement a turnaround plan for your organization?

Cat-scanning your business

7

Chapter 7
Cat-scanning your business

Legendary turnaround leaders supposedly can measure the corporate pulse even before they walk in the door. They grasp the problems, magically produce solutions to seemingly hopeless situations and as magically create a thriving enterprise. With turnaround veterans, evaluating a business is largely instinctive. Experienced corporate doctors who have walked through the doors of hundreds of troubled companies can instinctively tell what a bad company is all about. Instinct is valuable when time counts and your company is badly hemorrhaging.

Larger, more stable companies may require months of detailed analysis, but no crippled corporation can afford to linger over endless reports.

> **HOT spot** A company in crisis can't delay an evaluation.

Do not survey your business only at the beginning of the turnaround—make it continuous. How severe is your crisis? Is your company heading for cardiac arrest or recovery? How can the debt be restructured and what will the balance sheet look like at the end of the turnaround. More time will be necessary to make your business profitable. Some businesses never find the answer. Nor should you concentrate on profits early in the turnaround. Your objectives, then, are mainly to stay afloat and stabilize your business.

There is no one correct way to survey a sick business. It largely depends on who is examining the business and why. You are interested in your business' long-term prospects. Your creditors want to know whether your company will pay its debts. Your secured lenders have concern with their collateral. Your suppliers want to know whether you will pay future bills. Employees question whether you will downsize and cut jobs and salaries. Your stockholders worry about investment. Their one common objective, although for different reasons, is for your company to survive.

> **HINT:** Each group has different objectives and perspectives, so expect different conclusions about what can and should be done.

Fact-finding

Gather essential information. This information depends on the size and nature of your business, the cause and gravity of your problems and its apparent condition. Correct information gives you each piece of the overall puzzle.

note — You must piece the puzzle together. You may produce data never before compiled and implement controls you never thought necessary. You may get your first real look at your own business. The right information is more important than extensive information. You can get a quick fix with remarkably little information. Detailed information can come later.

Start with basic financial information: Balance sheet and profit-and-loss for three years. Also important is a monthly cash flow statement for the year ahead. Even scant financial and operating information must be current and accurate, and forecasts and projections realistic.

Key managers, employees, suppliers, creditors and customers can be sources of information. Each contributes a perspective of your company's strengths and weaknesses, with valuable insights beyond the financial statements and operating data.

Inspect the condition of inventory, fixtures, equipment and general housekeeping to get a "feel" for the situation. No company is accurately measured from an office.

> **E-Z TIP**
> Turnaround leaders kick tires!

Survey your staying power

The information must reveal the extent and urgency of your crisis and how rapidly and forcefully you must financially stabilize it.

The two most serious threats are:

1) Inadequate cash to continue operations

2) Creditor actions that threaten the company

Finding these problems usually takes a little detective work. Most companies tackle their problems only when creditors threaten bankruptcy, a lender forecloses or a tax agency padlocks the business.

While a troubled company can ordinarily block creditors, serious cash-flow problems are another matter. You must answer three vital questions:

1) What is your company's present cash position?

2) When will your company run out of money?

3) How can you raise money quickly to stay afloat?

In Chapter 8, I reveal many often-overlooked ways to raise cash, but the threshold question is whether your company can stabilize to rebuild, solve its creditor problems and become profitable. Make this quick prognosis before you decide whether you should attempt recovery.

You may answer these questions based on assumptions that may not be correct. You may assume certain sales next month, but can you rely on those sales? All planning and forecasting is "blue sky." Planning ahead, even a few months, is blue sky, although banks and other creditors still demand five year projections hardly worth their paper.

When you manage for profits, you must reorient to manage for cash flow. But when you're in trouble, go for cash flow—even if it produces less profits. Devise an alarm system for a future cash-flow crisis. Include a weekly or bi-weekly cash plan and daily reports against the plans. Can your business stay afloat? Even when the situation looks bleak, plan ahead. Once you are in the turnaround, you will find many opportunities to ease the cash crunch.

Survey for gold

To stabilize your business, protect its "vein of gold"—core assets and activities that are profit generators, and the foundation upon which to rebuild. They are your winners, not your losers.

Your short- and long-term plan must preserve your vein of gold, which may be a small, uninteresting part of your business. Dart Industries with sizable losses from its retail-drug (Rexall), real-estate and cosmetic divisions, counted on its tiny, but profitable, Tupperware division to rebuild. Penn Central railroads turned to the net worth and stability of its valuable Manhattan properties to rescue its long-ailing railroads. Continental Airlines' rescue came from rapidly identifying and preserving its most profitable air routes.

note — You may scour heaps of detailed financial and operating data before you understand what produces your profits and losses.

You may not have a vein of gold, that one definable business unit, product or activity that can stand apart as a future moneymaker. Small retail stores and service companies, as simple, unified organizations, cannot easily divide themselves into winners and losers.

Or, your vein of gold may have been forever destroyed. A company without a vein of gold has no potential and nothing worth saving. You won't understand your company unless you understand its strengths and weaknesses. Find the strengths. Preserve them.

Survey your financials

Numbers are concrete, unemotional and detached, and let you navigate accurately and objectively. Crunch numbers!

Start with 3 years of profit-and-loss statements:

- What is your break-even point?
- How far below or above break-even are you operating?
- What can your break-even point be reduced to? How quickly?
- What are your overall sales trends? By product? Line? Division?
- What are your margin trends? Expense trends?
- What factors caused your losses?
- What profits come from each product? Line? Division?
- Who are your biggest customers?

Don't focus on your profit-and-loss statement during the emergency stage. Only identify where and how much you are losing to shut down major cash drains. You can fine tune products when the company is stabilized and you can think about profits. Separating your winners from your losers demands precise, accurate income statements by company, division, product line or plant. With one identifiable cause for your losses, you fix what's broken.

A multi-problem company cannot initially do more with its profit-and-loss statement than to find significant ways to reduce expenses, without seriously affecting the business. Computerized financial models can help you project your bottom line under various scenarios. Income-statement manipulation is back-to-basics management to make money from your business.

Balance-sheet trends for the past three years show your financial strength from a different perspective:

- Are fixed assets valued accurately?

- Are accounts receivable verified and accurate?

- Do accounts receivable collections depend upon contract completions or continued business operations?

- Is the inventory accurate?

- Are the inventories salable, obsolete or slow moving?

- Are there valuable patents, trademarks, copyrights or other intangible assets?

- What assets are leased or financed?

- What equipment can be sold?

- What assets are unessential and can be sold?

- What is the amount and aging of each trade obligation?

Chapter 7

- Will slow-payment or non-payment of trade obligations affect continued supply?

- Do trade obligations need restructuring?

- How are overdue payables handled?

- What are the past-due tax obligations?

- What tax collections are threatened?

- Are secured debts and leases current or in default?

- Is foreclosure or repossession threatened on any secured or leased equipment?

- What is owed to pension plans?

- How insolvent is the firm?

- How illiquid is the firm?

CAUTION Uncover your dirty financial linen. You may find overvalued assets, obsolete inventories or capitalized expenses improperly valued to hide larger losses. The liabilities may include understated payables, unlisted contingent or disputed liabilities. Make your balance sheet tell the true story!

During the crisis stage determine whether you have primarily a profitability problem (requiring strategic restructuring), an insolvency problem (requiring debt restructuring), or both. Your liquidity should be short-term concern. Build cash reserves. Turn receivables, inventory and equipment into cash to keep operating.

Manufacturers and businesses with capital tied up in the plant and equipment must turn unproductive capital assets into cash operations.

129

Investigate:

- your present plant capacity

- your present and projected utilization of plant and equipment

- plant or equipment you can sell without hurting present or future sales or profits

- improvements or upgrades that can produce greater efficiency and productivity

A casual glance at your balance sheet will tell whether you need debt-restructuring. Yet, a business with liabilities two or three times its assets may be in no immediate danger if its creditors are patient. Look beyond the numbers to foresee immediate danger and threat.

Examine cash, receivables and inventory. Do you have sufficient current assets to maintain sales and positive cash flow? Excess debt can always be reduced, but assets cannot always be increased. Focus on one question—how can you transfer your assets and liabilities to stay afloat? That's what counts! Many ratios, comparisons and tests can help you fine tune your analysis. But you will know where you are going within five minutes, if you know what to look for! Or, hire a good accountant or turnaround consultant to make sense of the numbers. Your cash-flow statement is key. It can forecast whether you will have necessary operating funds for short-term survival.

> **HOT spot** You can lose money, be insolvent and still survive. But, you can't run out of money and survive.

Cash-flow analysis answers one central question: Does your company have the financial strength and stability to survive a workout?

Chapter 7

Survey your organization

Cat-scan your business from the top with a basic organizational survey:

- What is the organizational chart? What organizational changes have occurred in the past three years?

- What is the detailed job description for each executive?

- What is the composition of the board? How often does it meet?

- How active is it in managing the company?

- What are the staffing levels in each department?

- What are the line and staff relationships within the organization?

- Is management centralized or decentralized?

- What changes in the organization are necessary to carry out the turnaround?

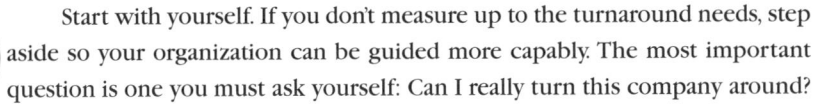

HINT: Start with yourself. If you don't measure up to the turnaround needs, step aside so your organization can be guided more capably. The most important question is one you must ask yourself: Can I really turn this company around?

If you won't honestly and objectively evaluate your own capabilities and performance, you won't honestly evaluate your employees. Even when you understand your shortcomings, you may not understand what the turnaround demands. It's not whether your employees can do their jobs, but whether they can perform significantly better. Improving results is never easy within a workout. Employees can also be judged too harshly. Replacements then arise arbitrarily. Junk the "yes men," who always agree. You can't afford them. You need free thinkers.

Hold candid, face-to-face meetings to evaluate key managers and employees. Deep-rooted employee problems include:

- high employee turnover
- recruiting problems
- employee theft
- employee protests or grievances
- poor morale
- reduced productivity

Employers must think twice before axing people, so you must assess not only each employee, but whether you can freely make changes.

- Will firings bring unfair dismissal or discrimination suits?
- Is there a union? Will the union cooperate or be hostile?
- What employment contracts are outstanding?
- What employees possess special knowledge, relationships or unique skills critical to the workout?

Meet with as many key employees as possible to answer one question: Are there the people on board that can put the business back together again? Several good employees are better than many mediocre ones.

You won't always have the time to hire and train new people. You may be too tired or stressed to build a new team; and you need people to lean on, not people who must lean on you to learn their jobs. Yet, people aren't numbers on a financial statement. A quick judgment is not always accurate.

A demoralized crew may spring to life through new leadership or be invigorated by the turnaround process. Employees who look strong may fall down on the job. Some will take advantage of the situation. You need competent and trustworthy employees, and it's tough to find these attributes. Unless you are an extremely good judge of people, you will have your disappointments.

Survey your competitiveness

To evaluate your company's competitive position, know where your company is now, and where it is likely to go. You ask whether your company has a future? Companies that never left the ground must decide if their business concept can work. It can. Just because a company never made money doesn't mean it can't. Many small, young startups have sound, even exciting and brilliant business concepts, but suffer problems most young companies face: A good business idea entangled in a badly designed or poorly managed business. Don't throw your baby out with the bath water. Evaluate not only your company but each product and service.

The mature company has no less of a challenge. There are many reasons for marketing slips but also countless strategies to regain competitiveness.

- Do you have a well-defined market niche?
- Do you follow industry trends?
- Can your company easily change and adapt?
- Who are its key customers?
- How profitable is each customer?
- Are relationships good with key accounts?
- Do others within your industry share your problems?

- Why are sales or market share shrinking?
- What products or lines are declining?
- What products sell well?
- Who are your key competitors? What are their advantages?

Carefully analyze each product, channel of distribution, end-user customer group and market area. You may see dismal innovation in new products, markets, promotions and other strategies. Also examine your company's marketing:

- What's your marketing strategy?
- Measure your marketing results. How can you improve those results?

A thorough product analysis helps you examine what you now sell and what you should sell. Downsizing through product elimination is common in a workout, when you must concentrate on those that produce cash. Companies with uncontrolled product proliferation can get into trouble.

- Which products or services produce your largest profits?
- Which products or services have the greatest growth potential?
- Which ones only tie up capital or lose money?

Survey your legal position

Most turnarounds create a legal maze that must be untangled early.

- Does your business have multiple entities?
- Can you protect the healthy entities from the sick entities?

Chapter 7

- What litigation disrupts the business? Is foreclosure, seizure or repossession of key assets an immediate threat?

- Is there current or potential litigation from shareholders, franchisees, customers or the government?

- Does the company have major claims against others? Can they be resolved quickly to raise cash to rehabilitate the company?

- What contracts or affiliations limit the workout strategy?

- How will outstanding warranties and service contracts be handled?

- What regulations or laws limit turnaround options?

- What other legal factors influence the workout strategy (such as whether Chapter 11 or a non-bankruptcy workout will work best)?

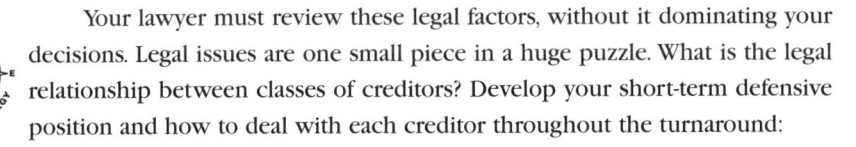

Your lawyer must review these legal factors, without it dominating your decisions. Legal issues are one small piece in a huge puzzle. What is the legal relationship between classes of creditors? Develop your short-term defensive position and how to deal with each creditor throughout the turnaround:

- Who are the major and essential suppliers?

- What debts are disputed?

- Are secured debts duly perfected?

- What payments within the past 90 days may be recovered in a bankruptcy preference?

- What debt has the company guaranteed? Have affiliated companies guaranteed company debts?

- What setoffs can be applied against debts?

- What are the loan renewal or expiration dates?
- What credit is available?
- What loans are in default?

note: Troubled businesses often become delinquent in their tax obligations (i.e. withholding tax, unemployment tax, sales tax, meal or room tax, etc.) owed the IRS, the state or the other local taxing authorities.

- Can tax arrears be rapidly paid from cash flow?
- Will existing or threatened tax liens impede a reorganization?
- Are there threatened seizures of the business by any tax agencies?

Also survey your leases:

- What is the remaining length of each lease?
- How important is each lease? Which can be terminated?
- Are important leases in default? Can they be cured?

Politics influence the outcome of a turnaround. Every business has a place within the community. Some are strongly supported because of community ties. Others are encouraged to close shop. Chrysler's workout was politics. Tens of thousands of less-known firms play political games. Is your company a small defense contractor? Minority-owned? Does it owe the government?

- Is your company a major employer?
- Does it supply important goods or services to the government?
- Do business groups or government agencies have special reason to support you?

Chapter 7

Answering the five big questions

You must synthesize the various surveys into an overall assessment and resolve these key issues:

1) How serious is the situation? Is your company critically ill?

2) How rapid is the downturn? How rapidly and forcefully must you start the turnaround?

3) What caused the downturn? Do the problems continue?

4) Does your company mostly need a strategic turnaround (profit improvement) or financial restructuring (debt reduction)? If you need both, which should you tackle first?

5) What are the major weaknesses and strengths? Can the business survive a turnaround? What weaknesses jeopardize it?

You must be in the corporate cockpit with one eye on your tailspin and the other anxiously scanning the instruments. Ask follow-up questions. Be skeptical. Never accept things at face value. Harold Geneen, former ITT chairman counsels: "Getting the facts—the unshakable facts—is one of the hardest parts of the turnaround." I will add, "It's always a bit harder to figure out what to do with the facts."

Checkpoint

1) How seriously ill is your business?

2) How rapidly and steadily is it failing?

3) What vein of gold must you protect?

137

4) What do your financials tell you about your business?

5) Are your employees an asset or liability?

6) How strong or weak is your competitive position? Can you effectively compete considering your handicaps?

7) What are your winning products or services? What are your losers?

8) What legal and political factors can you capitalize on? Which factors threaten you?

9) Can you spearhead the turnaround, or must someone else lead the charge?

26 ways to find quick cash

Chapter 8
26 ways to find quick cash

"Happiness is a positive cash flow." But it's more. Cash is your business' lifeblood. To stabilize your business, you must stop the cash drain and build cash reserves. Only cash lets you replenish inventory, advertise, promote and turn profitable sales. Only cash lets you bail out your debts. Cash is king, whether in a workout or a healthy company! Your business may fail, not because you can't become solvent or profitable, but because you can't stay afloat. When more cash goes out than comes in, you bleed to death.

Reverse events. Make more cash come into your business than goes out! You can't run on empty. Troubled businesses without cash become defensive. You no longer operate your business as you want, but as everyone else wants you to. Preoccupied with protecting yourself, you won't make money.

You must fight:

- Suppliers who tighten or eliminate credit, which drains cash reserves.

- Suppliers who demand override payments and charge higher prices, or take away valuable trade concessions.

- Lenders who boost their interest rates and shorten their terms.

- Creditors and lenders who push for faster payments.

Answer these three questions:

1) What can you do to immediately and significantly increase cash flow?

2) Which cash-raising actions will least hurt your business?

3) Which cash-raising actions can you best achieve?

Cash-Raiser Tip #1: Collect receivables

Every business has buried cash, even the poorest business. Where to look? Begin with your accounts receivable, which can produce the fastest cash. Don't let customers play with your money. Adopt a no-nonsense, aggressive collection policy. Antagonizing slow-paying customers is less important than getting your money. But first try positive motivators. Will a two-percent discount bring faster payment? Five percent? Talk to your customers. Give them deals to get them to write you a check, but don't appear desperate or customers may withhold payment, expecting to settle cheaply after you go bankrupt. When generous incentives don't succeed, immediately pursue collection. Forget collection agencies. Hire an aggressive collection lawyer to quickly sue and not waste time with collection letters.

> **E-Z TIP**: Make collecting overdue accounts everyone's responsibility, particularly sales staff and reps who best know your customer.

Cash-Raiser Tip #2: Sell receivables

Sell or factor your current receivables for quick cash. Factoring is a good cash-raiser when you have unencumbered receivables from solid business accounts. You will pay a factoring fee of six to eight percent. I turned $800,000 in receivables due a dress manufacturer into a fast $750,000. The $50,000 factor's fee was a big bargain, because the $750,000 rescued the dressmaker from certain bankruptcy.

You can factor receivables easier and faster than you can get an accounts receivable loan, because your financial condition is unimportant to a factor concerned only with the collectability of your receivables. Most factors prefer long-term arrangements, but you can find one-time factors. The Commercial Finance Association in New York has names of factors who routinely buy receivables from troubled companies.

Cash-Raiser Tip #3: Tighten credit

Avoid consumer charges. Use MasterCard, Visa and Amex. Every commercial account will buy C.O.D. for a better price. Ask your few key accounts. If they will, go C.O.D. for a one- or two-percent discount. Evaluate credit extended every customer. How profitable are they? How quickly do they pay? What are their long-term prospects? How can you get them to pay faster?

> Coax customers to buy for cash. Offer a small discount, or tighten your credit terms.

A credit policy must balance sales with cash flow, but unless you can comfortably finance your receivables, give cash flow top billing.

Cash-Raiser Tip #4: Trim inventory

Companies can easily mismanage inventories. How well do you control yours? Is your cash flow on your shelf or warehouse floor? Did you buy too heavily for extra discounts and bigger profits, but ignore turnover and cash flow? Slashing inventory is your

> If you are strangled with excess inventory, quickly sell it for a discount, even if you must dump it on a liquidator.

answer. Reducing inventory to free cash is only half the answer. Poor buying will keep you cash-starved unless you correct it. Adopt strict budgeting and rigid inventory controls. Liquidators buy merchandise of every type.

Cash-Raiser Tip #5: Dump idle equipment

Sell idle equipment, machinery or real estate for quick cash? Cash is also buried in fancy office furniture, fancy equipment or fancy cars. One insolvent publisher of children's books sat behind her lavish $8,000 marble desk. Her desk, designer lamps, oriental rugs and $200,000 in other nonsense trimmings are now history. She now sits behind a battered $50 metal desk—but with money in the bank. Dumping unessentials is essential for survival. Sell and leaseback essential equipment and real estate. Investors buy and lease back business assets for the tax benefits. One cash-starved plumbing-supply firm raised $165,000 through a sale-leaseback of its trucks to finance themselves out of Chapter 11.

An undercapitalized advertising firm unloaded little-used furniture for $80,000 and leased back a few essential items. The $80,000 paid their pressing bills and capitalized two profitable branch offices. Super-plush surroundings don't guarantee success. Money in the bank does!

Stroll through your business. What do you see? Computers? Manufacturing equipment? Cash registers? Airplanes? Bulldozers? What you're looking at is money!

Cash-Raiser Tip #6: Refinance

You may have equity or borrowing power in your assets. Refinance before your financial troubles destroy lending relationships and credit ratings. Conservative lenders consider credit and financial stability besides collateral; but even with severe financial problems, you may possibly squeeze more money from your assets.

With refinancing you fully encumber the equity in your assets, for a stronger bargaining position with general creditors and taxing agencies, who then have little or no equity to seize.

Cash-Raiser Tip #7: Exploit hidden assets

Can you sell or license your name? What about marketing rights?

> **HINT**: Your most valuable assets may be intangible product ideas, exciting technology or unique business methods which you can turn into cash.

An Indiana burglar-alarm company licensed its patented alarm system to an Arizona dealer for $70,000, and through nationwide licensing receives $850,000 a year in royalties from 32 licensees. Your imagination can open your mind and pocketbook to similar opportunities!

Time and time again, struggling, creative entrepreneurs turned intangible assets into great fortunes. Proprietary assets must be put to their highest and best use.

Cash-Raiser Tip #8: Tap pension plans

Employee pension plans have cash reserves, money you may legally borrow to get your business through the hard times. Companies routinely borrow from their pension funds. But move carefully, borrowing from your employees' pension accounts jeopardizes your employees' financial security. **CAUTION** This is not something to do without considering your responsibility to your long-loyal employees. You must have unshakable confidence you can repay the fund. Consult with your attorney and plan administrator. Pension law is complex, so you need good legal guidance.

Cash-Raiser Tip #9: Recoup detailed expenses

What pre-payments can you reclaim? Insurance is one cancelable prepaid expense that can get you a big refund check. A country-club membership was cancelled by a faltering commuter airline that couldn't afford to fuel its planes. The three-year, $15,000 prepaid membership had two remaining years, so $10,000 went back to their checking account. What prepaid expenses are not absolutely essential? What refund can you claim?

Cash-Raiser Tip #10: Rent idle space

What is idle space worth? A downsizing furniture manufacturer sublet 8,000 square feet of spare warehouse space for $80,000 annually—big money when you need pennies.

A cash-tight supermarket concessioned a tiny, high-traffic space, in each supermarket, to a branch bank for $100,000 advance rent. It's more than they ever earned from selling groceries. Swarms of bank customers now shop this supermarket. This same savvy supermarket operator leased his vacant basement to a local newspaper printer for another $40,000 a year. A Boston restaurateur shrewdly leased his high-visibility rooftop to a billboard company for $25,000 a year. Such cash-raising opportunities are tough to spot when you're in trouble, but unused, underutilized space is a potential cash-raiser.

> **E-Z Tip**
> Thousands of dollars can get into your empty coffers the day you sublet your idle space.

Troubled companies downsize products, employees, overhead and space! Give prospective tenants a 20-percent discount to prepay the first year's rent.

Cash-Raiser Tip #11 Coax cash from customers

Will your customers keep you afloat?

- A three-lawyer Philadelphia law firm sold prepaid legal services for $265,000.

- An enterprising Chattanooga druggist gave his customers 30-percent discount on their prescriptions if they joined his Golden Key Discount Prescription Program. He put $38,000 in the bank and boosted his prescription sales 40 percent.

- A Seattle movie theater peddled $165,000 in movie tickets through a "one-free-with-10" special. No-frills airlines hawk tickets the same way.

Cash-Raiser Tip # 12: Raise prices

You've probably cut prices to generate more business. That's usually the wrong direction.

Which products or services are least price-sensitive? When did you last increase price? If you need a big price increase to survive, then go for it. You may need higher prices to make the game worthwhile. Let your instincts and the economics of your situation—not what your competitors charge—dictate your prices. Competitors aren't always right.

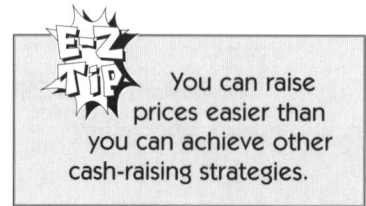

> **E-Z TIP:** You can raise prices easier than you can achieve other cash-raising strategies.

Camouflage price increases. Or give your products or services more perceived value than your competition's products. Charge for extra services and extended warranties. Push frills before you hike product prices.

Increase list price to consumers, but give bigger trade discounts to dealers and distributors. This encourages wider product distribution and maximizes sales potential.

Cash-Raiser Tip #13: Sell something

Selling brings in the fastest money. Troubled companies are often companies that can't sell. Concentrate on your most profitable products and largest customers. Limited time and resources make you prioritize on what will produce the fastest dollars. Give your salespeople incentives that tie performance to rewards. Pay commissions on additional sales. Reprogram your sales force. Push sales reps who only call on old, familiar accounts to land new, less friendly prospects. Replace salespeople and redefine territories, let your best sales people sell your most important accounts.

What other products or services can you sell? What upgrades would your customers buy? Can your sales reps carry complementary, non-competitive lines? Can you hold customers with special prices so you're guaranteed their next order? What special deals will they buy right now? A 10-percent greater selling effort may give you more than 10 percent income. Would that help your cash flow?

Penny-ante management

Every type and size business—whether a shoestring home-based venture or corporate giant—must slim down to shape up. How you spend is critical to cash flow. You cannot easily control income, but you can control expenditures. So cost-cutting is your surest, fastest route to stability.

> **HOT spot** Hunting cash is only one way to build your bank account. Cutting costs is another.

Companies usually slenderize only when their corporate flab becomes too noticeable. With smart organizations, cost-cutting is not a knee-jerk

147

reaction to poor profits, but a way of life. They realize watching costs only when business is bad is a recipe for bankruptcy. Cost-cutting can permanently and dramatically change how you do business. When you need profits and cash, you must lower your break-even point. Improving productivity, buying smarter, traveling more frugally and operating with fewer people are roads leading in the same direction. Cutting costs means getting more for your money—whether in accounting fees or copying costs. Turnaround businesses downsize to lower expenses, and belt-tighten the expenses they do have. Cost-cutting forces change, so expect resistance and opposition.

Sudden, tight-fisted policies are traumatic in lax companies. Unless handled correctly, they can cause less productivity and destroy employee morale. Counteract potential problems by getting your employees involved. Explain why cost-cutting is vital, and define new priorities. You won't salve all wounds from scrapped projects or fired employees, but your people will at least understand your reasons.

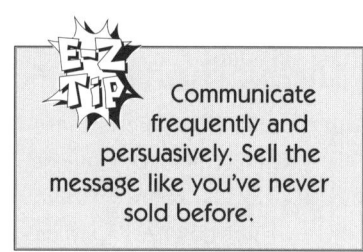

> **E-Z TIP:** Communicate frequently and persuasively. Sell the message like you've never sold before.

Every good cost-cutting program follows five steps:

1) Set specific cost-cutting goals (i.e. 20-percent). Set goals by department and for the entire organization.

2) Challenge every expenditure. Never assume you can't squeeze more savings.

3) Identify all areas in which you can cut costs.

4) Implement cost-cutting immediately. Don't procrastinate!

5) Follow up continuously on each cost-cutting measure to assess its impact upon your business. Cost-cutting must be continual.

Chapter 8

Cost reduction fails when you're weak-fisted. Stay tight-fisted. It's not what you do, but the extent to which you do it. Tweaking knobs won't save your business. Corporate graveyards are littered with dead companies that cut payrolls 10-percent when a 40-percent was needed. Survivors trim all the fat!

Try zero-based budgeting. Historical expenses don't tell you what to spend this year. A zero-based budget will answer three important questions:

1) Should we be involved in this activity?

2) Do we spend too much to perform this activity?

3) How much should it cost?

Cash-Raiser Tip #14: Shrink shrinkage

Theft, scrap and obsolescence can cause double-digit losses. Business owners can see huge profit jumps when they control shrinkage. If you can't stop your thieves, call in security pros who can. Their new computerized control systems can detect leaks effectively.

> ⚠ **CAUTION** Don't totally trust check expense records, invoices, purchase orders and other paper trails to tell you what's happening. Pay closer attention.

A supermarket chain plagued with losses in one of its stores discovered that its manager had added his own personal "extra" checkout, which funneled about 10-percent of the store's huge sales directly into his own pockets. They discovered this only on their third store inspection. Are your profits going out the door?

Cash-Raiser Tip #15: Buy better

You make money buying, not selling. Well-run companies demand the absolute lowest price and best deal from every supplier! When did you last hit

149

your suppliers? When did you last get competitive bids? How do you know you have your best possible deal?

Once you have your best price, try to beat it by another 5-percent. Bargain everything: Stationery, printing, freight, hotel rooms. Savings mount quickly, and you can usually haggle lower prices to create extra dollars.

> **E-Z TIP:** Sloppy buying costs you daily. Check new suppliers for new prices.

Cash-Raiser Tip #16: Rethink your products

Are you a manufacturer? Can you reduce material costs by reducing scrap or using less material to make your product?

A kitchenware manufacturer found out almost too late that he could easily substitute cheaper aluminum for copper on his kitchenware products. He used copper since he started in business, but would have another $1.5 million in his bank account, or four times what he now owes creditors, had he switched to aluminum!

Rethink every product. Can you use less expensive components? Would re-engineered production cut scrap and waste?

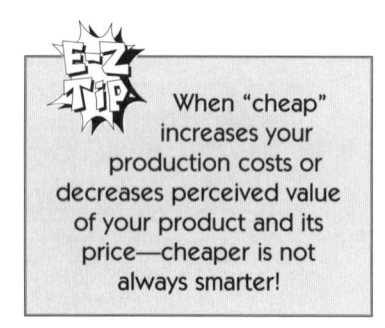

> **E-Z TIP:** When "cheap" increases your production costs or decreases perceived value of your product and its price—cheaper is not always smarter!

Cash-Raiser Tip # 17: Slash payroll

I cannot recall one troubled company where payroll could not be reduced 10-percent. Wouldn't a 10-percent payroll cut help your cash flow?

If you don't think you have a flabby payroll, you are contradicting Parkinson's Law: Work automatically expands to occupy these people to do it. The quickest, most common way to cut payroll is through layoffs. How much

Chapter 8

can you cut? Figure your labor costs as a percentage of sales. How do they compare to industry averages? What should they be following zero-based budgeting and strict job justification?

Don't hatchet good employees needlessly.

- encourage voluntary resignations, no-hirings and early retirements

- eliminate or reduce overtime

- reschedule work and paid vacations

- make full-time employees part-time, cut bonuses and benefits and reduce salaries

Understand the implications of every payroll-cutting strategy. Let your employees know your cost-cutting goals (in dollars and cents) and the alternatives you considered. Employees will endure great hardships if they see the hardships as necessary, and your policies fair and equitable. But they also want a light at the end of the tunnel, when they can again receive their just rewards.

Do you want more manpower for less money?

- Use temps to even out peaks and valleys. You'll pay more per hour, but have lower overall costs. You can't afford full-timers with too little work to keep them steadily and profitably busy.

- Hire apprentices and senior citizens—today's best labor buys! The young are anxious to learn. Senior citizens have experience, a strong work ethic and often work for less.

- Leasing employees cuts expensive fringe benefits. Employee-leasing companies in your area may save 10- to 15-percent by eliminating employee perks. You also avoid falling behind on your withholding taxes.

151

- Cut pension costs—use less costly alternatives: 401K plans and SEP or SARSEP programs. Age-weight your pension plan. Review these ideas with your pension advisor.

Cash-Raiser Tip #18: Slim down your own paycheck

If you run a multi-million-dollar business, you may not think saving your company a few bucks by reducing your own salary will count. Those few dollars may not be monetarily critical, but it's symbolic. When the boss won't sacrifice, why should his employees?

> **HOT spot** Sacrifice must start at the top. Before you cut your employees' paychecks, cut your own.

Greedy owners drain their businesses without caring what their business can afford to pay them. And it's an easy trap to fall into. A first-time owner swaps a $250-a-week job for a business with a $5,000 weekly cash flow. When you've never before had your hands on $5,000, it's tempting!

> *note* Your paycheck reveals your determination to save your business.

Sal's music store grossed a healthy $600,000, but had enough expenses to lose $68,000 (Sal's $50,000 salary, and another $30,000 off the books). Sal's wife drew $25,000, and seldom worked. What did Sal give his business in return?

Cash-Raiser Tip #19: Cancel perks

Chauffeur-driven limousines, wasteful "business" trips to strange, exotic lands where business is never conducted, lavish restaurants and hotels, personal magazine subscriptions or roses to the wife or girlfriend—all are business destroyers.

Playing the expense account game is okay when you make money, but not when you must hunker down. When you trade in your Caddy for a used Chevy, people will take you seriously. Until then, you're only the emperor without clothes. Eventually you will have no kingdom.

Cash-Raiser Tip #20: Talk to your landlord

Negotiate for rent! With rent 5-percent of sales, a one-third rent reduction boosts profitability nearly 2-percent. That's money! Troubled companies can sometimes negotiate dynamite rent concessions, as some recent successes prove:

- A large Denver software firm reduced rent $70,000 in a two-year workout.

- A struggling Boston floral wholesaler won a 25-percent-rent reduction ($60,000-a-year).

- A Boca Raton dance studio slashed $12,000 a year from its $30,000 lease.

Landlords aren't charities, but do lower rents when they have little negotiating power and fear that you will otherwise move out or go bankrupt, leaving them an empty space and no rent.

Take advantage of plummeting real-estate prices or your once-desirable commercial space will beg for tenants.

> **HINT:** You have bargaining power if you pay a high rent and your landlord has no prospective tenants who will pay what you pay.

Does your landlord have vacant space? Does he rent for less than you now pay? If you can't cut your rent, can you cut your space? A business-forms publisher downsized from 40,000 square feet to 30,000 square feet simply by rearranging storage racks, and saved $80,000 a year! Will your landlord let you sublet idle space? Can you avoid "soft" costs, such as merchants' association advertising? Can you reduce property taxes or insurance? Your landlord is only another supplier, and a lease can be revised to what you can afford to pay.

Cash-Raiser Tip #21: Stop insurance waste

Buy insurance to protect your equity in the business, not your creditors! When you are insolvent, and have little or no equity to protect, cancel product liability and public-liability (premises) insurance and other liability policies. You are now insolvent and judgment-proof.

Review your insurance coverage with other agents. Buy only the insurance you absolutely need to cut insurance costs.

- You can save up to 40-percent on employee health and disability policies by following a few simple safety procedures.

- Buy insurance cheaper through your trade or professional association, or Chamber of Commerce.

- Disability policies, an expensive type of insurance, can be dramatically reduced by extending the benefit waiting period to 90 days.

- A risk-management firm can survey your company for more ways to reduce liability and insurance premiums.

- Shop employee-health plans. Premiums vary by 50-percent. HMOs usually offer the best rates.

- Review your coverage. What does it cost? Do you really need it? How can you save money on it? Cancel unnecessary or overlapping coverages. Accept higher deductibles. Check premiums with other insurance companies.

Cash-Raiser Tip #22: Slash professional fees

note — Lawyers and accountants pillage and plunder bank accounts when you are in trouble.

Even healthy companies go broke from insane legal fees. You need good lawyers and accountants in a workout, but giving your cash to these professionals is not the way to save your business.

Bid legal and accounting work. Handle whatever you can yourself. Hire a law student for routine work. Avoid all litigation. Lawsuits are insanely expensive. If you must defend a lawsuit, hire a lawyer who will handle the case economically.

Demand detailed billing, and question suspicious costs. Some professionals pad their bills. Review each charge. Was it necessary? Is it reasonable? Could it have been handled by someone less expensive within the firm?

Arbitration, mediation and other litigation alternatives produce faster, cheaper and less stressful results. Write arbitration clauses into your contracts.

Don't overuse your professionals. Call your professionals sparingly. Time is money—right out of your pocket!

Cash-Raiser Tip #23: Save banking and finance charges

Banking is competitive, so shop banking services as you do other products and services to shave banking costs!

- Look for discounted or free banking services such as free or low-cost checking, free advice seminars, payroll services, cash "sweeps" to interest-bearing accounts and phone transfers.

- Negotiate lower interest loans as your company's performance improves and your loan status is less shaky.

Cash-Raiser Tip #24: Tackle travel and entertainment costs

You can frequently cut T&E 50 percent without losing a sale.

- Challenge every trip. Is it necessary? Can you use correspondence, telephone or teleconferencing? Few business deals require face-to-face meetings.

> Travel and entertainment costs are the most controllable costs.

- Can fewer people travel? Can you arrange trips more economically? Would multi-city trips avoid individual trips?

- Abolish expensive last-minute travel. Arrange Saturday night stayovers. Know the tricks when you travel, or get a travel agent who does.

- Traveling lean and mean on shoestring budget means you travel coach, sleep in budget motels and drive economy cars. You eat, not dine.

- Negotiate deals. Hunt bargains. A good travel club can save you money. Negotiate your own deal if you can do better. For instance, hotels routinely give 50-percent discounts if you book large groups or use them frequently. But you must ask.

Chapter 8

Cash-Raiser Tip #25: Economize on advertising and marketing

How much of your advertising and marketing budget is wasted? Economize without weakening your marketing clout. Become a sharper marketer by spending only on marketing that works for you.

- If you spend over $1,000 a year on Yellow Page advertising, read Barry Maber's *Getting the Most from Your Yellow Page Advertising* (AMACOM). It's jam-packed with good suggestions for bigger results from fewer dollars.

- Can your suppliers help you with ad costs? Co-op ad deals between manufacturers and dealers are common.

- Exhibit at trade shows? Test their value. Most trade shows give a poor return on investment. Choose trade shows carefully. Rent smaller booths with fewer frills, and spend more on pre-show publicity.

- Monitor each ad for results. Find out where your business is coming from.

- Your own in-house ad agency can save you 15-percent on your ad costs. It's practical if you spend even a few thousand dollars a year on advertising.

Cash-Raiser Tip #26: Call in the expense reduction pros

How many ways are there to save money? We only scratched the surface to sensitize you by pinpointing the few, more obvious opportunities.

Every expense has its own savings potential. While smaller expenses, such as telephone, delivery, postage and supplies, seem penny-ante, collectively they can waste enormous dollars. You won't know every trick to lower expenses, so you may be amazed to see how much money you can save following some simple strategies.

Nor should you become your own cost-reduction expert—you can hire these professionals. Expense-control experts scrutinize every expense, spot waste, and show you how to avoid it. These firms earn a percentage of what they save you.

Checkpoint

1) Can you collect your outstanding receivables faster?

2) What excess or idle inventory, equipment or real estate can you turn into cash?

3) What additional borrowing power do you have?

4) What hidden or intangible assets can you exploit for fast cash?

5) Do you have spare space to lease or sublet?

6) Can you coax your customers to prepay so their money is in your pocket today?

7) Can you raise prices slightly?

8) Can you sell more to more customers?

9) What must you trim to turn your flabby company into a lean-and-mean organization?

10) Do you need help achieving your cost-cutting goals?

How to jumpstart your employees and customers

Chapter 9
How to jumpstart your employees and customers

> **note:** Corporate plans, budgets, policies, strategies and objectives won't jumpstart your employees or customers.

It happens when you inspire your employees to achieve ambitious goals and deliver outstanding performance. It happens when you sway customers not to abandon you, but to support you because your company is user-friendly. It happens when you convince creditors and lenders that your past problems will remain in the past. It happens when you make stockholders applaud your small gains, confident that yours is not just another company destined for the trash can. It happens when you make positive things happen.

As you must create financial stability, you also must create organizational stability. Which is considerably more difficult than regaining financial stability, because you need a "people" philosophy. Managers fail when they deal with people as "things," eroding their relationship with employees and customers, two groups most needed in good times and bad!

Destroy these relationships and you have nothing with which to rebuild. Each group has its own stake in your success, and each good reasons to support you. But when you ignore this, you lose their support and usually your company.

> **E-Z TIP:** Pull together your employees and customers. Win their support. Make them essential to your comeback.

Chapter 9

John Mahoney, an old college friend and fellow-turnaround pro, tackled a classic case of organizational dry rot when he came aboard as president of a fast-failing, $20-million-a-year women's clothing retailer. Mahoney recounts: "Employees were jumping ship or just didn't give a damn. Suppliers cut our credit, dwindling our inventory, causing lost sales and evaporating goodwill. Customers who see empty racks don't come back. Competitors hovered like vultures. Some awaited our auction to pick up our inventory and two others solicited our best employees, while others besieged landlords at our best locations to steal our choice spots. It was crazy as hell!"

Sound familiar? When you operate defensively, it either pulls you, your employees and your customers together, or it pushes you apart. Creating a climate for success is never easy, but always necessary. You must deal in hope!

Motivate your crew

> **note:** The right attitude lets your employees know their company will succeed.

All companies want and need motivated employees for improved productivity, but in a turnaround company morale is usually rock-bottom. You can eliminate extra people and cut salaries, but for real success turn your people around, so they don't just work for you, but with you!

During the crisis stage, when you first come to grips with your problems, your employees are most demoralized. Employees care less about their work than their own security. They never know when they'll be out of a job. A manager for a large catering firm in Chapter 11 asked me, "How can I be excited about my company, when I may get a pink slip or a 20-percent pay cut next week?"

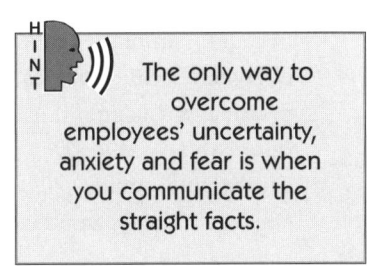

> **HINT:** The only way to overcome employees' uncertainty, anxiety and fear is when you communicate the straight facts.

161

Motivation suffers when cutbacks must be made, so get your firings done quickly and simultaneously. Let your remaining employees feel secure you have no further cutback plans. Rumors abound in a troubled organization, so give your employees the facts.

You may not need to terminate employees; your best employees may voluntarily leave. You must then achieve a turnaround with fewer, less capable people. To keep your best people, offer them more responsibilities in the turnaround and attractive incentives when the turnaround succeeds. Identify those few key employees most vital to the business.

Perhaps offer 20 percent of a deferred bonus, if the company attains its performance goals. Make it significant, specific and tied to measurable performance. But never offer ownership in the company. You don't want your employees as minority shareholders or partners who can cause you major headaches later. Should you cut pay to preserve jobs, or sacrifice jobs to maintain salaries? Sometimes the answer is to do both. Pay cuts must be temporary.

> **E-Z TIP:** Develop an incentive program that ties critical employees to the business throughout the workout.

Layoffs are best for long-term savings. A $30,000-a-year employee won't hang on long for $25,000. Employees better tolerate fringe benefit cuts than salary cuts.

Winning bargaining concessions from a labor union is always difficult because unions expect sacrifice elsewhere before salaries or jobs are touched. A Chapter 11 can wipe out oppressive collective bargaining agreements and is sometimes employed against an inflexible union.

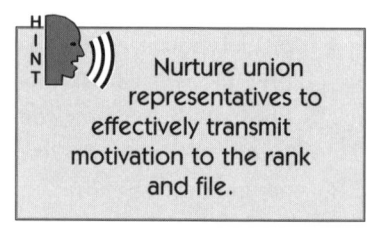

> **HINT:** Nurture union representatives to effectively transmit motivation to the rank and file.

Chapter 9

Labor unions can enormously influence how employees react. Chrysler, the first major corporation to appoint a union official to its corporate board, understood union power.

How employees react to layoffs and salary cutbacks is psychology as well as economics. A 10-percent salary rollback sells easier when you and other executives take a 40-percent cut and creditors lose 70-cents on the dollar. Your employees must truly see an "equality of sacrifice." And must perceive it as equality. A $25,000 employee cut to $20,000 is hardly sympathetic to a CEO whose $250,000 salary is hacked to $200,000. The sacrifice must be functionally equal.

Employees expect top managers to take it hard on the chin. If it doesn't revitalize morale, it neutralizes antagonism. But spilling executive blood won't always appease employees who must shed their own. Employees can least afford to sacrifice for the organization. A clerk-typist who loses $10 a week can't relate to lenders and creditors who are losing millions.

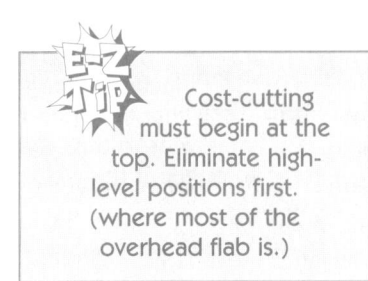

> **E-Z TIP:** Cost-cutting must begin at the top. Eliminate high-level positions first. (where most of the overhead flab is.)

Stabilizing morale is never enough. Shock your troops into positive thinking, people redirected from failure toward success. Their attitude will mirror your own.

Recondition employees to think opportunity, profits and growth, not only problems. It won't happen overnight, but it must happen if you want to go from a defensive to a forward-moving company. And it will be far tougher for you than for the manager of the healthy firm. Few employees relate their work to profits. Employees want a more prosperous employer but will seldom work harder to make their employer more prosperous.

Substitute wage-and-benefit cuts with recognition rewards as a benchmark of recovery. Bonuses are justified as conditions improve, and

> **HINT:** For results, employees must see a direct benefit to themselves through financial incentives tied to performance.

restore salaries and benefits as soon as possible. Sales commissions and productivity incentives will produce much better results than across-the-board incentives. Establish incentives before your cutbacks so that employees see the upside as well as the downside.

Incentives are your carrot. Also carry a bigger stick. Be less tolerant of poor performance and quickly terminate employees who perform poorly. Your employees must realize they will either yank their oar harder or they're out.

Turnaround companies must be people-sensitive, and even more performance- and survival-sensitive. Terminating a poorly performing, but loyal and long-standing, employee is an unhappy duty in corporate downsizing. You need the best. Ignore affirmative action and other red-tape laws and policies that restrict your ability to hire good employees rather than those Washington wants employed. Forget welfare programs when you're a step away from your own welfare check. Monetary rewards are vital, but never create the crucible of enthusiasm you need.

Encourage an open atmosphere and a teamwork approach through a collegial management style, new compensation policies and personal example.

A client, Jon Humphreys, takes the crew of his cabinet shop to lunch whenever something positive happens, such as a sizable new order or a sales increase.

Another company on the rebound from slumping sales raffles off a free vacation to a lucky employee whenever sales hit a certain mark. These are only symbolic gestures, but symbolism lifts spirits. Shortly after the devastation of

Chapter 9

Pearl Harbor, General Jimmy Doolittle launched a stunning bomb raid on Tokyo. The raid inflicted negligible damage, but Americans now had cause to smile. Victory can come with small, symbolic punches!

Honest, open and frequent communication is the cornerstone of this new corporate climate. Don't communicate through fancy corporate bulletins or memos filtered through five layers of management. Meet face-to-face with your employees. Roll up your sleeves and talk *with* your people. Don't talk *to* your people. Your employees have a great stake in your company's survival, so don't callously leave your employees in the dark about corporate events.

> **note**
> Nothing alienates employees more than a distant and unresponsive boss.

I hear employees say, "We gave this place years of work, and we depend on it to feed our kids and keep a roof over our heads. We damn well have a right to know what's going on!" They're right. Telling your employees what is going on is good communication and what courageous managers are all about. And tell them the bad news. Involvement creates jump-start organizations.

You may think you communicate effectively but only give employees lip service. Your employees will naturally be cynical to whatever you tell them, particularly when your company is in deep trouble and the truth may encourage employee defections. Even rats have the good sense to abandon a sinking ship.

Still, good managers accept the right of employees to share the bad news with the good, even if tempered with optimism. Meet frequently. Try to learn from them. In troubled times, your natural instinct to insulate yourself from your employees is fatal in the bad times, when you critically need constant feedback from employees.

Don't tell your employees merely what is happening—explain why. You may understand why things are the way they are, but do your employees? A

165

small Pittsburgh wrought-iron accessories manufacturer couldn't obtain credit from the manufacturer of a brass-assembly screw, so he switched to an alloy screw available from a supplier who would extend credit. The alloy screw didn't work as well as the brass screw, and employees wondered why the company suddenly switched to the alloy screw. Employees figured the boss lost his mind, until he told them why. Suddenly, the boss became an innovator and survivor, not an imbecile. Unless your employees understand your reasoning, you may also look like a dunce.

Divide employees into task forces. Assign each a specific project. Let key employees rotate on a special workout committee. Giving employees a role in corporate governance is hardly novel, but what better time to implement it than in a turnaround, when employees sense the need to more strongly control their own destiny.

> **E-Z TIP:** Motivation builds when employees actively participate in the turnaround.

End bad politics

Enthusiasm, cooperation and unity can't happen with internal feuding, back-stabbing and politicking. A polarized company is a company divided, and nearly impossible to save.

> **note:** Your best intentions and best efforts are neutralized when your organization is riddled with bad politics.

In tough times, politicians become totally disruptive. From top managers to warehouse clerks, everyone must work together closely. Without that basic harmony, you must make changes.

A larger business may have a board of directors that's either too passive or too domineering. It either fails to control, or stifles the flexibility needed. Politics, regardless of form, must be avoided when it impedes changes necessary for survival.

Chapter 9

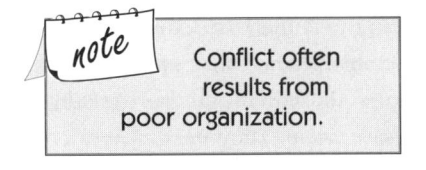

> **note** — Conflict often results from poor organization.

Your company may be too top heavy, or give employees too little support. You must reshape your organization so that necessary changes can be swiftly implemented, and results accurately and quickly measured and communicated back to the top.

You also need the right people in the key spots, people who take direction from the top, and force it to the bottom of the organization. But the answer is not to play with neat little boxes on a piece of paper.

You have a five-point strategy to get the most from your people:

1) Demonstrate strong, optimistic leadership.

2) Establish clear goals and strong incentives.

3) Communicate constantly and honestly.

4) Encourage employee participation in the turnaround.

5) Eliminate organizational politics and roadblocks.

Create a user-friendly company

Survivors romance their customers, and give them more than ever before. Of course, customer-driven firms less frequently fail because they believe their customer is their lifeblood and run their business accordingly.

Penn Central, Baldwin-United Corporation, Rolls Royce and W.T.

> **E-Z TIP** — In troubled times, you must put your customer on the pedestal.

Grant are four corporate relics who turned their backs on customers. Yet, firms play ostrich and hide from customers when they are in trouble. They have a bureaucracy-driven philosophy to serve their needs before their customers. Cosmetic changes won't save them. They need a new corporate philosophy, where the customer truly comes first.

Distressed companies are vulnerable to more aggressive competitors who can better satisfy the always-fickle customer. You will lose the battle and let your customers and sales disappear if you succumb to pressures to "de-market" rather than market. Cash poor companies almost always cut back first on advertising, promotion and other marketing efforts, seen as less vital to their survival. To save cash, they slash customer service and cut product quality.

Sales seem secondary when you're fighting so many other problems. Yet customers dump suppliers when they no longer get the products or services they want, when they want them and at good prices. Customers shop winners, not losers. Strong competitors will trade on your vulnerability. Counteract your vulnerability. Develop even more powerful marketing programs and better customer service, so they know your company is alive and well.

> **HOT spot** Customers must not believe you can no longer properly serve them.

A large, long-established, Boston drug wholesaler, slogging through Chapter 11, had five competitors stealing its retail accounts. They dangled more lenient credit, extra discounts and even free vacations. The firm's sales manager recounts: "In the first two months, we lost 60 of our 465 accounts. To strike back, we designed our own re-energized marketing program, and added three new salespeople to stay close to our customers. Despite cash problems, we invested $60,000 for a promotional campaign to win new customers. Our competitors, convinced we were down for the count, couldn't believe we could bounce back and grab their customers! We thought we had too many financial and operational problems to worry about sales, marketing or customer retention, and became sloppy. We took our customers for granted. But, when you're in business, you can't become sloppy despite other problems."

Sometimes you do it with mirrors. Years ago, a client's printing firm was failing fast, and his competitors, like vultures, hovered for the kill. "XYZ Printers won't be around long, so why not send us your printing?" was their war cry. Soon a $600 billboard prominently placed beside XYZ's plant announced: "Under Construction—New and Expanded Facilities for XYZ Printers." Of course it wasn't true: XYZ could barely scrounge up the $600 for the sign. But the story worked. We sent pictures of the "construction site" to every customer. Customers believed it. After all, seeing is believing.

> **HINT:** Look successful, even if you are not successful. You need guerrilla marketing when you don't have the big bucks.

Make your advertising and promotion more effective and economical and also match your turnaround plan. Replace "smother 'em" marketing. Pareto's law says 20-percent of your customers generate 80-percent of your sales. Target that 20-percent—even if you must neglect smaller, less profitable accounts. You can't be all things to all people. Once you identify customers vital to your future, then marshal the shrinking resources to forge stronger relationships with them.

Through downsizing you will lose your marginal accounts. However, that can be healthy if it helps you hold those few big customers. Avoid public relations, community image-building, institutional and other "soft" advertising.

> **E-Z TIP:** Each advertising dollar you spend must produce direct, measurable and very profitable results.

169

Selling in troubled times

Adopt precise cost to sales evaluations. Sales compensation must match performance. Switch salespeople from salary to commission, if only to eliminate non-producers who never earned their salaries. Salespeople sell more aggressively with their paychecks on the line. Surviving corporations stay market-oriented, and direct their managerial energies to satisfying the important customers. Misguided organizations harness large sales forces to replace the now-lost valuable customers. Keep the customers you have, not the customer you may get. Sell through sales reps? You will probably need to re-energize your rep groups. How are they now performing?

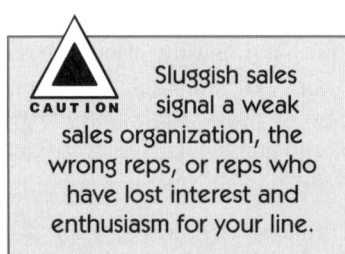

> **CAUTION** Sluggish sales signal a weak sales organization, the wrong reps, or reps who have lost interest and enthusiasm for your line.

This happens when a client company gets into trouble. Good reps want winners and don't like handling the losers within their trade. New products, promotions and services can help with your rep organization.

Good communication is as important with your rep groups as with employees. Your reps must know your plans and how you will correct problems they must deal with (late or spotty shipments, poor quality, weak sales support). Your reps also are concerned whether they will be paid. Pay commissions more frequently, so there is one less obstacle between you.

E-Z TIP: Your sales reps are your goodwill ambassadors to your customers. They must field the complaints, handle embarrassing rumors and convince them that yours is a good company to do business with. Your job is to tell them why.

Chapter 9

Hold your prices

Too many companies get into trouble by underpricing, which is as common an error as overpricing. Pressures to boost sales and keep customers happy leads to lower prices. The fallacy is that low-profit sales are profitable when added to your present sales. But, low-profit sales seldom cover their costs.

Reduced prices force competitors to retaliate with even lower prices. Victory inevitably goes to the company with the greatest staying power, seldom the turnaround company. Cut costs instead. Most turnarounds should increase prices, which, if well-timed, rarely hurt sales—but can greatly add to profits.

Marketing 101

Energizing customer relationships needs a new commitment to product quality and customer service. You can't lower product quality or service and get away with it.

> **HOT spot** Customers react badly to shoddy products and service.

Surviving companies teach us that the turnaround is one last opportunity to look at your products and services as your customers do. It also may be your last opportunity to build that better mousetrap. Focus on your key products or services.

Downsize to your core products. Few care to shotgun a wide variety of goods or services. Don't waste precious resources on the unimportant. Simmons Mattress shrunk from 8,000 dealers to 5,000 dealers they could profitably support. They concentrated their resources on building stronger dealer relations, and stepped up promotional programs to boost sales, while they improved quality and increased prices. Theirs was a basic survival strategy: "Thick on the best, to hell with the rest!"

171

Answer these six questions:

1) On which customers should you concentrate?

2) On which products or services should you concentrate?

3) What marketing (advertising, promotion) most effectively and efficiently reaches your customers?

4) What new services, products or programs can strengthen key customer relationships?

5) What can you do right now to look like a survivor?

6) What resources can you commit to your marketing program?

If the purpose of business, as management guru Peter Drucker suggests, "is to create a customer," or, as Stanford's Harold Levitt puts it, "to buy a customer," then energizing these philosophies is on your shoulders as the turnaround leader. You have primary responsibility to your customers. Energize your employees and your customers, and create a link between them through which flows improved products, services, systems and policies.

> **HINT:** Show every employee how to acquire new customers, keep existing ones and rebuild on a foundation that acknowledges the customer as the source of everyone's paycheck.

Employees who truly care about the customer are important for any company, and doubly important for troubled companies, where employees and customers must both be adaptive and flexible because they have limited resources.

Business survivors keep their customers happy by staying close to them, very close. Winners listen to their customers, service them and make sure they always feel important.

Chapter 9

If you believe that the business of business is customer service and satisfaction, then energize your business in that direction. You achieve this when you:

- Develop a sense of purpose and a shared view of what your company is about.

- Instill a sense of pride that your company is the best at what it does.

- Create a success climate by navigating your people away from problems and toward opportunities.

- Build the motivation machine that inspires ordinary employees to perform extraordinarily.

- Energize your organization with a user-friendly, customer-first, service-driven philosophy.

- Fashion new products, services and programs to regain the competitive edge and to show that your company has a real future.

Where, when, and how do you begin? Start now. "Where" is not difficult. Don't send a letter or another catalog. Don't even phone. Get in your car or hop a plane, but see every important customer—and when you're in trouble, there are few customers who are not important.

Possibly you only need to walk the floor of your own retail business, or stop at a few tables, if you're a restaurateur. There's no substitute for frequent, meaningful contact. Let your customers know you appreciate their business. Discover the problems they may have with you and how you can better satisfy them. But satisfying customers is never enough. Listen to complaints. From the seeds of discontent, implement change. It

> **E-Z TIP:** Give your customers more than they expect, more than they paid for and more than your competitors give.

173

won't depend as much on the nature of their problems with you but on how you handle them. Customers are understanding if you explain reasons for the problem, how you will remedy it, and sincerely express concerns for how it affects that customer. Most unsatisfied customers will give you another try. Stabilizing relations with an unhappy customer must be a high priority.

An example: A mid-sized manufacturer of household items in Duluth became surrounded by cut-throat competitors. This manufacturer with the smallest share of the market had its rough spots. Deliveries were late, product quality uneven, billing errors too common, and customer complaints rampant. The sales staff avoided or ignored complaints. Rather than face the problems, they less productively hunted down new customers to replace lost customers. Their policy changed. Customers who complained were called by a sales rep the same day. Every effort was made to resolve all complaints within three days; and to salve wounds, complaining customers were given a small concession (an extra discount or some free goods) on their next order. Soon sales rebounded. Mostly from customers who had previously complained!

A customer-first system won't develop overnight. Bind yourself to your customer slowly and deliberately, but listen to your customers. Customer satisfaction is not measured by you. It's measured by them. You must support them both. When you do, you have the foundation for a very successful business.

> **E-Z TIP**
> If you want your customers to support your business, your employees must support your customers.

Checkpoint

1) Do your personnel policies promote good morale?

2) Do your employees perceive you and other top managers as sacrificing to save the business?

3) What incentives can you offer your employees to increase productivity?

4) How well do you communicate with your employees?

5) What bad politics pollute your business? What can you do to end them?

6) Are you paying the most attention to the customers critical to your survival?

7) Have you primed your sales organization to sell even more for you in troubled times?

8) Is your marketing cost-effective? Targeted to the key accounts?

9) Have you created a user-friendly, service-driven philosophy?

How to turn your business into a creditor-proof fortress

10

Chapter 10
How to turn your business into a creditor-proof fortress

Vulnerable businesses stand the best chance to fail. Well-fortified, creditor-proof enterprises usually survive. That's how I see it!

If you reviewed my 1,000 cases, you would find it amazing how resilient a well-protected business is compared to those that are exposed and unprotected. That is why this chapter preaches this important rule: You, not your creditors, must have the upper hand and the strongest bargaining position. That happens only when you turn your business into a creditor-proof fortress.

You may not see the need to protect your business even when creditors breathe down your neck. You may think your business needs no protection. You may think there's nothing you can do to protect it. You may think it's too late to protect it. You may think incorrectly on all counts!

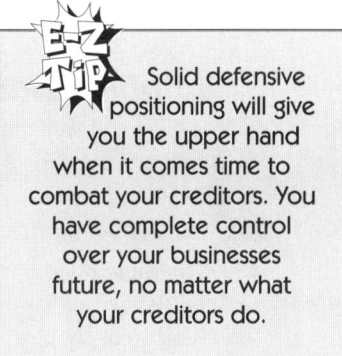

> **E-Z TIP** Solid defensive positioning will give you the upper hand when it comes time to combat your creditors. You have complete control over your businesses future, no matter what your creditors do.

Without defensive positioning you are exposed and vulnerable. Your creditors control the show. You must dance to their tune. Is that the way you want it? Not if you are a survivor!

Survivors do everything possible to creditor-proof their businesses. Survivors protect themselves before they go into business. Survivors continuously fortify themselves once in business.

Building your fortress

note

Timing is critical. Building a strong financial fortress takes time, and you build the strongest fortress when you defensively position your business before serious problems arise and you have angry creditors chasing you. Still, it's never too late to try.

Fortifying a client's business is always one of my very first objectives. I know that I'll eventually go eyeball-to-eyeball with creditors. When I do, I want them boxed in so they must accept our deal. You can achieve this only by convincing creditors they will get far less—perhaps nothing—if they refuse your deal. To be truly convincing you must show your creditors that you can stay in business regardless of what they do. You, not your creditors, must have the options.

How can you turn your business into an impregnable, creditor-proof fortress? With these six vital building blocks:

Building Block 1: Use a corporate shield

Building your fortress begins with the right business organization. There are over 15 million businesses in America. Four million are unincorporated. Their owners sit on a literal time bomb. When they fail, as most will, their owners may lose not only their businesses, but everything they own personally.

Using a corporation to operate your business is essential today because only a corporation protects your personal assets from your business creditors. Only the foolish, naive or unknowing jeopardize their personal assets. Don't be among them. Limit your creditors' recourse to your business only. Don't let them follow you home. It will cost you dearly. Even if you have no personal assets to lose, why subject yourself to a personal bankruptcy when it is so easily avoided?

It costs only several hundred dollars to incorporate and a few extra dollars for accounting and maintaining corporate books and records. There are commercial firms that will incorporate you for under $50. Investing those few dollars is a tremendous bargain when you consider how effectively a corporation protects your personal wealth from business failure.

Early in my legal career I represented a young pharmacist who had just gone bust with his two un-incorporated drugstores. When the smoke cleared, Joe and his family had lost their $300,000 home, two cars and a host of other personal assets to their business creditors. "You don't need the hassle of a corporation," his naive lawyer had counseled when he set Joe up in business. Dumb, dumb advice. Don't you fall for it!

> **E-Z TIP**
> A corporation is the best insurance you can buy today! Don't discover that too late.

What can you do if your business is unincorporated and heavily in debt? Act fast. It may not be too late to protect yourself. Quickly incorporate and transfer both your business assets and liabilities to your new corporation. Then gradually pay down the debts that belong to your unincorporated business. You will have the cash flow, as your new corporation will simultaneously build its own liabilities. Once you've fully paid the debts of your unincorporated business, you are left only with corporate creditors, and your personal wealth is no longer endangered. This takes careful planning and good legal advice to make certain you do not violate any laws.

I can tell you about one chap who incorporated his Reno, Nevada, surgical supply store only several weeks before liquidating it under an Assignment for the Benefit of Creditors. Nearly all of the debts predated his incorporating, 'so the creditors had the legal right to collect from the owner personally. But the creditors never checked to see if the business was incorporated when the debt was incurred. They simply assumed it was incorporated from the start and never pursued it further.

For purposes of liability protection, it does not matter whether you use a regular "C" corporation or an "S" corporation. They differ only in their taxation. Your accountant can guide you on this. You also may consider

> **note** If you're not incorporated, do it immediately. Confining your creditors to the fewest possible assets means they can look only to the business for payment—not to you!

forming a limited liability company. But never operate as a proprietorship or partnership.

A corporation limits your liability only when you avoid personal guarantees on the corporate debts. This can't always be avoided, because banks and other lenders rarely lend to small businesses without an owner guarantee. But you can escape most guarantees on other corporate obligations if you follow the strategies in Chapter 19.

Building Block 2: Isolate winners from losers

If one corporation is sensible, then two, three or ten corporations may make even more sense. If you own several businesses, incorporate each separately. One failed business won't endanger the other healthy business. It's the smart way to creditor-proof a growing conglomerate. Only fools put all their eggs in one basket.

Beware the law of probability: Even the clever businessperson eventually saddles himself with a loser. That one loser can easily destroy everything.

Here's another lesson learned too late. Joan and Harry, a young Texas couple, once owned three thriving Mexican restaurants in the Dallas suburbs. Their fourth restaurant? A disaster. Enormous losses from this poorly located fourth restaurant soon

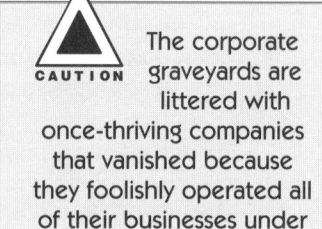

> **CAUTION** The corporate graveyards are littered with once-thriving companies that vanished because they foolishly operated all of their businesses under one corporation.

tumbled the three profitmakers because all of the restaurants were in the same corporation. A common mistake? Sure, but don't you make it!

Chapter 10

note — Your goal is to isolate your potential losers from your present winners. If you incorporate each business separately, you can safely shed your losers while building on the strength of your winners. This gives you maximum protection when you're small and most vulnerable. Larger companies can't as easily shed their losers. Tax, financing, creditor and operational factors may require a one-corporation structure. But you may never become big unless you do isolate your sick ventures from your healthy enterprises while you are growing!

You may find it equally smart to split your existing corporation into separate corporations! Confine your liability-prone activities to one corporation and have your more valuable assets owned by the less vulnerable corporation.

Think! What is the heart of your business? Where and how are you most likely to incur liability? How can you separate one from the other? Think very carefully. This survival-thinking saves businesses! Plenty of Main-street ventures are organized precisely this way. A Tampa superette chain operates each of its 16 stores through a separate corporation. Each fully stands on its own with no financial or legal entanglements with the other ventures. This is smart, defensive positioning.

I encouraged a $12-million-a-year Denver electrical component manufacturer to become two separate corporations. One would serve the industrial market, the other the consumer market. This too is smart defensive positioning!

Smart operators function through multi-corporations, even when they operate small, simple businesses. Saving an ailing business then requires only minor surgery to remove the few sick parts.

> **E-Z TIP** If your business is in the first stages of a downturn, see how you can legally spin essential assets into a new, debt-free corporation. Confine creditors only to the least important, most expendable part of your business.

181

Building Block 3: Shelter key assets

The building-block strategy, by using corporations, limits your creditors to the assets of your business. Multiple corporations isolate your sick businesses from the healthy business.

Here is your third creditor-proofing strategy: Keep your operating company asset poor so creditors stand to gain nothing when they go after you.

note — Real estate is an important asset that should never be owned by an operating company. Why needlessly expose a valuable building to business creditors? Own real estate personally or title it in a separate real estate trust, corporation, limited partnership or another entity that keeps it beyond the reach of your business creditors.

Good advice? You bet!

Unfortunately, Lucy didn't think so. A once-prosperous owner of a thriving restaurant on the beautiful intracoastal waterway in Fort Lauderdale, Lucy wisely snapped at the chance to buy the building from her landlord. Contrary to my advice, she titled the property in her restaurant corporation. When Lucy's restaurant fell from grace as Fort Lauderdale's fashionable dining spot, her restaurant failed. But her trade creditors, owed about $600,000, had few worries. They grabbed the big equity in her real estate.

Lucy will never again give her creditors that opportunity. Now $600,000 smarter, Lucy owns her real estate outside the operating corporation and safe from creditors. A still smarter Lucy similarly titled her chairs, tables, furniture, equipment and even her valuable liquor license to another outside entity. Any future creditors could chase only empty space. Too bad Lucy hadn't taken my advice before she lost $600,000.

Nobody wants to hurt creditors, but it's nevertheless more comforting when you can lose nothing, and your creditors can gain nothing should push come to shove. That's the real world!

Chapter 10

Does your corporation hold assets that would be safer titled outside the corporation and beyond creditor reach? Real estate? Expensive equipment? Patents? Trademarks? Copyrights? Distributorship or franchise rights? If you want protected assets, title them outside your business and lease or license their use to the operating business. That's savvy strategy!

Building Block 4: Debt shield your business

I love big, friendly mortgages. They are high on my creditor- proofing list and a great tool to help save your business. A business, heavily encumbered to a friendly lender can become a debt-free business overnight. Magic? No. Only some basic law turned to your own advantage.

Assume your business's assets are worth $100,000, and your brother has a $100,000 mortgage secured by those same assets. Suppose you also owe general creditors $200,000. Because your brother's mortgage has priority over all other creditors, including your general creditors, there would be absolutely nothing left for your general creditors if they seized your assets or pushed you into bankruptcy. Your unsecured creditors then lose their bargaining power, and you have precisely the business-saving leverage you need to survive.

> **E-Z TIP**
> A friendly mortgage or debt shield offers you enormous survival power. This one strategy has helped me save hundreds of once-troubled businesses.

> **Definition:**
> A *friendly mortgage* has a "friendly" mortgage holder willing to protect you and cooperate with you so the mortgage becomes a defense shield. It may be a relative, a friend, a loyal supplier, a friendly bank or an affiliated company.

To work, your friendly mortgage must cover the liquidation value of your business assets. Too small a mortgage leaves your creditors equity to chase, and you do not have adequate protection.

183

How do you create your friendly mortgage?

- If you loaned tons of money to your business, why not secure your loan with a mortgage on your business? (See your lawyer to structure this correctly.)

- Do you owe a friend or relative for loans, wages or fees for services? Why not secure these obligations?

- Do you have a favorite supplier you want to protect and who in turn will, protect you?

- Do you owe your banker on an unsecured line of credit, or have you secured your loan by a mortgage on your home or other personal assets? Is it a banker you can work with? Why not also give him a hefty mortgage on your business?

Understand a little law, and you'll see how effectively you can shelter your business with a friendly mortgage. You can never lose control because your friendly mortgage holder can legally foreclose and resell your business assets, perhaps to a new corporation you organize. It's one way to solve nagging, unsecured creditor problems, when less extreme measures fail. Later, Chapter 5 explores this strategy in greater detail.

Building Block 5: Control your lease

If your location is vital to your business, your lease may be your most important and valuable asset.

One good way to protect your lease: Have a separate corporation be the tenant in your lease. This corporation can then sublet the space to your operating company as a tenant at will.

You are vulnerable when your troubled business holds the lease because the bankruptcy court can sell your lease; even without landlord approval and

Chapter 10

even if your lease prevents an assignment or a transfer to a new tenant. So in bankruptcy it's easy to lose control of your valuable location, and with it your business.

I learned that costly lesson as a green legal pup trying to bail out a client's fashionable gift shop perched in a very popular Boston mall.

My business-saving strategy started by protecting the business with a hefty friendly mortgage. I figured I could then negotiate a great deal from the creditors, who were owed more than $300,000, as they then had no equity in the business to chase.

Boy, was I wrong!

What I blindly overlooked was the fact that my client was paying a bargain $20,000-a-year rent on retail space worth more than $60,000, And the lease had twelve more years left.

Before I could catch my second wind, the creditors threw the gift shop into bankruptcy, and sold the lease to a competitor for a whopping $200,000. The creditors were nearly fully paid, and my client was out of business!

I never again made that mistake!

Now when I come across a business with a valuable lease, I rush to protect it. I write the lease to one corporation set up for that purpose and sublet to their operating company as a tenant at will. They can then evict their failing business and sublet the space to a new startup corporation. Or they can sell the lease and pocket the profit if they don't want to go back into business. Or they can negotiate with their creditors, assured the creditors can't put a big value on their lease.

When your lease is not an asset of your troubled business, your creditors can neither claim the lease nor sell it. Your creditors only option is to liquidate your other assets at public auction. They cannot sell your business as a going concern for those bigger dollars. When creditors must settle for those few auction dollars, you gain bargaining power, an important building block for your creditor-proof fortress.

Building Block 6: Shelter the goodwill

note — The guts of any business is not its machinery, inventory or receivables. It's the relationship of a company with its customers.

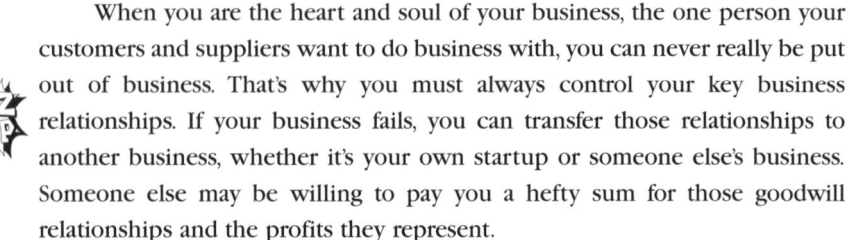

When you are the heart and soul of your business, the one person your customers and suppliers want to do business with, you can never really be put out of business. That's why you must always control your key business relationships. If your business fails, you can transfer those relationships to another business, whether it's your own startup or someone else's business. Someone else may be willing to pay you a hefty sum for those goodwill relationships and the profits they represent.

A key rule is to avoid long-term customer contracts when you're in trouble. As with a real-estate lease, customer contracts can be sold by a bankruptcy court to a buyer willing to assume them. Without a long-term contract, there's nothing to sell; your customers can discontinue business with your defunct company and transfer their business to any place you designate.

note — Developing strong relationships with key customers and suppliers is always good business, but it is essential to survival when you're in trouble. Goodwill is the cement that holds your fortress together!

Who are your key accounts? Your vital suppliers? When they want to do business with you, and only you, you are indeed the heart of your creditor-proof business!

Now, let's put our various fortress-building strategies into perspective. Imagine for a moment approaching your creditors and challenging them to take everything you have.

Sounds silly, doesn't it?

With a creditor-proof fortress, you literally can offer creditors everything, because there's nothing to take. Why?

- Because your business is incorporated, your creditors can claim only your business assets, not your personal assets.

- Because your businesses are separately incorporated, your creditors can claim only assets owned by your ailing enterprise, and they must leave untouched your flourishing businesses—because your most valuable assets are safely titled outside your failing corporation, your creditors have few assets to claim.

- Because those few assets are encumbered by a friendly mortgage, creditors can claim no equity in those assets.

- Because your lease is securely held by another corporation, you creditors cannot make claim to it or sell your business as a going concern.

- Because you are your businesses most valuable asset, your key customers and suppliers will take their business wherever you go, not wherever your creditors say to go.

The six fortress builders give you, and not your creditors, total control. You must be in control when you want to turn your debt-saddled business into a debt-free money machine on your terms!

Blockading creditors and bill collectors

Entrenched within your creditor-proof fortress, you can deal with your creditors from a strong position. Begin your defense by freezing payments to creditors on past-due bills to plug your cash drain. You must stonewall creditors so you don't bleed to death. You know how it is. Creditor A, owed $4,000, pushes for $500 a week. Creditor B, owed $7,000, hassles you for $350

Troubleshooting Your Business Made E-Z

a week. Creditor C squeezes $1,000 a month on your long overdue bill. To recoup his $6,000, Creditor D withholds your trade discounts. You are soon repaying creditors two dollars for every dollar you earn. You can't stay in business when you try simultaneously to pay loans, replenish inventory and pay operating expenses, and settle back bills.

Dribbling payments to creditors on past-due bills accomplishes nothing. It's a fool's game. You'll repay your creditors thousands of dollars and still be in debt. Since you can as easily restructure $500,000 in debts as $400,000, what do you gain by squandering $100,000 to pacify creditors before you seriously tackle your problems?

You must be equally tough with lenders who will try to drain you of what they can before your bankruptcy. Of course, lenders who hold your assets as collateral can more easily coerce payment than unsecured creditors, who can only sue to collect. Still, secured lenders, who accelerate payment on shaky loans, also drain your business and must be resisted.

Prioritize your debts and expenses: Suppliers, utilities, professional fees, back rent, insurance, loans, taxes. What do you owe each? How overdue is each? What debts are personally guaranteed? What debts are secured?

> ⚠ **CAUTION** You won't win popularity contests by dribbling those payments. Creditors will still call you an S.O.B and deny you credit.

Your objective is to pay no more than what you absolutely must to keep your doors open. Pay expenses in the following order:

1) payroll and payroll taxes

2) rent and utilities

3) Secured loans and leases on essential assets

4) Purchases of essential supplies and inventory

188

Chapter 10

Use common sense. For instance, pay a few dollars to a small, nuisance supplier if it helps you concentrate better on your larger creditors. Or pay personally guaranteed debts if it frees you of personal liability.

Put on a bullet-proof vest

You may fight creditors for months before you finally pull the trigger to escape your debts. This is your final window of opportunity to fortify your business before your big battle. The trick is not to let creditor pressures get the best of you, so you can focus on the main objectives of the turnaround.

You can't think positively or work creatively when preoccupied with protecting your butt from the searing heat of creditors. But a thick-skinned employee, whose life savings are not wrapped up in the business, can leave behind emotion. Find someone with the stomach and the cunning to play the game! The title of controller or vice president/accounts payable allows your employee to interface authoritatively with creditors. Find someone who can pacify creditors so they won't harass you, and yet has the good judgment to warn you about particularly onerous threats. Where do you find this character? It may be one of your employees, or you may need to look outside your business for the right individual. I have a ready roster of battle-hardened veterans ready to don bullet-proof vests for my clients. They are worth their weight in gold.

> **E-Z TIP**
> Preserve your sanity by hiring a hardy soul with a deaf ear, a bullet-proof vest and a fast tongue to handle the creditors. Don't you "dance" with the creditors. Nothing is more time-consuming and depressing than to listen to clamoring, hostile creditors.

One memorable case of mine involved a defunct travel agency that stranded hundreds of tour travelers when it didn't pay the hotel bill. Bombarded with scores of threatening phone calls, my clients, Jan and Pat, barely escaped nervous breakdowns when one of my veteran "accounts-payable specialists" answered their telephones and took control of the situation.

189

Protecting clients from creditor hassles is one of my firms most important functions in a turnaround. I insist creditors call me, not the client. Creditors will talk to me because they know I will give them straight answers. My accounts-payable staff logs hundreds of creditor calls each day. These are distracting phone calls our clients avoid in order to give their businesses the attention and positive focus they badly need.

> **E-Z TIP**
> Guide your business with a clear mind and a positive attitude. Find a sterner soul to handle the guns so you can steer the ship.

Seven rules to tame creditors

Follow some basic rules, and you can effectively handle hundreds of hounding calls from angry creditors seeking one simple answer to one simple question, "Where's my money?" Violate these rules, and you make costly mistakes, lose creditor confidence, pay what you shouldn't, or grant costly concessions. Post these seven rules by your telephone and inside your checkbook:

Rule 1: Forget phony excuses

No, your check is not in the mail. No, your accountant does not have your checkbook. No, your dog didn't eat the bill. You can't pay because you don't have the money and you need time to put together a workout plan that's fair to all creditors. Now, that wasn't too difficult, was it? Your creditors will respect your straight talk and won't badger you every day. You will be spared making lame excuses and losing credibility.

Perhaps you don't want to save your business, but need time to pay back taxes or guaranteed debts, recoup your investment or only need to grab a few more paychecks until you can find a job or start a new business. Your promise of a workout plan is still not a misrepresentation, because your workout can be, and often is, a plan to liquidate your business.

To defuse creditor pressure, I routinely ask creditors for a 60-day collection moratorium while I analyze my client's situation and formulate a workout plan. Most creditors agree because our request is reasonable. When 60 days pass, I inform creditors that a plan is nearly completed and will be on their desk within 30 days. This wins me 90 hassle-free days. Creditors may eventually receive an unacceptable plan, but it's a plan, and that's all I promised. If they reject the plan, I request 60 days more to modify the plan hoping it will be more acceptable. You can stall for several months without ever using the tired, "I-lost-your-invoice" cliche that nauseates creditors.

Rule 2: Don't let creditors intimidate you

Most creditors are reasonably patient, but more than a few will try to intimidate you into a fast payment.

They may threaten to push you into bankruptcy (they almost never do). They may threaten lawsuits (you can tie them up in courts for years). They may threaten to report you to the credit bureau (haven't you lost your credit already?).

Ignore creditor threats! Let pushy creditors know they will be paid after more patient creditors are paid. This counterthreat works! Collection agencies and attorneys play roughest because their client has already been tossed around. These professional collectors are unconcerned about your goodwill and future business.

No matter who chases you for money, fight back and refuse payment. You need to protect yourself and your more cooperative and patient creditors who are waiting in line for their fair due.

Rule 3: Refuse override payments

Creditors have their own tricks. They may try to deduct earned discounts, promotional allowances or other purchasing incentives from your overdue bill. As a C.O.D. customer, always demand the same price and allowances as cash customers receive. Credit returned goods against future purchases, not your past bill.

Trivial? Hardly. Override dollars can mount up mighty fast. Pay no override or extra payments toward your past-due bills. A troubled stationery retailer let his wholesaler apply more than $1,000 a month in trade discounts to his past-due $90,000 bill. In three years, the wholesaler recovered $36,000 more than other creditors. This was neither fair nor smart. Insist your suppliers give you every dollar in trade concessions, and pay nothing on arrears unless it's part of an overall settlement.

Rule 4: Don't give your creditors security

Never secure creditor obligations with a mortgage or a guarantee. Creditors who hold a mortgage on your business or your personal assets are in too powerful a position and can only hurt you.

Creditors may wave a big stick and threaten a lawsuit, or dangle the carrot of leniency in exchange for security. Refuse! The only time to give a creditor a mortgage is when it's a friendly mortgage that defensively shields your business.

An "unfriendly" mortgage only protects your creditor, ties your hands and limits your options to rescue your business.

Rule 5: Ignore business termination threats

I laugh when suppliers say they won't sell on C.O.D. terms without payment on account. Few suppliers enjoy a monopoly. And even when they do, it's poor economics to pay more on your back bills than the new goods can produce in profits. Nor should you favor important creditors over less vital suppliers.

I often hear how vital certain suppliers are, and why they "must" be paid during the workout. The product or service is vital, not the supplier. There are always other suppliers. When suppliers threaten to discontinue business, I need only call their many competitors who are anxious for business.

Rule 6: Listen. Don't talk

CAUTION: Loose lips sink ships and businesses! Watch what you tell your creditors. You may unwittingly say things that will later hurt you. For instance, admit that you are insolvent and your creditors can throw you into bankruptcy. Nor should you reveal who your other creditors or suppliers are to a disgruntled creditor, who may solicit their aid to throw you into bankruptcy. Tell your creditors only four points:

> **E-Z TIP:** No supplier wants to lose your business. Reduce your fears about losing an important supplier by shopping for replacement suppliers in advance. Shop carefully, and you may find even better deals!

1) You are now experiencing problems and cannot presently pay.

2) You will pay C.O.D. on future orders.

3) No unsecured creditor will receive preferential payments; all general creditors will be treated equally.

4) You will offer your creditors a fair and equitable plan to resolve your debts within a month or two.

Rule 7: Follow these rules

Conspicuously post these rules. Read them daily. My clients do, I closely monitor their checkbooks to make sure they play by these rules. Those who don't lose their checkbooks. It's that simple. It's a necessary discipline, because every wasted check to creditors hurts your chance for recovery. Yes, it's you on the firing line, and you must face the hostile creditors day after day, so it will be tempting to write a check to get rid of a pushy creditor. But survivors say no.

Treat creditors fairly

While you must keep your creditors unpaid, you must be sensitive to their position and respect their rights. Your creditors are only businesspeople like yourself; they too are trying to make good in their own business. They extended you credit in good faith, and you must treat them fairly if they are to cooperate with you. Even unpaid, angry creditors can be turned into friends if you:

Show loyalty

Nothing angers a creditor more than ignoring their bill while you buy from someone else for cash. Let your suppliers know immediately that you will continue to buy from them–but only if they remain competitive on price and terms and cooperative with you on the workout. Creditors won't take your loyalty for granted.

Avoid preferences

Creditors rightfully get angry when they discover that other creditors are being paid while they are not. Assure your creditors that if they are going without payment, so are your other creditors. Remind creditors who demand payment that you will treat all creditors equally. That's only fair.

Your secured lenders may not let you pay your unsecured creditors during the workout, so your cash goes to them rather than to your unsecured creditors. If payment in violation of this order only causes your lender to foreclose, you have a credible reason for not paying general creditors. Why not make your secured lender the bad guy who won't let you pay your bills? It's a strategy that has worked for me many times.

note: Creditors stay patient only when other creditors stay patient and when they are not losing the upper hand through their patience.

Chapter 10

Stay 100-percent honest

Creditor cooperation is earned only when your creditors trust you and believe in your honesty. Thirty years in this business has given me an opportunity to rub shoulders against plenty of cheats and crooks who lost their companies only because their creditors distrusted them.

Bad checks are dishonest. Don't juggle an overdrawn checkbook. Bounced checks always spell trouble. So do false credit applications. The truth may lose you credit, but lies only invite fraud charges. Obtain credit honestly, or go without it.

Don't buy heavily on credit when you know you can't pay. Hustling credit from new and unsuspecting suppliers, or loading-up before you go belly-up, is bad business. Not only will it destroy your business, it will destroy your reputation and can get you into serious legal trouble.

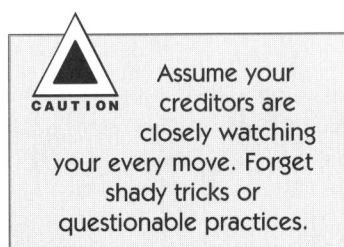

> **CAUTION** Assume your creditors are closely watching your every move. Forget shady tricks or questionable practices.

Don't move inventory or equipment suspiciously. Even innocent transactions can be misinterpreted, and the smallest transgression magnified.

How to outwit collection agents and lawyers

Stalling your creditors won't work forever. Eventually you will deal with collection agencies and lawyers representing creditors who believe that fast action is the best action, and that the squeaky wheel gets the oil.

Large, impersonal, automated corporate creditors move quickly to collect. Their computers have no ears. You must instead find a real person you can talk to when you're not paying because:

195

- The goods were defective, late or were never received, or the service was unsatisfactory.

- Your payments were not properly credited.

- You have merchandise for return,

These claims can stall your account for 60 to 90 days while your claim is investigated.

Turning your account over to a collection agency or attorney joins the battle. Collection agencies are far less threatening than attorneys, and also are more easily handled. Collection agencies may be national firms such as Dun and Bradstreet, or local agencies. They may serve all industries or just one industry, such as the jewelry or the garment trades. Whether big or small, collection agencies skillfully extract money from recalcitrant and unknowing debtors who are easily harassed and intimidated.

Collection agencies succeed mostly through their ability to intimidate by creating an illusion of enormous power. In reality, collection agencies are as powerless as their clients. Nasty letters and harassing or angry phone calls are their only weapons.

I'm relieved when a creditor hires a collection agency. I know the account will be tied up for several months before I must contend with a still nastier lawyer.

Consumers are well-protected from abusive collection practices by federal law. Commercial accounts are less protected. Collectors, for instance, may badger you at home, evenings and weekends. Slamming the phone in the caller's ear is one practical remedy. Report illegal notices that look like lawsuits to the Federal Trade Commission. Others may threaten to forcibly repossess unpaid merchandise. Goods once sold to you remain yours whether paid for or not. The bill collector may show up at your business and can stay there until you ask him to leave, which you should do quickly.

A lawyer, whether hired by the creditor or a collection agency, will soon appear. A good collection lawyer can be a pesky thorn in your side, but lawyers vary greatly in style and effectiveness. Passive lawyers write collection letters. Aggressive lawyers sue with little or no warning and push their claims aggressively.

> **E-Z TIP**: Don't let a bill collector intimidate you into writing a check.

You will then need a lawyer to stall the lawsuits inexpensively! Find a young, lawyer smart enough to tie up cases without costly legal maneuvers. A $5,000 legal bill to defend a $10,000 claim destined to go absolutely nowhere is nonsense.

My law firm defended countless troubled business clients against garden-variety creditor suits. My computers constantly pumped out inexpensive, but efficient boiler-plate defenses. My clients would eventually straighten out their financial problems or go bust while the case stagnated, so why needlessly run up legal fees? Use common sense with your lawsuits, or your legal fees will kill you faster than your creditors!

How swiftly can events unravel for you? If your creditors are now sending you dunning notices, you can probably delay matters for many months. Pesky collection agencies and lawyers can consume a few more months. How much more time do you need to turn your headache business into a debt-free money machine?

Workouts and cramdowns: tackling your problem loans

Chapter 11
Workouts and cramdowns: tackling your problem loans

Your objectives in a debt restructuring are to keep creditors at bay and reduce debt through a "voluntary" debt-restructuring to avoid either a Chapter 11 reorganization or bankruptcy. Digging out from debts accumulated from years of unprofitable operation can be tricky.

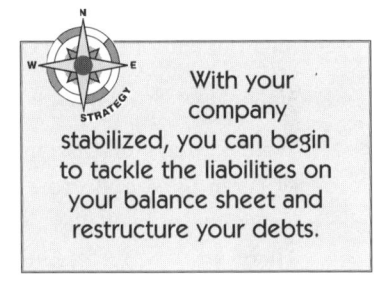

> With your company stabilized, you can begin to tackle the liabilities on your balance sheet and restructure your debts.

You must convince creditors they will be treated fairly and equitably in relation to other creditor groups. Your creditors also must be treated fairly in relation to others who must sacrifice when a business goes bad, such as stockholders and employees.

note — With debt restructuring, understand your options and the alternatives. Also know the concessions to bargain for and how to negotiate debt relief you need.

Workouts can be long, tedious, complex affairs, and exhaust you. While you fight creditors, you must simultaneously hold your business together with too few assets. Big corporations organize in-house teams to handle their debt restructuring. Smaller companies rely on professional advisors who understand workouts and can design objective, workable financial arrangements.

⚠ **CAUTION** Debt workouts demand good negotiating skills. Similar situations produce markedly different results because of the parties' abilities to handle an adversarial situation.

The best deals happen when all parties negotiate in good faith and understand the other parties' interests and options. Still, debt workouts differ from most other business and legal negotiations. They usually involve many parties with conflicting interests and rights. Polarization within creditor groups often jeopardizes reorganization and forces companies to resolve their problems within the more stable environment of Chapter 11.

Less experienced debtors also avoid open discussion of their situation, or won't disclose information critical to a well-planned workout. There are few secrets in a workout, and secrets bring a predictable and unpleasant reaction, as do surprise or unexplained moves. Poor communication may spur your opponent to act against you.

> ⚠ **CAUTION** Creditor groups, hostile to each other as well as to the debtor company, will each fight for their share of the spoils.

Debt restructuring usually involves three major groups of creditors:

- secured creditors

- unsecured or general creditors

- taxes

You must handle each creditor group differently, because each has different rights, alternatives, concerns and options. This chapter tackles secured loans. The following chapters will give tips to handle general creditors and taxes.

Reshaping your debts

Even when you reach your goals, you must become and stay profitable to survive.

Begin with your secured obligations, those debts where the creditor has a mortgage or a pledge of your company's assets as collateral.

> **HOT spot** — You must restructure your overall debts to fit your assets. It also must match what you can pay and when.

Bank loans, government or SBA loans, acquisition loans from sellers of a business or loans from other asset-based lenders are common examples. Equipment leases technically differ from secured obligations but are treated similarly.

Tackling the secured creditors is a critical first step in a debt workout, because secured creditors can foreclose on their collateral and close your business. Your unsecured creditors can only sue to recover their debts. So secured lenders must be handled carefully because of their enormous self-help power.

> **E-Z TIP** — Lenders don't want your business, only their money.

Secured lenders have a strong bargaining position, but may cooperate when you can't pay. Lenders hate foreclosure hassles, and a foreclosure reflects poorly on a loan officer. No lender, however, will sit idle while your loan falls further behind.

Adopt the right attitude. Be cooperative and realistic with cooperative, realistic secured lenders.

> **HINT** — Never avoid lenders when you have financial problems. Lenders can forgive a defaulted loan, but not an irresponsible borrower.

Some lenders are unreasonable. To survive, you must know when to cooperate, when to fight and excel at both.

Take a "no-nonsense" look at your "no-nonsense" loan

You may be victimized by a nonsense loan that you can never repay. The loan may never have made sense, and was doomed for default from the beginning. It also may have been a sensible loan that became unworkable as losses mounted. Most troubled loans are unsound from the start. There are hundreds of examples: A seller unloads her $100,000 business to an unwitting buyer for $300,000, and finances $250,000. The seller later wonders why the buyer defaulted. A hungry supplier overloads a new account. A venture capitalist finances a hi-tech start-up built on an overly optimistic business plan. Each of these are self-victimized lenders who will find themselves in a workout, hoping to recoup a tiny fraction of what is owed.

My files are loaded with SBA blunders. The SBA only makes loans smart banks turn down. The SBA's too-lenient lending policies put as many people out of business, as into business.

Nonsense loans have no winners or losers. Borrower and lender both lose. The business owner loses the business and perhaps personal assets. The lender loses on the loan. You and your lender must think clearly so that you both come out as well as possible. Within those parameters, you carve your deal.

Tear up your loan and start fresh with an entirely new deal if that's what it takes for you and your lender to come out winners.

Definition:
Winning, for you, is saving your business. Your lender wins if he ends up with more than if you had failed.

A three-step master strategy can reshape any nonsense loan:

Step 1) Convince your lender he will receive more through a restructured loan than foreclosure.

Step 2) Cut your loan to about the liquidation value of the collateral.

Step 3) Repay what your business can afford to pay and grow a future.

How to defang your lender

Lenders with problem loans are defensive. They want to secure past-due payments, protect their collateral, shore up their loan with more collateral, and liquidate the loan at the first opportunity. Take the initiative. Forewarn lenders of upcoming problems.

Take the initiative and you can win concessions denied delinquent, uncooperative borrowers.

But cooperative or not, your lender must decide:

- Should he foreclose now, or cooperate, and hope for a larger recovery later?

- Temporary and permanent loan concessions he should grant?

> **You may negotiate your loan workout with your lender's workout team, including your loan officer, and the lender's legal counsel.**

Your first objective is to buy time to start your turnaround with lender cooperation; a grace period of reduced or canceled payments until your cash flow improves and you stabilize. You can then negotiate an entirely new loan arrangement.

Troubleshooting Your Business Made E-Z

Workouts require legal guidance. Most importantly, the lender's attorney adds a somber tone to the situation, a reminder that your lender takes your loan problems seriously.

Your lender must initially decide whether to work with you or foreclose. If your lender's collateral is chiefly inventory or accounts receivable, he may worry that you will deplete these assets during your workout, and he will lose more if he forecloses later.

Lenders foreclose for different reasons. Your lender may be uncooperative if regulatory agencies are pressuring them. Or huge losses this year may be better absorbed this year. A new loan officer may want to charge your bad loan to his predecessor. Lending institution politics create irrational decisions.

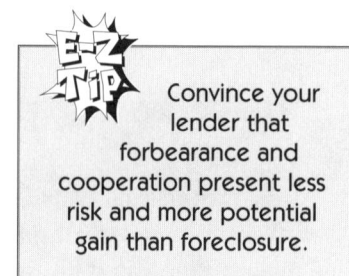

> **E-Z TIP:** Convince your lender that forbearance and cooperation present less risk and more potential gain than foreclosure.

Your role as a guarantor is another important consideration. For example, a bank suddenly foreclosed on a furniture manufacturer's $300,000 loan, barely one month overdue, because the owner was divorcing, and the bank wanted to attach his home before he lost it to his wife. Convincing your lender that you will remain financially strong as a guarantor is as important as demonstrating your company's continued financial strength. If your lender has recourse to other strong guarantees (such as the SBA), it may prefer to collect under these guarantees.

An IRS lien will give the IRS a first lien on accounts receivables generated 45 days after the lien. The bank must foreclose to protect its rights to the pledged receivables unless you file Chapter 11. Fraud, embezzlement or other dishonesty also invites foreclosure. Lenders won't cooperate with thieves.

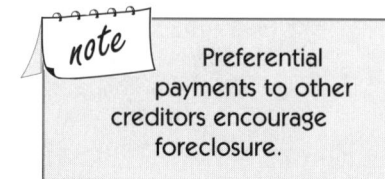

> **note:** Preferential payments to other creditors encourage foreclosure.

204

Despite these strong reasons to foreclose, you can turn any lender into an ally. Prior relationships are important. Trade on it, and your lender's may be more lenient and reasonable. Lenders are people and unpredictable. Attitudes and policies vary within the same bank.

Start out with a positive attitude, and anticipate cooperation. Consider many factors in your favor. Lenders dislike adverse publicity from closing a business. Nor is your lender certain that with time you won't repay more than through immediate foreclosure. You must convince your lender that cooperation offers more long-term benefit than risks. Your lender must believe your company can be quickly stabilized without draining collateral. Make your case.

Will outside financing cover your deficits? Give the lender frequent asset appraisals to monitor its collateral. Set benchmarks by which you and your lender can determine whether your company is recovering to your mutual satisfaction. Show your lender why he has nothing-to-lose and everything-to-gain proposition. Show why time and patience will help him as much as you.

> Give your lender cash-flow statements to demonstrate how your company will finance itself, without depleting the lender's collateral.

That's the formula that turns lenders into allies!

Deal collectively with secured lenders. Don't shield your lenders from one another or conceal other loan defaults. Successful workouts need coordination and cooperation between secured lenders, especially when they share the same collateral. Secured creditors are concerned when lenders are paid when they are not. Collectively, you design a more unified and equitable solution.

Preparing for battle

Be smart. Battle your lender only when your personal assets are fully protected. Otherwise, your lender may attach your assets without warning, or want them pledged in exchange for his cooperation.

> **note** Money deposited with your lender is vulnerable.

Your bank can automatically grab funds in your checking and savings accounts, and funds from other loan guarantors with monies on deposit.

Lenders try to shore up shaky loans with collateral, more business assets, personal assets, or additional guarantors. If your lender thinks your present collateral won't cover the loan, it probably won't. So why jeopardize more assets to only improve your lender's position and weaken your own? Refusing more collateral won't bring faster foreclosure. Well-secured lenders foreclose faster because they know a foreclosure will get them fully paid. Under-collateralized lenders need patience. Expect your lender to dangle attractive concessions for more collateral. Temporarily suspended payments, lower interest or fresh advances are common. A well-secured lender will foreclose instantly.

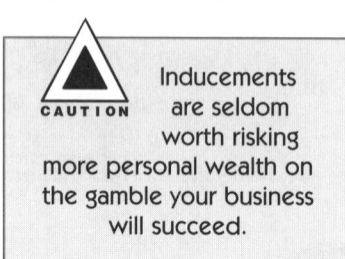

> **CAUTION** Inducements are seldom worth risking more personal wealth on the gamble your business will succeed.

Politely say "no" to a pushy lender? Title your property with your spouse. Your spouse will be uncooperative, and refuse to encumber marital property. You be the nice guy. Make somebody else the "heavy." Whatever your tactic, arrange your financial affairs so you no longer control assets your lender wants pledged as collateral.

Chapter 11

Loan-shrinking strategies

Lenders won't readily cut their loans, but you must shrink loans when your business is over-financed or when the loans exceed what your business is worth.

An example: A small meat-processing business, with assets worth about $100,000, owed its banks $240,000 and its general creditors $150,000. We renegotiated the bank loan from $240,000 to $135,000. The general creditors, in poorer bargaining position, accepted $15,000, or about 10 cents on the dollar. The company finally had a sensible balance sheet.

Downsizing debts to match what your business is worth is common sense, but even veteran business owners struggle with loans they can never fully repay. They struggle for as long as their creditors let them. They build neither equity nor net worth in their businesses. Their future, in reality, is only a paltry paycheck, never a debt-free, valuable business.

What is your business worth? What would you pay for it as a buyer? Forget book or liquidation value. The workout is your opportunity to buy your business back from your creditors at a price another buyer would pay.

This is your maximum debt. But try to cut your debts to their liquidation value. Overly indebted business owners don't always see this point. If your home, worth $100,000, was mortgaged for $200,000, you would see why you must reduce your mortgage by $100,000 to see equity. You also would agree it would be smarter to abandon your house to the bank and buy another house where you could immediately build equity. You don't always see this as quickly with a business.

Where do you start? Estimate your assets' liquidation value. Asset appraisal involves guesswork, and there is always margin for error. The nature and condition of your assets and location and seasonal demand are several factors that influence this value. Raw material, unfinished goods or questionable receivables are most difficult to value.

207

Troubleshooting Your Business Made E-Z

> **E-Z TIP**
> Negotiate when your assets have the least value. Accounts receivable, for instance, are worth more to your lender than finished goods, which are worth more than raw materials.

Leases, copyrights, patents, franchise rights, customer lists and other intangible assets may be worth more than tangible assets. Few lenders can capitalize on these assets whose value is destroyed in liquidation. Liquidation costs, auction and attorneys' fees and other foreclosure expenses, will reduce a lender's recovery. Factor these costs into your negotiations. Prolonged lender negotiations gives your lender time to scout buyers who will pay more for your going business. Lender's cooperation may last only until a buyer appears who will pay bigger dollars.

> **HOT spot**
> Smart lenders won't auction troubled borrowers. They get more for them as going businesses than as distressed assets.

Turn choking payments into bite-sized installments

note

Reducing debts is one objective. Also restructure loan payments to what you can afford. Over-financed businesses usually fall behind on payments, and must reduce their debt and realign monthly payments. But even modest loans can choke you. Your loan payments must leave you adequate working capital and cash to rebuild your business.

What can you afford to pay on your loans? What do conservative cash-flow projections show?

To reduce strangling payments, try these three propositions:

1) **Extend your loan.** Extend short-term loans to long-term obligations. Extending loans to seven or even ten years is common in a workout. The loan may be "ballooned," or fully due in three to five years, but you gain breathing room.

2) **Defer principal.** Pay interest, but freeze principal payments until your business is back on its feet. Principal payments may be significant.

3) **Suspend loan payments.** Well-collateralized lenders resist because they can fully recoup by foreclosing. Shaky lenders will play the waiting game if they see brighter prospects ahead and a small recovery from pressing collection now. Well-collateralized lenders also are patient if they have a comfortable cushion to cover accruing interest.

> **HOT spot** Winning a temporary moratorium on payments is a tough sell, but lenders go along if it is the only way to save their loan.

More workout tips

> **note** Coaxing a lender to restructure your loan takes arithmetic, psychology, bluff, luck and know-how. Lenders have their own tricks.

Caught in a cross-fire between losing some of their loan or a foreclosure that will yield them even less, some lenders push the patience pill. "Stick with it," they chant. "Someday, somewhy, your business will succeed." Catch the hidden message?

209

Lenders will do most anything to save their loan. They will extend payments to get fully paid. Extending loans endlessly, of course, is reasonable to the lender. Virtually any loan can be repaid if you choose to spend your life in serfdom, working for your lender.

Your lender also may see a brighter future for your business, a day when it can fully repay the loan. Perhaps next year, or in five years, you would be a big success. The bank could then hold out for full repayment. Strike with poverty on your side. Give your lender a win-win deal: The lender gets more than through foreclosure, and you get a loan you can live with.

Lenders are motivated to go when you wave money. The shakier the loan, the less cash you wave. I've negotiated loan buyouts for as little as 10 cents on the dollar, even when the lender may have realized 70 or 80 cents on the dollar through foreclosure. Perhaps the lender wanted to avoid foreclosure hassles. Offer about 30 percent below what you think the collateral is worth at liquidation. Your lender will negotiate for more if he thinks he is in a stronger bargaining position. Arrange financing before you approach your lender, so you have a firm cash offer. Watch the risk factor. Don't pledge more personal assets or incur greater personal exposure for the new financing. Don't only cut your debt, also limit your exposure.

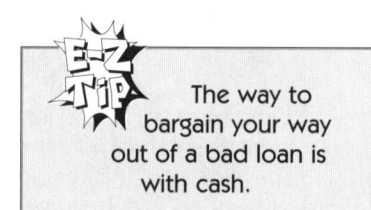

> **E-Z TIP:** The way to bargain your way out of a bad loan is with cash.

DEFINITION *Larger companies may swap debt for equity.* The lender gets shares in the company and cancels part of the loan. "Puts" and "calls" allow either the lender or the company to later sell or buy back the shares for a set price. A lender who becomes a shareholder benefits from future upturns in your company's fortunes. You gain a manageable loan. Your lender avoids an immediate loss. You avoid foreclosure and a lost business. Converting lenders to partners works well when your company is over-leveraged and needs more equity.

A highly leveraged New York bioengineering firm cured its defaulted $1.5 million bank loan when their bank converted 70 percent of their loan for 35-percent of the promising company. It was a smart deal. In foreclosure the lender would recover only 20 or 30 cents on the dollar. Why kill a business with such strong growth potential? Today, the bank's interest is worth $25 million. It was a very smart deal for both parties. But don't act too hastily. You can give away too much of your business to a pressing lender. You usually can do better with third-party financing to buy out the lender for a discount. Had the bioengineering firm shopped for new financing, it may have borrowed $1.5 million to buy out the bank's loan for perhaps 10 percent of the company.

Negotiate with your lender as if it were a third party, not someone with the power to padlock your door. You don't get the best deal when you're frightened.

If your business has a strong future, trading shares for less debt can ease your financial problems and win you even more financing. Last year, a fast-growing California software company convinced its lender to accept 40 percent ownership in the company, cancel $1.2 million on a $2 million loan and advance another $1 million. These deals happen daily!

Can you interest your lender in a piece of your company? Give it a try. Your deal will depend on the viability of your loan, your growth potential, your lender and your ability to negotiate a deal.

There is symbolism when a lender turns stockholder. Other creditors, employees and stockholders see it as a sign of confidence, a signal that you have a future!

Wave the big stick

Waving wads of money or stock certificates to appease a pushy lender isn't always the solution. With an unreasonable lender you sometimes must wave a big stick.

Lenders are painfully aware that a bankruptcy court can force reasonable lender settlements. Of course, your lender can still collect on personal guarantees, or foreclose collateral not owned by the Chapter 11 company. So whether your lender gets hurt in Chapter 11 depends on whether it has good recourse outside the corporation.

> **HOT spot** Two big sticks can bludgeon a stubborn lender. One is a Chapter 11, which lets you reduce your loan to the collateral's liquidation value. But don't rush quickly into bankruptcy for the reasons in Chapter 13.

The lender-liability lawsuit is another powerful weapon in your arsenal. Lenders who mistreat borrowers can lose bundles. You can sue your lender for considerable damages and have your loan canceled if your lender:

- Committed fraud or misrepresentation.
- Changed your loan terms without your consent.
- Exercised unreasonable control over your business.
- Failed to make promised loan advances.
- Made adverse comments about you as a borrower.
- Defaulted your loan without good cause.
- Negligently disposed of your collateral.

Threatening a lender liability suit can often persuade a lender to settle. Have a good lender-liability lawyer review if you suspect lender liability.

> **E-Z TIP** Common legal defects frequently render a lender's mortgage, but not necessarily the obligation, entirely worthless.

You may have other good defenses. For instance, never assume your lender has a valid mortgage.

Defects can, at the very least, delay foreclosure and require your cooperation to correct. Have your lawyer carefully review all loan documents. Serious defects create bargaining power!

Lender cooperation can be used advantageously in a workout. When your secured lender controls your assets, he can help you extricate your business from nagging tax and trade claims.

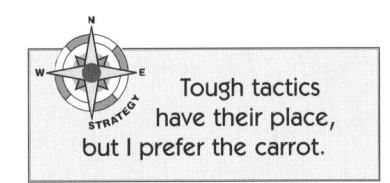

> Tough tactics have their place, but I prefer the carrot.

Parlaying lender cooperation saved a large New Hampshire textile manufacturer, who owed its lender about $4 million and its trade creditors $8 million. With the liquidation value of the business under $3 million, I was confident I could negotiate the lender's loan down from $4 million. Rather than attack the lender, we waited for the lender to foreclose on the business and resell its assets to my client's new corporation, to eliminate the $8 million due the unsecured creditors. My client, through his new corporation, assumed and repaid the entire $4-million loan. It was another win-win situation. The manufacturer regained solvency, and the cooperative lender gained.

Winning ways to get more money

Lenders loan you money when you are at the threshold of bankruptcy.

Advancing you a few additional dollars now may keep your business alive to repay those dollars later. A timely infusion of additional capital can get your distressed business through its financial crisis and be a shrewd move for you and your lender if:

- The additional capital is vital to your survival.

- Your lender is satisfied that the new loan will be repaid.

- Your lender will lose money if your business fails.

- The additional loan is small compared to what the lender can lose if you fail.

Your lender may not advance you more funds if he has no more funds to advance, or your lender cannot advance more against a defaulted loan for regulatory reasons. But, these lenders may subordinate their security interest on your collateral to allow new secured financing. Subordinations should be part of your grab bag of concessions when you meet with your lender.

Trade creditors, particularly larger creditors, have more to lose if your lender calls your loans, and are your best loan candidates. If your general creditors won't give you a loan, they may pay your loan to keep you operating and increase their own chance of getting paid.

A wholesale-grocery advanced more than $80,000 to keep a struggling Florida restaurant afloat until its peak-selling season. The restaurant survived and repaid the wholesaler the $80,000 and more than $150,000 in past-due bills. The wholesaler would have lost, had the business failed. A creditors pool similarly loaned a boat-repair shop $50,000 to cover note payments in the slow winter months. Over the next two summers, the boat yard repaid the $50,000 and the other outstanding bills due its supporting creditors.

> **HINT:** Your creditors have a big stake in your business, maybe more than you. They may decide their stake is worth protecting with a few extra dollars.

A successful loan bailout involves more than numbers, or even legal and financial one-upsmanship. Loan workouts are very much a people game. Personalities and psychology are important. A borrower and Lender must work together in good faith.

Chapter 11

Checkpoint

1) Do you have too big a loan in relation to your assets? A loan you cannot repay?

2) How must you restructure your overall debts to shape a healthy balance sheet?

3) Are you fully protected from your lender?

4) What loan concessions do you need?

5) What defenses or counterclaims can you use as leverage against your lender?

6) How can your lender help you in your debt restructuring?

7) What is that cooperation worth?

8) What do you really know about how your lender will react to your problem loan?

12
How to settle with creditors for pennies on the dollar

Chapter 12
How to settle with creditors for pennies on the dollar

If you can restructure your secured loans—then tackle excessive unsecured debts, trade payables and tax obligations. Handling these creditors may be more complicated than your problem loans, because you will have many unsecured creditors which are a less manageable situation than one or two secured lenders.

note — Unsecured creditors are relatively powerless compared to secured lenders. Unsecured creditors accept pennies on the dollar to settle, because pennies are better than nothing. What you owe is a statistic when you are in trouble. What you can pay creditors is reality. And you can negotiate such settlements, whether in Chapter 11 or through a non-bankruptcy workout.

Negotiating settlements with unsecured creditors can be a challenge, because these creditors are numerous, represent a variety of relationships with your business, and they seldom share the same stake in whether your business survives.

Evaluate the politics of your situation, key relationships between you and your creditors, and between creditors:

- How many creditors must you deal with?

- What do you owe each?

- Which creditors are critical to your business?

- Who are the largest creditors, and will they control the outcome?

- How friendly or hostile are relations between you and your creditors?

- Which creditors will benefit most from your survival?

- How cooperative or adversarial are the creditors with each other?

- What credit associations or law firms are involved in the workout, and what is their usual approach in a workout?

Only with this information can you see settlement negotiations as cordial or hostile, whether one or two creditors will dominate events, or whether one creditor will lead other creditors to follow. You'll better sense how to approach your creditors.

Start with an out-of-court settlement

Too few businesses attempt to restructure their debts outside bankruptcy.

If the out-of-court workout fails you can file Chapter 11 strategy. But I try for an out-of-court settlement because non-bankruptcy arrangements are usually more advantageous than a Chapter 11 reorganization.

One advantage is that you can keep your financial problems private, and avoid the public announcements that accompany Chapter 11. This is important when your customers will drop a supplier with financial problems or your employees will abandon an unstable job. Customers and employees are less aware of out-of-court workouts.

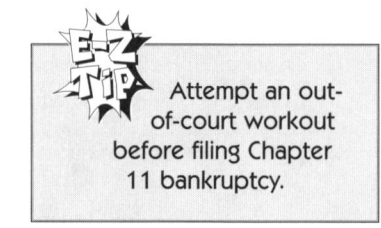

> **E-Z TIP:** Attempt an out-of-court workout before filing Chapter 11 bankruptcy.

Chapter 12

You are also unconstrained by the many rules and restrictions of a Chapter 11. A workout gives you greater flexibility to shape deals with your creditors. A Chapter 11 requires a rigid reorganization plan that treats all general creditors equally.

Privacy, creativity and economy are three compelling reasons to work a deal with your creditors without bankruptcy. Still, an out-of-court workout may not be your solution. Because a workout is a voluntary arrangement between you and your creditors, it won't stop lawsuits from holdout creditors. Nor will it stop a bank foreclosure or tax seizure. Chapter 11 also is necessary when too many unsecured creditors reject your workout proposal. A Chapter 11 will force your plan on holdout creditors when accepted by a majority of creditors.

> **note** — The major advantage of a non-bankruptcy workout is that you will save a fortune in legal fees. A Chapter 11 bankruptcy creates enormous fees.

The number of unsecured creditors and what you owe each greatly influences whether an out-of-court workout will succeed. With fewer creditors your odds improve, because you can manage few creditors without Chapter 11. Chapter 11 produces a more orderly process and brings the holdouts into line, when you have many creditors. What you owe each creditor also changes the outcome of your workout. If you have 100 creditors, but owe the five largest creditors most of your debt, your out-of-court workout may involve only these five large creditors.

Always try an out-of-court workout first, particularly if you don't have tax or secured creditor problems. We have successfully negotiated out-of-court deals for companies with hundreds of creditors, because we are well-experienced in debt-restructuring.

219

The pennies-on-the-dollar formula

Your workout plan must convince creditors that it is:

1) **Feasible:** You can pay what you promise.

2) **Fair:** Your plan treats all general creditors equally and proportionately.

3) **Equitable:** Your plan gives creditors at least what they would receive by liquidating your business.

DEFINITION

Out-of-court workouts also are called compositions, which include consolidations and extensions. Under a debt consolidation, creditors receive a fraction of their obligations. An extension extends payments. A composition may, for example, give creditors 20-percent as full settlement, payable over 24 months. The two key negotiating points then are:

- How much will you pay?

- When will you pay it?

What will you pay? As secured lenders must consider the liquidation value of their collateral, so must unsecured creditors.

What would your general creditors receive if your business were liquidated? Estimate the liquidation value of your assets, and deduct all secured debts, unpaid taxes, accrued wages, attorneys' fees, liquidation costs and other priority claims that must be fully paid before your unsecured creditors. You can then approximate what your unsecured creditors would share.

For example, if your business would liquidate for about $300,000 and you owe $200,000 to your secured creditors and other priority claims (including liquidation costs), then your general creditors would share about

$100,000. If you owe unsecured creditors $1 million, each would receive about 10-percent of their debt. Your plan must offer these creditors more.

This shows you the minimum amount to offer. How much higher should your offer be? Start negotiations by offering creditors about 5-percent more than they would receive through a forced liquidation. In the above example, creditors would share $100,000 (10-percent of the $1 million they are owed). A sensible first offer may be $150,000, or 15-percent. Always offer creditors more than what they would get under liquidation, but don't be too generous!

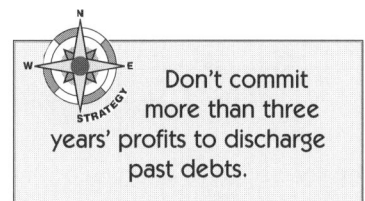

> **Don't commit more than three years' profits to discharge past debts.**

How high can you afford to go? How long you are willing to work for your creditors? Your most generous plan pledges to your creditors all profits for those years. Why mortgage your future for longer?

Creditors may disagree on other points

Creditors may disagree with your estimate of your business' liquidation value. Obtain liquidation appraisals from recognized commercial auctioneers, and value your receivables and intangible assets, such as trade names, leases, copyrights, and patents. Your attorney or accountant can schedule the priority debts.

If your general creditors would receive absolutely nothing under a forced liquidation, offer them 15 percent on their claims. I've negotiated a few 5 and 10 percent plans, but they are rare.

Creditors in larger cases may challenge future profit projections and the profits that should be earmarked for creditors. Creditors also may want you to invest more money to boost the dividends for creditors. Refuse, even if your business is recovering and the risk

> **CAUTION: Confine creditors to business assets. Don't expose your own.**

221

of loss negligible. Creditors who question profit projections may also question expenses. Big owner salaries, fancy-fringe benefits and other costly perks catch a creditor's eye. Conversely, your creditors may see high profits for your company, and commit you to an unrealistic dividend. You too may become too optimistic about your future. Be conservative.

> **CAUTION:** Overly eager creditors can project future earnings two or three times greater than what you may project, defeating a settlement.

Who can accurately project what any company will earn or can comfortably pay two or three years ahead? It's more difficult with the more volatile workout firm.

Offering general creditors a stock dividend can help resolve this problem. As stockholders, your creditors then share your future fortunes. Your creditors may accept an ownership interest to cancel debts if your company has a bright future and a marketable stock.

Offer a formula plan. Guarantee your creditors a minimum dividend plus a bonus dividend based on a specified sales or profits. Formula plans can produce serious problems. Your formula may not reflect cash available for dividends. Or you may intentionally avoid performance levels to avoid creditor dividends. Or you may encounter difficulties in drafting, interpreting or enforcing your formula.

For greater dividends, creditors may force the sale of valuable assets, or entire "cash producer" divisions or subsidiaries. Resist when these assets are the foundation of your future. Creditors see no sacred cows. Chrysler was nearly forced to sell its highly profitable tank division before its creditors relented. The tank division rejuvenated Chrysler. Airlines forfeit their best air routes for creditors. Many wither and die.

> **HOT spot:** Fancy company cars, idle computer systems and other symbols of corporate flab, are obvious targets for alert creditors anxious to wring more from the ashes.

Less significant points are negotiated with creditors. For instance, if you extend payments will creditors want interest? Remind creditors that if your business goes bankrupt, they will wait years for a check from the bankruptcy court—without interest.

Smart creditors may demand a mortgage on your business to give them a priority over future creditors—should you fail. The mortgage also lets them more easily enforce payments.

For most general creditor workouts, the debtor company negotiates to pay a percentage of the total indebtedness over time. Treating creditors equally is essential, but you may offer creditors alternative plans. For example, you may give creditors the choice of a 10 percent immediate cash dividend or a 20 percent paid over three years. Letting creditors choose among options boosts your chances for acceptance. Creditors no longer see it as "take it or leave it," but instead "which offer should I accept?" Psychology is all-important.

Creditors owed under $500 are usually fully paid, as their involvement makes settlement too cumbersome. Small creditors with little at stake are less inclined to accept settlement and spoil a successful workout. Larger creditors routinely buy the claims of smaller creditors to avoid their obstructing the workout.

DEFINITION
Compositions or informal out-of-court workouts are generally conditional on acceptance by creditors owed at least 90 percent of the debt. Fewer acceptances leaves too many unresolved claims. Holdouts may have their claims defended against or acquired by other creditors to protect the company and the plan. If you can reach agreement with most creditors, but too many holdouts still remain, then a Chapter 11 can force your plan on your few dissenting creditors.

If you only need time to pay creditors, propose 100-percent, either on a stand-by or extension basis. Stand-by means your creditors suspend collection for this time. With temporary stand-by, creditors agree to a moratorium on their claims until settlement is accepted or rejected.

Head-to-head

Open communication with creditors, early in the workout, to set procedures for negotiating the settlement plan. Negotiations need not be complicated. If your company is small, send your creditors a letter outlining your financial problem and include a proposed settlement (the plan) to accept.

You need direct creditor negotiations. On larger cases, creditors are represented by a committee of three to twelve large creditors. The size and complexity of the workout determines the composition of the committee. The creditors' committee has several roles:

> **note:** Creditors usually won't pursue lawsuits because there's not enough at stake.

- Determine your company's financial condition.

- Audit your company for fraud, embezzlement or other dishonesty.

- Review your cash flow and profit projections to negotiate settlement.

- Consider alternatives to a workout, such as bankruptcy or forced sale of your company.

- Identify special problems or cash-raising opportunities.

- Negotiate the final settlement plan.

- Recommend the negotiated settlement to other creditors.

- Monitor your company's progress.

- Enforce compliance with the plan.

Work exclusively through the steering committee, which in turn will communicate with other creditors. You are then spared the pressures of general creditor contact. Creditors will await the outcome of negotiations if kept abreast of events by the creditors' committee. Settlement negotiations involving heavy debts are usually long, tedious and frustrating. Creditors bring to the bargaining table anger, suspicion, irrationality, doubt, desire for vengeance and emotions.

Twenty creditors each see your situation differently. The "Cynic," is convinced you pillaged, plundered and raped your business, until you prove differently. Explain how your business got into trouble. Point out problems that caused losses. Diffuse creditor suspicions. Invite them to inspect your books. Creditors usually decline, but resist inspection, and creditors push harder to discover what you are hiding.

The "Moralist" chants, "You owe me $1,000, I want $1,000. Anything less is immoral and unconscionable." His tune is "what ought to be" never "what is." Be patient. Present the facts until they finally sink in.

The "Avenger" is upset about the $50,000 you owe him, but demands vengeance for the $500 bounced check on your last order. To handle the avenger, adjust the small, irritating items.

A credit manager of a big supplier may only worry how to explain to his boss why he is losing the $80,000 you owe.

The lawyers in the crowd are wondering how they can Make more fees under a bankruptcy. These and other stereotypical characters are on every creditors' committee.

When you negotiate with your creditors:

1) **Play for time.** Creditors, like fish, must tire before you reel them in. Anger and emotion run high at first. In time, your creditors will move on to new problems and fresher losses. As yesterday's news, creditors

225

settle more favorably. You may need to wear the creditors down for a few more months. Persevere. Creditors need time to recover from the maddening thought that they are losing money.

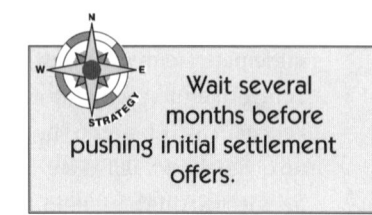

> **Wait several months before pushing initial settlement offers.**

2) **Recruit friendlier and more influential creditors** to support you, to neutralize opposition and win converts to your cause.

3) **Meet with your holdouts individually** to find out why they oppose your proposed settlement. Directly confronted creditors must tell you why he won't accept your settlement. When objections are known, you can deal with them.

4) **Bypass obstacles.** Don't let a credit manager or another middle manager nix your proposed deal. Jump heads when someone representing a creditor on your workout is unreasonable. Reach the ear of someone higher. Don't stand on formalities and protocol.

> **If your lawyer can't strike a deal with the creditor's lawyers, go for a quick agreement from the creditors.**

5) **Use your professionals**. Your lawyer may have better luck with the creditor's attorney. If negotiations strike out at your level, switch negotiations to your professional. Or, reverse events.

Sell future dollars

To get your deal, you may need more powerful motivators. Sell the future profits your creditors will reap by doing business with you. How much business do you do with your creditors? What future business can they anticipate from you? Make your creditors see your business as an important future asset to them!

Creditors generally cooperate with honest, hard-working troubled-business owners. Creditor distrust and resentment forces liquidation for viable businesses that offer creditors generous settlements. Did you antagonize or alienate your creditors? Did you issue bad checks?

Misleading financial statements? Con credit long after it was obvious you could not pay? Will creditors believe you embezzled from your business or were too casual in your concern for your creditors? There is ample opportunity for the breakdown of good relationships between you and your creditors during the workout. One trouble spot is switching to a new, competitive supplier. Or your creditors may not see your sacrifice as you continue to draw a high salary and big perks.

Small things rankle creditors, like showing up at your creditors' meeting driving a new Jaguar. You won't appease creditors about to lose hundreds of thousands of dollars behind this symbol of wealth.

Creditors won't settle if they lack confidence in your management. A poor or non-existent turnaround plan, unmet projections or continued operating losses don't inspire creditor confidence. Creditors then think they will gain more by immediately liquidating your business.

Larger companies can recruit a new chief executive or financial officer for a fresh perspective, credibility and vigor to the restructuring effort. Someone who can say, "I did not create this mess, but can clean it up," develops a very different relationship with creditors than those who created the mess.

Tackling your one large creditor

Perhaps you have only one or a few troublesome creditors.

Deals with one creditor can be more imaginative because you no longer need an "equal" deal. You negotiate with one creditor as you will under a general composition, but your personal relationship with that one big creditor, usually decides whether you will succeed.

note: One-creditor settlements can be creative.

I recently settled with a major creditor for a large New York fabric store that owed $125,000 to a Danish textile manufacturer. The manufacturer realized that in bankruptcy he would receive about $25,000 or a 20 percent dividend. Through hard bargaining, we settled for $50,000 with $10,000 paid immediately, $35,000 over two years and $5,000 in inventory returns for credit. The debt cancellation also was conditional on the retailer buying $250,000 a year COD from the manufacturer over three years.

9-point debt settlement checklist

Use this checklist when you negotiate:

1) **How much will you pay?** Offer 5 percent more than what your creditors would get in a bankruptcy. Gradually raise your offer in 2 percent increments.

2) **How much now and how much later?** Pay immediately what your business can afford without investing of your own money. Limit future payments to what the business can comfortably pay.

3) **What length of payments?** Don't commit to longer than two to three years. Payments to creditors should not exceed cash on hand plus two or three years' surplus cash flow.

4) **What about return goods?** Merchandise returned to suppliers for credit should be bartered the same as a cash payment.

5) **What about a mortgage to secure future payments?** A mortgage on your business assets is a reasonable creditor demand, and a bargaining tool for other concessions. Require your creditors subordinate their mortgage to any future financing.

6) **What about interest?** Two or three year payouts may require a reasonable interest.

7) **Will you personally guarantee the payments?** Refuse!

8) **What about future purchases?** Creditors may condition settlement on your future business, but buy at the same price as cash customers and can use what you agree to buy.

9) **What about giving creditors' shares in your company?** Don't give creditors more than 25 percent of your company. Negotiate a buyback option to reclaim 100 percent ownership.

Always ask yourself tough questions: Is your business really ready for that fresh start? Can your business survive and prosper?

Resolving tax problems

If you owe taxes to the IRS or state taxing authorities, you're not alone. It's an easy trap to fall into. You may have used withholding or sales taxes to cover operating expenses. Financially troubled companies sometimes owe many of thousands of dollars in back taxes. Eventually, the IRS padlocks their doors or levies their bank accounts.

Troubleshooting Your Business Made E-Z

The right strategy against the IRS depends on several factors: How much you owe, the severity of your finances, your personal exposure and wealth, your workout plan and, how closely the IRS is to closing your business.

If you owe the IRS a substantial amount and want to stall collection, pay the oldest quarters first. This delays IRS detection and gives you time to implement a workout plan and final resolution of your IRS problems. Because you will pay current quarters late, you will incur further penalties. If you only need a few months to pay back taxes, then pay the current quarters to avoid more penalties.

How much do you owe? If you owe significantly and have little personal wealth, you may never fully pay the IRS. Whether you owe the IRS $2 million or $1.9 million is academic, when you have no personal assets or income. Your best strategy may be to sink your company, pick up its few assets for pennies on the dollar and begin anew with a new corporation.

If you want to avoid personal tax exposure, as you should, and cannot fully pay, then pay the employees' withholding or "trust fund" taxes. As an officer or owner of your business, you are personally liable for unpaid trust taxes, but not the employer's contributions. To ensure payments are applied to the trust portion, clearly mark this on your checks. Trust taxes average about two-thirds of the total taxes, so paying the trust taxes only saves you money. For instance, if your total taxes are $6,000 weekly, you would save $2,000 a week by not paying employer's contribution and save about $25,000 if you closed your business in three months.

You may avoid payment or filing returns for several quarters, but eventually the IRS will catch you.

To slow down the IRS:

1) Give a good excuse for your tax delinquency. Sickness? Business interruption? Other casualty? Business reversals beyond your control? Make your case. IRS agents are human.

230

Chapter 12

2) Is your business heavily encumbered? Will the IRS get little or nothing under seizure. IRS guidelines discourage seizure of overencumbered businesses, but agents still seize or threaten seizure to frighten you into payment. The IRS will not seize your business if you post a bond or pledge assets equal to the equity in your business. Never pledge collateral worth more than the business, nor pledge personal assets.

If you can't agree on installments with the IRS, file Chapter 11 before IRS seizure. Filing 11 later is usually a hollow victory because your business may have been seriously disrupted by the IRS.

If you do owe excessive taxes, an out-of-court deal with your secured lenders and general creditors is futile unless you simultaneously solve your tax problems.

A business is never safe when it owes the tax collector. The IRS will levy bank accounts. The IRS will levy your receivables and devastate your cash flow and customer relations.

State-taxing authorities can be equally tough. You may owe your state even more than you owe the IRS. Most states follow IRS procedures for enforcing their tax claims, and you need a similar counterstrategy.

Do you or your business have tax troubles, read my *How to Settle with the IRS for Pennies on the Dollar* which reveals the strategies, tactics and tricks to defend yourself against the tax collector. But don't play games with taxes. Pay taxes on time because the tax collector plays roughest.

Checkpoint

1) Can an out-of-court settlement with your general creditors be your best debt-reduction strategy?

2) What would be a fair settlement with your creditors?

3) What problems may hamper a settlement. Why may creditors object to your proposition?

4) What arguments can you make that would most persuade or convince creditors to accept your offer?

5) What is your strategy on back taxes?

Bewitched, bothered and bewildered about bankruptcy?

13

Chapter 13
Bewitched, bothered and bewildered about bankruptcy?

Troubled companies and a Chapter 11 bankruptcy go together like a horse and carriage. Too many failing businesses think their solutions are in the halls of bankruptcy, and they usually are wrong.

Don't file bankruptcy too fast. Understand its pitfalls. Know when to file Chapter 11 and when to avoid it. To improve your odds of surviving Chapter 11, understand its features.

Here's a quick primer: A Chapter 11 lets you rehabilitate your business by reorganizing debts owed creditors. Under Chapter 11 you can reject contracts, and oftentimes raise fresh credit and capital.

The few companies that survive Chapter 11 are usually larger companies. Fewer than 10-percent of the survivors are small firms. Most will usually disappear within three years. These companies never really resolved their problems in Chapter 11. Because of these dismal results a Chapter 11 is usually the wrong medicine for small, sick businesses. Still, most small business owners hastily jump into a Chapter 11 as their solution when it's nearly always fatal!

> **note** Only 15-percent of Chapter 11 companies successfully reorganize, while 85-percent fail.

Business owners are too easily prodded into Chapter 11 by a bankruptcy attorney unfamiliar with more effective cures for a sick business. A Chapter 11 spells the big fees, but also can be the wrong medicine for your business.

When a Chapter 11 can be your best friend

A Chapter 11 has downsides, but there are five situations when Chapter 11 can succeed:

1) To stop creditors from seizing, repossessing or foreclosing

note — Chapter 11 is the only way to stop secured lenders from foreclosure. Unsecured creditors cannot sue a company in a Chapter 11, and secured creditors are similarly enjoined from foreclosing on a Chapter 11 company without court approval. The bankruptcy court will protect you from foreclosure if it believes the lender is adequately protected. But, you must show that your lender will not be hurt by delay in foreclosure.

About a third of my Chapter 11 cases are to stop lender foreclosure. We may have no difficulty with unsecured creditors, but lenders can be more pushy. A Chapter 11 won't resolve problem loans or permanently stop foreclosure, unless your lender can convince the court that its collateral is losing value, or you are falling further behind. Delay will then hurt your lender.

Chapter 11 can cool a lender and create the calming atmosphere to negotiate lenient loan arrangements. You can give your lender other concerns in Chapter 11 under threats of "cramdown," which reduces your lender's loan to the liquidation value of its collateral. The cramdown is to restructure the overfinanced company with uncooperative lenders.

It's preferable to negotiate a more workable loan without Chapter 11. Why endure the expense and hassle when you can as easily and less expensively and amicably reach the same agreement a bankruptcy judge may force upon you?

You may cut a deal with a recalcitrant lender and avoid Chapter 11, if the lender is convinced we otherwise will file Chapter 11.

2) To stop the IRS

HINT: Chapter 11 stops the IRS dead cold, and can tame the IRS. Once you file a Chapter 11, the IRS (and other taxing agencies) must:

- Stop all further collection efforts.

- Cancel all seizures or levies against your property.

- Return seized property still in its possession,

Chapter 11 gives you up to six years to repay your back taxes. Consider Chapter 11 if you can't repay. It is technically possible in Chapter 11 to settle with the IRS for less than what you owe If you owe a small tax bill, resolve it without a Chapter 11—if you have no other creditor problems. Don't spend $10,000 or $15,000 in legal fees to file Chapter 11 to resolve a $25,000 tax bill. Borrow, even at high interest, and pay the IRS.

Use common sense. Don't borrow against personal assets to pay the IRS (or other creditors) if you doubt the survivability of your business. For your Chapter 11 to succeed, you also must have the financial ability to pay delinquent taxes within six years. If you continue to lose money, you lack that ability. If you fall further behind on taxes after you file Chapter 11, the bankruptcy court will quickly close you down.

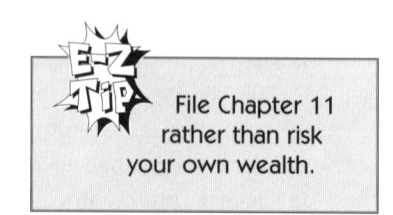

> **E-Z TIP**
> File Chapter 11 rather than risk your own wealth.

Chapter 11 cures state tax ailments as it does unpaid federal taxes. Filing Chapter 11 to stop the tax collector is common. Many small-business Chapter 11s are caused by serious tax problems.

3) To resolve general creditor problems

You can't always successfully restructure trade debts as out-of-court. Creditors may be too hostile, unmanageable or numerous.

If you have only a few creditors and good relationships, then out-of-court debt restructuring should work. You then avoid the long, complex and costly Chapter 11. If you have many hostile creditors or complex financing involving different creditors, then a Chapter 11 may be necessary to control competing claims and create order from chaos.

You may reach a settlement with most creditors but still have holdouts. A Chapter 11 reorganization plan approved by a majority of your creditors, will bind holdouts to the same plan. A Chapter 11 forces creditors to face the unhappy reality they will never get fully paid. Time diffuses emotion and is a forum where you and your creditors can negotiate. Out-of-court workouts are frequently achieved against the threat of Chapter 11. Creditors aware of your financial problems will quickly and aggressively try to collect, so your workout must be rapid and controlled. However, the threat of Chapter 11 may coax hostile creditors to bargain. Bluff Chapter 11, but be prepared to follow through. For Chapter 11 to succeed, you need approval of your plan from a majority of your general creditors owed at least two-thirds of the total unsecured debt. For instance, if 100 voting creditors are owed $100,000, then 51 creditors collectively owed $67,000 must accept your plan. You

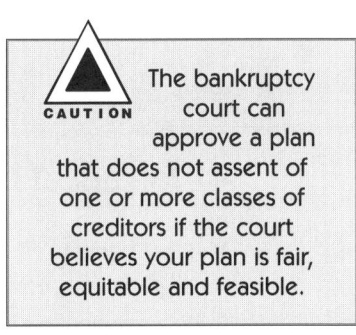

> The bankruptcy court can approve a plan that does not assent of one or more classes of creditors if the court believes your plan is fair, equitable and feasible.

may need to boost your offer to gain the necessary votes. You need similar approval from other classes of creditors, secured creditors, taxes, and priority claimants. It is usually easier to gain their approval.

In contrast to Chapter 11, out-of-court workouts need virtually 100 percent creditor acceptance. Settling with creditors collectively owed $500,000 is meaningless if you have other creditors owed another $500,000 chasing you.

You can combine Chapter 11 and an out-of-court workout into a pre-packaged Chapter 11. First attempt an out-of-court workout. In the earlier example, if 51 creditors assented to your plan and collectively were owed $67,000, a similar "pre-packaged" Chapter 11 would bind the 49 non-assenting creditors owed $33,000 who could otherwise sue for full payment.

A pre-packaged Chapter 11 starts with an out-of-court agreement, where assenting creditors confirm they will assent to the same plan in Chapter 11. If you gain enough assents to confirm your plan in Chapter 11, but too few for a successful non-bankruptcy workout, file Chapter 11. The plan of reorganization will offer creditors the same plan the majority of creditors agreed to in the out-of-court workout. You have the necessary assents in hand. You can quickly exit Chapter 11 with your out-of-court plan forced upon all creditors.

The pre-packaged Chapter 11 lets you attempt a non-bankruptcy workout, with nothing to lose. If you later need a Chapter 11, you can conclude it quickly. This can save you considerable aggravation and legal fees of a prolonged, costly Chapter 11.

4) To cancel burdensome contracts

You can extricate yourself from unprofitable supply contracts, a lease on outdated equipment, or real-estate lease. You can cancel oppressive collective bargaining agreements causing your troubles.

You can reject or cancel any lease or contract that the court finds burdensome or detrimental to your financial rehabilitation. Without the ability to shed bad contracts and leases,

> **E-Z TIP:** Chapter 11 lets you terminate burdensome contracts and leases.

238

many companies cannot regain profitability. Many fast-growth chains eventually go into a Chapter 11. They start with two or three profitable stores and rapidly expand. Predictably, many locations are mistakes, which they shed through Chapter 11.

Some cases where Chapter 11 allowed cancelled leases and bad contracts to save a business:

- A Connecticut clothing wholesaler canceled an order for 20,000 winter coats when he decided more profitable leisure wear should be the cornerstone of its turnaround.

- An Iowa electronics firm terminated twelve costly executive employment contracts and saved more over $1.3 million in salaries.

- A Massachusetts oriental-rug importer, using mail order rather than retail distribution, filed Chapter 11 to escape sales rep contracts.

- A Florida ambulance service in Chapter 11 became profitable after it canceled unprofitable emergency service contracts with three cities.

Because Chapter 11 usually comes on the heels of big losses, it's not surprising that most firms must undergo radical change in Chapter 11. The ability to wiggle out of bad contracts allows that change.

5) To get credit

note Many troubled firms get more credit after they file Chapter 11 than they had before.

Suppliers know when you are in financial trouble. Suppliers correctly reason that what they sell you on credit today may become 5 or 10-cents on the dollar several years from now. Creditors seldom recover pre-filing debt. But when they extend you credit after you file Chapter 11 your supplier is in a more secure position to get paid when due, because creditors get paid before general creditors owed pre-filing debts.

Chapter 11 also lets you refinance more creatively. For instance, with court approval, you can safely lend to your own company and grant yourself a mortgage on your business assets. Affiliated companies can similarly pledge assets to secure new financing. Many other money-raising options, not usually possible or safe without Chapter 11, become available because bankruptcy grants new lenders and creditors priority over existing lenders. Unconventional financing arrangements may be vital when your business needs fresh cash.

Three Chapter 11 pitfalls

A Chapter 11 dims considerably when you consider three big pitfalls:

1) You may scare away customers and suppliers

What will long-term customers with warranties or extended contracts think about your Chapter 11? Will they want an orphaned product or a deal with a potentially dead company?

A machine shop that manufactured one critical part for a Detroit automaker considered Chapter 11. But the automaker would switch suppliers at the first hint of bankruptcy. Could the automaker rely upon a supplier who might disappear? Our answer was a quiet, out-of-court workout. Despite the potential loss of important customers, a Chapter 11 may be unavoidable. If so, a fast and effective public-relations campaign can blunt customer concerns and rebuild confidence in your future.

note — Word of your Chapter 11 will get around, no matter how small you may be. Competitors quickly publicize your problems to your customers, suppliers and employees.

2) You can lose control of your business

Creditors can ask the court to appoint a trustee to run your business if they can prove gross mismanagement or fraud. The creditors' committee, or the court, also can set your salary or control daily decisions. Many business opportunities will be missed because you're in bankruptcy, and the court will require biweekly financial reports and mountains of red tape which takes time way from rebuilding your business.

> **CAUTION:** You need court approval for anything outside the ordinary course of business.

Bankruptcy is a hostile environment where different players can make life difficult. Managing your business through creditors and the court is a bitter pill to small entrepreneurial business owners.

3) It is costly and time-consuming

Chapter 11 is a hotbed of legal maneuvers, ploys and counterploys, which cost time and money. It is more involved, expensive and cumbersome than less legalistic, out-of-court creditor arrangements. Good employees will become frustrated and may move on to more free-wheeling companies. These complexities and bureaucratic inefficiencies encourage high legal fees and boost Chapter 11 beyond the financial reach of all smaller companies.

> **note:** A Chapter 11 can take several years (one to two years is average).

You need a big company, big money and the organizational stamina to withstand the endless red-tape nonsense. Fees in out-of-court workouts pale against the whopping Chapter 11 fees. This is why many troubled smaller companies either attempt out-of-court workouts or simply close up shop rather than file a Chapter 11.

The advantages and disadvantages of a Chapter 11 are greatly magnified between large and small companies. Small companies can sometimes trade on more personal relationships with suppliers and lenders. Still, larger corporations fare better in Chapter 11. And unlike the large corporation whose failure can sink smaller suppliers and unemployed thousands, your small business has little impact on those it does business with. A Fortune 500 company will be kept alive by a benevolent Uncle Sam or dependent suppliers and creditors who cannot afford to let it sink. Your small business is expendable!

> **HINT:** Small companies lack the big corporation's clout and leverage with creditors.

How to survive a Chapter 11

A Chapter 11 is strong medicine for any sick business, perhaps too strong. Few companies can finance themselves through Chapter 11. Chapter 11 can ease credit and cash flow. Cash shortages nevertheless are a serious, chronic problem. You must know how you will stay afloat in Chapter 11, if your secured lenders resist new financing or interrupt your cash flow.

Chapter 11, to stop a foreclosure, is short-lived if your lender can convince the court your collateral won't sufficiently protect him. Chapter 11 chiefly fails for the same reasons out-of-court workouts fail. Creditors stay hostile and uncooperative and sabotage you whether in or out of Chapter 11.

Chapter 11 companies essentially fail because they get chopped up in the meat grinder and bureaucratic mine field. Bankruptcy judges bend over backward to keep larger companies alive, but small businesses clutter a busy docket. Chapter 11 offers only a temporary, safe harbor to redirect and rebuild your company. Chapter 11 is only an opportunity to rid yourself of creditors. Your problems aren't over until you make money. Few companies that emerge Chapter 11 are profitable. The rest only gain a second opportunity to snag a new round of creditors before they finally fail.

Chapter 13

When you are overly optimistic and anxious to get the ordeal over with, you and your creditors can reach hasty deals and ignore hard, dismal facts. Companies that succeed in Chapter 11 share six common characteristics:

1) They go into a Chapter 11 with sufficient cash and a nucleus of assets.

2) They have a solid business plan of how to become profitable and rebuild.

3) They enjoy creditor cooperation and support.

4) They maintain a positive cash flow during the Chapter 11 and thereafter.

5) They cure their underlying problems.

6) They get out of Chapter 11 quickly.

Even then, this doesn't necessarily suggest a Chapter 11 should not be attempted. Some ingredients for a successful outcome can be found only after you file for reorganization as a safe harbor, get your second wind and calmly see what you have to save, and how to save it.

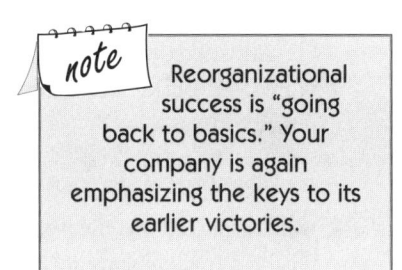

> **note** Reorganizational success is "going back to basics." Your company is again emphasizing the keys to its earlier victories.

How to bury your dead business without bankruptcy

HOT spot Perhaps you prefer to quietly and discreetly bury your company. Don't file bankruptcy! Chapter 7 gives you nothing but red tape, legal fees and a bankruptcy trustee who will look for every reason to sue you.

What is the right way to bury a dead business? Make an Assignment for the Benefit of Creditors (ABC). Where you transfer your assets to an assignee, who liquidates your business and pays creditors their share of the proceeds. The process is similar to bankruptcy, but an ABC offers you several important advantages:

- ABCs are simpler: An ABC avoids complex, formal court proceedings. You simply sign a paper and give your assignee the keys and a creditor list.

- You usually incur no fees with an ABC. The assignee takes his fee from the liquidation proceeds of your business.

- ABCs are less troublesome. With an ABC, you have fewer concerns with preference claims against yourself, as in bankruptcy. Assignees are unlikely to pursue fraudulent transfers, not like bankruptcy trustees. You appoint the assignee, although the assignee must protect creditors. Creditors can still petition your business into bankruptcy, but seldom do.

Most creditors prefer an ABC to bankruptcy because they get paid faster. Liquidated businesses (such as in a bank foreclosure) can make an ABC to notify its creditors.

We have assignees who will handle assignments in every state and are well respected by the IRS, lenders and creditors. They can liquidate your business quickly, smoothly and usually without a cost to you.

Checkpoint

1) Do you understand that as a small business owner you have less than 10-percent chance of surviving a Chapter 11 ?

2) Is a Chapter 11 the remedy you need to stop bank foreclosure or tax seizure?

3) What efforts have you made to resolve your creditor problems without a Chapter 11 ?

4) Can a pre-packaged Chapter 11 work for you?

5) To what extent do you need a Chapter 11 to rebuild credit or obtain new financing? What about canceling unfavorable leases and contracts?

6) Would a Chapter 11 cause you to lose essential customers?

7) Do you understand the disadvantages of a Chapter 11 ?

8) If you are planning a Chapter 11, do you have the ingredients to survive and succeed?

9) If you are planning to close your business, have you considered an Assignment for the Benefit of Creditors instead of Chapter 7 bankruptcy?

Dump-buybacks: the fast track to a debt-free business

14

Chapter 14
Dump-buybacks: The fast track to a debt-free business

The fastest route to a debt-free business? Dump your company and buy back its assets at a bargain price. You are back in business, and your pressing debts are gone.

DEFINITION — Sound too simple or devious? It can be your most practical strategy. Hundreds of companies do it every year! It's not complicated. You "dump" your business by voluntarily liquidating. You set up a new corporation and buy from the liquidator those assets you need to restart your business. You're back in business, at the same location, with your same assets, but without the haunting debts.

Barbara "dumped" her way to a debt-free business. Tired of jostling with creditors pressing to collect $600,000 in long overdue bills, Barbara, with the stroke of her pen, made a voluntary assignment of her home-accessory store for the benefit of creditors. Several days later, the assignee sold Barbara's newly formed corporation the assets of her former business, free of creditor claims. Barbara paid only $45,000 to buy the assets from the assignee. Barbara again opened her doors for business, while her nagging bills disappeared—gone forever!

Ken had a similar story. His furniture outlet owed a local bank about $200,000 for a loan and $1 million for suppliers. Ken had the bank foreclose on its long-overdue loan. The bank sold Ken's newly-formed corporation $350,000 in merchandise and fixtures from his foreclosed business for the assumed $200,000 debt due the bank. A simple foreclosure wiped out $1 million in trade liabilities. It was a smart deal for Ken's bank, because Ken mortgaged his home to the bank as additional collateral, while Ken had a debt-free business except for the bank loan.

Dump-buybacks save businesses like yours every day.

The perfect solution

> **note** A dump-buyback is an ideal solution for a business with few assets and heavy debt.

Why waste time and effort with creditors when it's easier, faster and cheaper to restart your business by buying back its assets from your creditors, leaving your liabilities behind? Rest assured it's 100-percent legal. Creditors come out at least as well in a dump-buyback as in an out-of-court workout, Chapter 11 or a Chapter 7 bankruptcy. It can be a win-win situation for you and your creditors. You avoid the fanfare and risks of other debt-reduction strategies, and your creditors get more money faster than through bankruptcy.

Dump-buyback companies range from large manufacturing plants to small service firms. In each case, a bankruptcy trustee, receiver, Assignee for the Benefit of Creditors, the IRS, state tax collector, bank or finance company agreed to sell the assets of the defunct business back for a bargain price. Because the deal was quickly orchestrated, some businesses never closed their doors. Employees and customers never discovered the business actually failed.

> **note** Bankruptcy judges routinely review and approve dump-buyback cases because the deals are fair and equitable to creditors and their best deal under the circumstances.

Chapter 14

Why can the dump-buyback be your best bet?

> Dump your business problems fast, so you can concentrate on making money.

- It is simpler and less costly—you need only to form a new corporation and negotiate to buy back the assets of your failed business. Why feed your lawyer money you will need in your business?

- It is faster. You can be back in a debt-free business in a few days. A Chapter 11 or an out-of-court workout can drag on for years.

- You control the disposition of your business. You control the timing method of liquidation and liquidator. Chapter 11 puts your assets under the total control of the bankruptcy court and your creditors.

- It avoids the need to resolve contested creditor claims. The liquidator pays each creditor from the proceeds and resolves disputed claims. You must resolve disputed claims in Chapter 11 reorganization or out-of-court workout.

Consider how practical a dump-buyback was for a small Pittsburgh health club struggling with $50,000 in new fitness equipment and loans of $30,000. The club's former landlord sued the health club for $200,000, claiming breach of lease.

Jim, the club's owner, argued that since his former landlord neglected the premises he could legally move on and ignore the lease. But for Jim to fight his ex-landlord would cost thousands in legal fees. Winning could ruin Jim financially.

Sinking his health club was a more practical alternative. An equipment-supply company held the mortgage on the fitness center's equipment and agreed to foreclose and sell the equipment to Jim's newly formed company at

249

public auction. It was the high bidder at $30,000, swapping the loan from Jim's former corporation to his new corporation. Jim restarted his health club without closing his doors, and with less than $3,000 in fees.

Jim's old landlord soon won a default judgment against Jim's former corporation, but can no more squeeze money from Jim's former corporation than blood from a turnip.

Large, publicly owned corporations can't do a dump-buyback. They have legions of stockholders, high visibility, complex financing and restrictive securities regulations. Bigger firms must solve their financial problems through Chapter 11, or more traditional debt-restructurings. While large companies can't vanish today and open again for business tomorrow, small corporations can, because they are simple, low-visibility and nimble.

HINT: Be practical to save your business. As in many cases, practicality is folding one tent and pitching another.

Dump-buybacks aren't only for nickel-and-dime ventures. Few Fortune 500 corporations can try it, but it can work even for multi-million-dollar operations.

The dump-buyback blueprint

The dump-buyback takes professional skill, creditor cooperation and some luck to work. You must walk a narrow line: You must be scrupulously fair and honest with creditors. You want your business back as cheaply as possible. Within these conflicting goals are two basic steps:

Step 1)   Liquidate your business.

Step 2)   Acquire the assets you need to start again—at the lowest possible price.

You can liquidate in several ways. A creditor or lender with a mortgage on your business can foreclose on, and resell the assets at a foreclosure. Another way is the Assignment for the Benefit of Creditors. Most states allow a debtor to assign or transfer assets to a representative of the creditors—the assignee—who then sells the assets and distributes the proceeds to creditors. An Assignment for the Benefit of Creditors seldom involves court proceedings, so it's quick and efficient.

You also can petition the court to appoint a receiver to liquidate your business. Or, your creditors can request a receiver, who, like an assignee or bankruptcy trustee, liquidates your business, sells its assets and distributes the proceeds to creditors.

Finally, you may file for a Chapter 7 bankruptcy and have the bankruptcy court appoint a trustee to liquidate your business. This is least desirable, because a bankruptcy trustee must go through a cumbersome court process to sell a bankrupt business. This delay destroys goodwill, as your business can be closed for months. You need a fast liquidation.

You also can file Chapter 11, and have the bankruptcy court approve the sale of your assets to your new corporation. This is a "liquidating Chapter 11," and is sometimes used on larger cases, but can be as cumbersome and risky as a Chapter 7 liquidation. A liquidating Chapter 11 can be a good strategy when you have an overencumbered business. The bankruptcy court can order a sale of assets free and clear of all creditor claims, including liens and mortgages. You can then buy the assets free of the mortgage. Every liquidator has one function: Sell your assets quickly and for the best price.

How do you buy back your assets for pennies on the dollar?

Your liquidator must sell your assets in a commercially reasonable manner, whether by public auction or private sale. Assets under a distress sale sell for a small fraction of their cost.

HINT: When you want to buy back your own business, you enjoy a distinct advantage over other bidders: You can afford to pay a premium to start again because you don't see odd lots of merchandise or equipment to be trucked away. You see a new and revitalized business emerging from the ruins of one that's been temporarily dismantled to shed creditors.

Most liquidators will sell you back your assets at private sale if the deal is unquestionably fair to your creditors. Offer your liquidator about 20 percent more than what creditors would receive if the assets were auctioned. Base it on a professional appraisal. Your deal must be honest and fair in every respect. Avoid impropriety. Liquidators will rightfully refuse to sell privately to the principals of a distressed business unless the deal can withstand close scrutiny. Don't hide in your new corporation. Your creditors will eventually find out that you're the buyer, so why raise suspicions that you acted improperly? You must disclose your personal interest in a buyer company when you buy through the bankruptcy court. Let your lawyer guide you on these technicalities to avoid serious legal blunders.

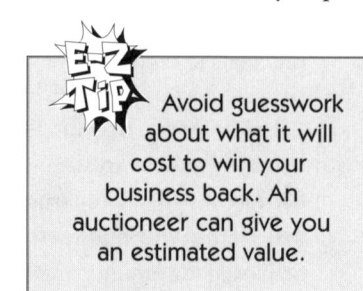

> **E-Z TIP:** Avoid guesswork about what it will cost to win your business back. An auctioneer can give you an estimated value.

A well-orchestrated dump-buyback is as fair to your creditors as it is practical and beneficial to you. It's a sensible way to get creditors the most money, and the chance to restart your business.

Directly sell your assets debt-free

You may not have to transfer your assets through a liquidator to buy them back debt-free.

Bulk sales laws are intended to prevent a business owner from selling his business assets outside of the ordinary course of business without paying his

Chapter 14

> **HINT:** You can sell the assets of your troubled business directly to your new corporation, free and clear of all liabilities, through a "bulk transfer."

creditors. Creditors must be notified of the intended transfer ten days before the transfer. Creditors not notified can later reclaim the assets sold to the buyer.

Bulk sales laws do not require the seller's creditors to be fully paid, they need only be advised whether they shall receive full payment from the sales. Creditors who won't be fully paid must receive detailed information about the intended sale. Creditors who do not object (usually through a lawsuit to prevent the sale) cannot later claim the assets sold to the buyer. Bulk-sales laws do not apply to sales by a secured party, assignee, receiver or trustee in bankruptcy.

How can the bulk sales laws help you if your objective is to restart your business? If you own Company A and want to transfer its assets to Company B free of Company A creditors, you must first notify Company A's creditors. If Company A's creditors do not stop the sale, then Company B receives clear title to the assets, even though Company A's creditors receive less than full payment.

Minimize creditor opposition. Sell creditors on the deal. Your bulk sales notice should include two or three professional appraisals that show a considerably lower auction value than what your new corporation will pay. This is key. Creditors must get more than if your business were liquidated.

> **E-Z TIP:** Build a strong case why the sale is in the creditors' best interests.

> **note:** A bulk sale can be ideal if you only have unsecured creditors. Secured debts and tax liens automatically follow the assets to your new business, so a dump-buyback or Chapter 11 is necessary to shed these liabilities.

253

Fadeouts and walkaways

If you own a small business with few assets, then why even bother with a buyback? Set up a new shop from scratch.

Beginning again with a brand-new company makes much more sense than wrestling with creditors. A local landscaper, with about $10,000 in equipment and no receivables or other assets, considered Chapter 11 to restructure $100,000 in secured bank loans, $90,000 owed the IRS and $160,000 due general creditors.

Instead he bought back his equipment for a few dollars at auction, yet replaced his equipment with new gear for a fresh start. The gardener's loyal customers would certainly patronize his new landscape business. Why not walk away from a few thousand dollars in landscaping equipment when you also walk away from $300,000 in liabilities?

Restarting your business gradually is the "fade in/fade out." Build up a new company while you wind down your defunct business.

> **HOT spot** The fade out gives you time to develop your startup when it's operationally difficult to simultaneously close one business and open another.

The fade in/fade out certainly worked for a Tampa employment agency saddled with more than $200,000 in debts. When the creditors breathed fire, the owner simply opened another agency across town using a similar name, and gradually weaned his many accounts to his new agency. The creditors finally auctioned two old desks for a few dollars to apply to their $200,000 debt.

CAUTION The fade in/fade out requires meticulous planning to avoid creditor claims that you misappropriated assets from your defunct business to start your new venture. Your accountant and attorney should guide you so you start clean.

Chapter 14

Guarantee your success with a backup plan

When one tactic fails, switch to another. Stay two steps ahead of the creditors. Develop a total game plan. Include every contingency. When you cover the bases, you play the game more enthusiastically and optimistically, because you know exactly where you are heading and the many routes to get there.

> **E-Z TIP**
> You don't rely on one strategy alone to save your business. You need backup strategies.

Checkpoint

1) Can a dump-buyback be your ideal debt-busting strategy?

2) Have you well-fortified your business so it's defensively positioned for a dump-buyback?

3) Can a cooperative, secured creditor help you with a friendly foreclosure?

4) Would a bulk transfer of assets to a new corporation be workable?

5) Would a fade in/fade out or walk-away be the right strategy to solve your creditor problems?

6) Has your professional advisor reviewed these strategies with you? What is your total game plan?

255

Making your money machine 15

Chapter 15
Making your money machine

Making money is the ultimate purpose of any business. It may be great fun working, but if you can't make money, you have a hobby, not a business. If you lose money—you have an expensive hobby. You didn't want an expensive hobby—you wanted a profitable business.

Everything you've read so far has brought you only to the point where you are well positioned to make money. Your business is stable. Your creditor problems are behind you, or soon will be. Now your business must make money. How do you turn your business into a perpetual money machine? There's no simple formula; strategies, like snowflakes, are never identical.

Set solid profit goals

It's not enough to hope for profits. Set profit goals. Think big! Modest expectations create underachievers.

> **note** Profits prove your competitiveness.

Profits allow your business to grow, attract better employees, develop new products and services, invest in more efficient plant and equipment, and market more aggressively. Profits signify a healthy future; losses mark an ailing or dead enterprise.

Shoot for profits that can let your business grow by 20-percent a year. This conservative number is for a mature business in a stable industry. Seek higher profits for a young, entrepreneurial venture with growth potential.

Businesses must double in size every five years or lose momentum and slide backward.

- at least a 30-percent return on your equity. Without this return on your money, it's smarter to sell your business and invest in stocks. A smaller return is acceptable if reasons other than money motivate you.

- 50-percent more than your competitors' profits. When you wring 15 cents profit for every 10 cents of what your competitors earn, you are a super-manager.

- at least 20-percent above last year's, outperform your own prior performance. Ask a sprinter how it feels to beat her best time around the track. She'll mop her brow and smile. Making more money than before is your gold star!

These goals can happen! Many companies with small profits—and even losses—became incredible money machines that outstripped wildest expectations. How did they do it?

Down the yellow brick road

The Wizard of Oz had his yellow brick road. You have your own yellow brick road to profitability: A strategic and operational bottom-line strategy to more income at less cost. That moneymaking formula is obvious and basic. But is it basic? You have lost sight of how to make money, and it's not central to your planning. Answers won't quickly appear. Your opportunities may be hidden.

Profit Strategy #1: Back to the future

Did you make money years ago? Make this your starting point for making money today.

Chapter 15

If your business never earned a dime, you must invent your blueprint. But if you once made money, you already have the blueprint. Perhaps you strayed too far, or in the wrong direction, or moved too rapidly from what worked in the past. Retrace your steps. What was your business like when it last made money? What changes caused the profit decline?

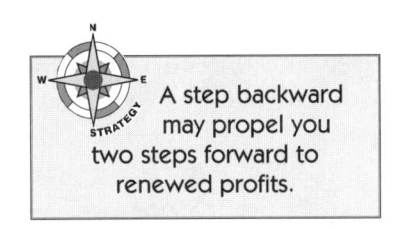

> A step backward may propel you two steps forward to renewed profits.

Reversing direction seems contrary to growth and progress. Perhaps it is, in terms of sales. But, you need profits—more than ambitious expansion that causes more unaffordable losses. Small losses today that produce bigger profits tomorrow are okay—if you can afford temporary losses and are certain of future profits. Your company may be in trouble because it went in the wrong direction. A new product line or new retail location may have failed. Reverse course to erase those missteps. Returning to your past gives you a temporary, profitable foundation from which to re-direct your business toward another yellow brick road.

Profit Strategy #2: Shrink

Downsizing your business is like returning to your past, but is different. Just because a business is reshaped it doesn't necessarily produce a smaller business. Sometimes, you may change the products, pricing, or expand your business.

> **HOT spot** Downsizing rids your company of everything that destroys profits!

- Which products/services are unprofitable?
- Which retail locations, divisions or branches lose money?
- What marketing programs don't pay?

259

When you don't constantly ask yourself these questions, you lose the way. When you have your answers, act decisively. You can't wait, because you can't afford to lose more money!

> **E-Z TIP:** Fast-growth companies frequently downsize to shed their losers. Be invigorated by your winners, but never overlook your losers.

Downsizing may require radical surgery, not merely shedding a layer of skin. You want to build muscle. Sacrifice flabby, unprofitable products, services, functions, locations or assets.

A Detroit machine-tooling firm downsized from $22 million in sales and $3 million in losses. They cut 35 unprofitable items. Two years later, they grossed $10 million, but earned $1 million in profits. A common story!

Profit Strategy #3: Atomize and synthesize

DEFINITION Never made a dime? No proven profit center? Your answer may be to atomize and synthesize! You *atomize* by tearing your business apart. You *synthesize* by building a brand new business.

Fed up with Connecticut's low Medicaid reimbursement, Bill and Martha Simon turned their failing nursing home into an alcohol-dependency treatment center. Same building, same beds, but a different business. That's atomizing and synthesizing. Bill and Martha now earn $200,000 a year in profits from their new venture, while they lost $120,000 operating a nursing home.

Synthesize and atomize? It worked for Henry Wybel, whose Fort Lauderdale boat dealership got stuck on the shoals when stiff competition, a recession and a luxury tax on boats all rocked the boating industry in the early 1990s. What could Henry do with his huge used boat inventory and boatyard on Florida's famed Intracoastal? Rent boats of course! Henry rents plenty of boats and operates a growing water-taxi business for sightseeing and ferrying hungry tourists to popular waterside restaurants.

This is rethinking your business. You think less about the business you're in and more about the business you should be in. If you think your business is a born loser that can never be turned into a winner, meet Charlie Silberling, a Connecticut street-smart entrepreneur. His life centered on his old movie theater, a loser when he bought it and a bigger loser when I met him. It featured old reruns and empty seats. "The business lost $40,000 every year. Face it, Charlie, you've got a loser on your hands." Charlie could see beyond what he had, and ripped out the seats, sold his projection equipment and cleverly converted the tired, old theater into a beautiful new consignment-art gallery. Charlie's "Wintergate Art Galleries" exhibits 800 paintings from local artists, and is always swamped with art lovers. Charlie now makes plenty of money, and couldn't be happier.

Profit Strategy #4: Fast-forward

How do you make a near-bankrupt chain of eight sunglasses kiosks profitable? "Quickly expand to 20 kiosks."

With only eight outlets, Jim and Harry could never buy sunglasses to be competitive with the large chains. Fashionable manufacturers only sold directly to volume retailers. With about 20 stores, Jim and Harry would have volume and buying power. They now buy their sunglasses at rock-bottom prices from the best manufacturers. They also have the clout to get locations at the more successful shopping malls.

> Big isn't always more beautiful, but it can be more profitable!

Fast-forward is your strategy when your basic business is sound, and you need scale economies. You can grow internally, acquire other businesses or merge. Most fast-forward companies expand. A retailer multiplies its outlets. A manufacturer produces more products. A publisher publishes more books. But you may grow even faster through acquisition. And merging two businesses can produce enormous profits.

Profit Strategy #5: Focus

Your business may make more money by focusing and you no longer will be all things to all people.

Niche marketing is not a new idea, and small businesses usually do best monopolizing small, profitable and less competitive niches. And they thrive! Even big companies now chase small-market segments once beneath them.

But Fortune 500 companies lack entrepreneurism, operational flexibility and a love for the field. These attributes belong to the entrepreneur.

- What market segments or customer groups should you target?

- How can you bundle products or services to target this market?

Plenty of niche markets are available for you to tap. Whether you sell shoes, publish books or operate a dental clinic, don't be a stumbling generalist. Focusing on a niche is critical when you have few resources to scatter in all directions.

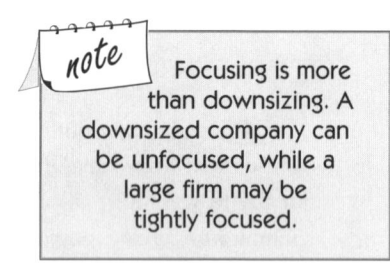

note: Focusing is more than downsizing. A downsized company can be unfocused, while a large firm may be tightly focused.

Profit Strategy #6: Knock on doors

Some businesses need only knock on a few more doors to get new customers. Maybe you never hustled customers, or opened your doors but never figured out how to get a prospect to walk through. Perhaps your marketing was too sporadic, unprofessional or ineffective.

Hundreds of books tell how to market and sell. Read some. But now, answer four questions:

- What sales do you need to become profitable?

- What new customers do you need to generate these sales?

- What have you done to get these customers?

- What more can you do?

Find the right answers, and you'll find profits.

Fundamentally sound businesses go bust only because they can't push their sales above break-even. They have the right product, right market, right prices and right location; everything but the know-how to get buyers. Business owners don't always know how to promote and sell. Techniques can be taught. We can't help the individual who won't try to sell. You must go after customers aggressively, no matter what business you're in. Customers won't automatically come to you. Success may require a few extra knocks on the door.

Profit Strategy #7: Hike prices

Even small price hikes can produce significant profits. Add 5-percent more income to your income statement. How profitable would you be?

You may lose a few customers with higher prices; even if you lose a few customers, it will usually put you ahead. Pricing largely depends on your product, service and competition. Each must be carefully considered. But many businesses are in trouble only because their prices are too low. You can increase prices so your customers won't leave you. Improved service, add-ons, bundling and services and similar tactics build perceived value, reduce price resistance and, most importantly, add dollars to turn a profit.

Manufacturing firms usually lose money because they price their products to match a competitor's. If their competitors are larger, more efficient or can produce the product more cheaply, they must outflank their competitors through product differentiation or superior service, or both. You can charge higher if you are different.

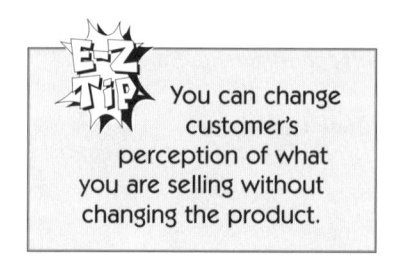

> **E-Z TIP:** You can change customer's perception of what you are selling without changing the product.

Gino Paulucci, of Papa Gino's, tells a great story of how he unloaded a truckload of discolored bananas for twice the price of unblemished bananas. Gino, then a kid working in a Duluth, Minnesota supermarket, was told by the boss to stack the speckled and discolored (but perfectly edible) bananas in front of the store and close them out for 15 cents a pound, or half the usual 29-cent price, Instead, Gino hung a sign announcing the arrival of the famed "Argentine banana." In two hours, he sold the entire lot for 49 cents a pound!

Profit Strategy #8: Cut costs

Look at your expenses. How can you build profits? If you hold your sales steady and cut expenses 5-percent, what are your new profits? There's 5-percent fat in your expenses? You're kidding yourself. Even skinflint businesses can squeeze another 5 percent from their cost column. Businesses once squeezed can be squeezed for another 5-percent. You must constantly cut when you are desperate to survive! Nickels and dimes become profit builders. Two cents more per widget and 5 cents less on production and overhead costs, and, you have 7 cents additional profit per widget! Sell enough widgets, and you'll have a profitable widget factory. High overhead costs are frequently profit destroyers. The business slowly chokes to death on operating expenses that constantly creep a bit higher.

If you want a money machine, radical surgery on unnecessary overhead costs can make it happen faster. Cut, cut and cut. Let nothing escape your scalpel.

Chapter 15

Profit Strategy #9: Build mile-high sandwiches

Building a mile-high sandwich isn't a strategy from the Harvard Business School. That good advice came from my dad, who never went to Harvard.

But my dad's "mile-high sandwich strategy" was his only profit strategy! After World War II, my dad scraped together $500 to open a tiny delicatessen in Boston. He twice expanded and soon had 40 bustling employees and legions of salivating customers crowding his small deli. Starting with almost nothing, my dad built the second largest deli in New England! As a youngster, I was his chief busboy and observed customer after customer eat only half their sandwiches and "bag" the other half to take home. Of course, dad's sandwiches were about a mile-thick, so customers with only one stomach could never finish one, no matter how tempting the challenge.

I once asked my dad why he didn't put less in the sandwich? He then taught me my most valuable business lesson. "Son," he said, "Give your customers more than they expect and more than your competitors give them. When you do, they will come back again and again—and bring new customers with them! My sandwiches are the biggest in town to give my customers more!"

My dad was right. The best, most enduring path to profits is through a bigger sandwich. Give your customer more! It's your turn. Rethink product quality. Rethink service. Do your customers get more than they expect? Listen to my dad. Building a profitable business may be as easy as a few more slices of corned beef between the rye.

Eight profit-planning tips

Turning a profit strategy into profits is the heart of the turnaround. No matter how brilliant the scheme, you must start with a profit concept and action plan.

Tip #1: Get a sense of what is going on

You can become so immersed in daily events that you lose touch with new trends within your industry that pinpoint opportunities and new directions for your business.

> **E-Z TIP**
> Get your head out of the sand. Read trade journals. Visit or spy on the successes in your industry. Analyze. Ask questions. Steal ideas!

Tip #2: Brainstorm

Make profit-planning a group sport. Brainstorming. Bouncing ideas around synergizes the process, and creates a sounding board—particularly if you have free thinkers, not yes men, in the group. Encourage a free, open flow of ideas. Review every possibility and its potential. Involve people within your organization who must implement your plans.

Tip #3: Prioritize strategies

We discussed a few possible profit strategies. There are others, so consider them all. You may adopt one or two primary profit strategies with many secondary strategies. Prioritize so you know the resources and attention each deserves.

Concentrate first on business changes that can happen fastest and produce the most definite, significant and immediate profits. Clamp down quickly on your big losers. Start with a cost-cutting program and find product lines or operating divisions that constantly lose money. Follow a concentric pattern of hitting hardest and fastest at those areas that bring the fastest results.

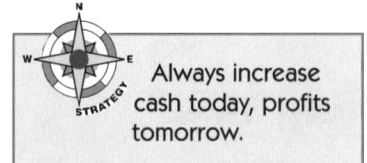

> **STRATEGY**
> Always increase cash today, profits tomorrow.

Tip #4: Set realistic profit goals

Your profit plan must work! A realistic plan has detail, hard numbers, and clearly shows how each change will increase profits. Long-term planning is less precise and predictable. Lack of reality is a major stumbling block. Your idea may sound intriguing, but lack operational practicality. You cannot afford more mistakes. Your future plans must work. Electing a safer course that generates modest profits is better than a big-potential, big-gamble plan. Safety is part of reality.

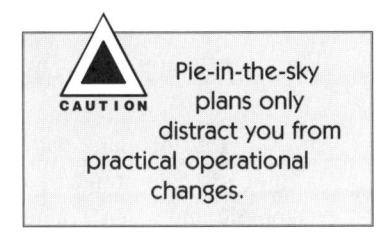

> **CAUTION** Pie-in-the-sky plans only distract you from practical operational changes.

Does your plan fit your financial, organizational and logistical capabilities? Do you have the money and resources for the plan? Work with what you have or can obtain. A plan that goes beyond that is only an idle and costly dream.

Tip #5: Stay flexible

> **note** You may find profits at the end of a path you never intended to travel. What seems logical at first takes you to alternate routes.

Few plans follow a straight line. Most zig and zag with new, unexpected opportunities and roadblocks. If your initial tactics don't achieve results, switch strategies. You can look only so far ahead, and the path to profitability can be long. Proceed step by step, and measure the impact of each step.

Tip #6: Act quickly

First cure serious operational problems and fend off creditors. Building cash flow and protecting what's left of your business then takes priority. Focus

267

on profits after the emergency stage, when you have operational matters under control. Then take a hard look at your business.

Tip #7: Implement decisively

Profit planning without good implementation is only a gesture in the right direction. Implementing your profit plan will be considerably more complicated when you must change how you do business. Some profit plans are less ambitious, but even modest business overhauls consume considerable time, effort and resources. Take it in small bites.

> **HOT spot** Stay open to new ideas and modifications because profit planning is a continuous process

What will you do first? How will you implement each step? Who will be responsible for each task? What is your timetable? What are the overall costs and costs per activity? How do you know whether your profit strategy is working? Even the best plans may not sufficiently improve profits. Bad plans can produce even greater losses! With good financial monitoring you know quickly whether your plans are working.

Tip #8: Produce enough profits

Some businesses never produce decent profits. The bankruptcy courts are loaded with profitable companies who make money, but not quite enough money to cover their obligations.

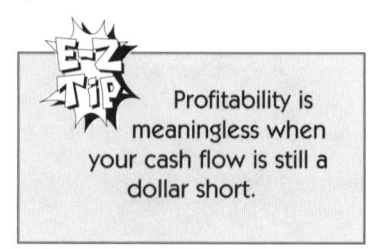

> **E-Z TIP** Profitability is meaningless when your cash flow is still a dollar short.

Checkpoint

1) Can your business make the money you need? The money you want?

2) What are your profit goals?

3) What is your vision for your business? How can it be changed to produce a profit?

4) Was your business once profitable? Can it be made profitable again by reshaping it to what it was?

5) Can your business become profitable by increasing prices, cutting costs or selling more effectively?

6) Are you giving your customers real value for their money or are they shopping elsewhere, where they find more value?

7) What is your plan for achieving profitability? Is it realistic? Attainable?

8) Can you earn sufficient profits to cover all your obligations?

Secrets of second-hand financing

16

Chapter 16
Secrets of second-hand financing

"Successful companies live within their incomes, even if they have to borrow to do it." These words from humorist Josh Billings also apply to unsuccessful companies.

You may need new financing to muscle your way through the turnaround so cash-flow shortfalls won't force you to shut down. You may later need financing to recapitalize your business and grow. Many failed businesses could have found money with more savvy refinancing strategies, but, ". . . a dime short and a day late."

When your business is hard pressed for money, your thoughts run in a hundred different directions. Get more money from present lenders. Borrow from long-standing customers. What new money sources can you tap? What assets can you pledge for additional loans? Will the government bail you out? Should you throw more of your own money into the business?

Answers to these questions rest on many factors: the size and type company, relations with lenders and creditors, whether your problems are behind or ahead of you, and what you can offer a financier.

Regardless of your business, fresh financing for a stricken business never comes easily or cheaply, when you're competing for money against bright-eyed entrepreneurs with slick business plans for another Dell Computer or McDonalds. Also competing for money are about 12 million healthy companies with solid track records. Why should they lend to your tarnished and faltering company, which may have neither a spectacular future nor a successful past?

I know what it is like. Lenders ask you to close the door quietly on your way out and spray their office with Lysol. Borrowing money is not all gloom and doom. Turnaround companies do get refinanced. You can too. Forget conventional financing strategies. They work for start-ups and stable enterprises, but not sick companies. You need more patience, perseverance and old-fashioned shoe leather to find someone who will open his pocketbook.

How much money do you need?

How much money do you need? Set a minimum and a maximum. Few lenders will overfinance you. Borrow what you need to make money! Anything less is still a dime short.

> **CAUTION** You can easily underestimate the cost to put your business together again.

Don't refinance in stages. You can't refinance too frequently. Many turnarounds first borrow to pay creditors, then find money to recapitalize their business. These short-sighted financing strategies seldom succeed because the business has been pledged in the first financing round, exhausting borrowing power.

note

Lenders prefer to cautiously advance. They may give you a few dollars to nurse the company through the turnaround, and advance more as the company progresses. But arrange loans so you know what your lender will do in the future. For financing, prepare a business plan that shows how your loan will be used. Do you need money to:

- Pay creditors?

- Reinventory your business?

- Buy or refurbish equipment?

- Undertake new marketing?

- Finance receivables?

- Replenish working capital?

What will you need for each? What are your minimum and maximum needs? Can financing come in stages? What will you pledge for collateral? How do you propose to repay?

Turnarounds, like startup ventures, must be projected cautiously. Extravagant, grandiose plans won't win financing. Faulty financing plans, like faulty turnaround plans, don't bring success. A shoestring mentality is healthy. It forces innovation. You question every purchase, slash every cost and pare dollars you thought you needed into dimes you do need. That drill builds self-discipline.

> **E-Z TIP:** Frugality and a tightwad mentality are essential to good planning.

Close-to-the-vest financing

So where do you find money? Don't head for the bank yet. Most turnarounds are bankrolled by "close-to-the-vest financing," money that comes from your own pocket!

> **note:** Business owners are usually the only ones with the interest and confidence in their business to keep it alive.

Don't finance your business until you exhaust your business' resources. And don't reach into your pocket if you can't find money elsewhere.

Parent companies nurse sick divisions or ailing subsidiaries for only so long, and stop throwing good money after bad. No company forever feeds its losers. Corporate graveyards are littered with broken companies too slow to cut losses, and shed poor performers.

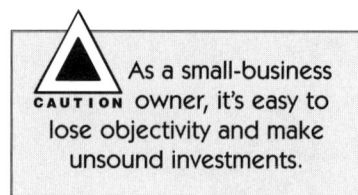

> ⚠ **CAUTION** As a small-business owner, it's easy to lose objectivity and make unsound investments.

Be objective! You are emotionally involved in your enterprise, which can be dangerous to your pocketbook! You will make sounder decisions if you answer four questions:

1) How much can you invest?

2) How much should you invest?

3) How much will you invest?

4) When will you invest more?

With the first question you know the additional financial risk you and your family can safely absorb without jeopardizing financial security. What you should invest is determined by what your business can justify as an investment, assuming it can be turned around. Your business can consume massive capital, but does its profit potential measure up?

The final question challenges you to set performance standards and benchmarks to measure recovery. Advance more funds only when you pass each benchmark.

> **HOT spot** The amount invested must be limited to what you cannot internally finance or borrow.

It's difficult to deprive your struggling business those few extra dollars from your own pocket when it needs dollars. But throwing money at your business won't solve its problems. Never throw fresh money into the business until you have a turnaround plan taking hold. Feed your business slowly with funds for contingencies and growth.

Borrowing from a bank by mortgaging your house is not a bank loan. It's your loan. If the business fails, the bank simply takes your house. Yet, business people foolishly mortgage themselves to the hilt to keep their businesses alive.

Chapter 16

These entrepreneurs first empty their savings, then their life insurance and finally their kids' piggy banks in the blind pursuit for survival. They eventually find more money is not the cure, only when nothing is left to throw into their business.

Loansmanship 101

It is easiest to throw more of your own money into the business, not smartest to throw in someone else's money.

1) How long you look

> **note** Don't get discouraged. You will eventually find money if the loan proposals are sound.

Check your staying power. You will knock on 100 doors before one opens. But, it may take time. So start early. You may look for permanent financing too soon. The time is when your company is stable, and you have profits to repay the loan. Financing also may force you to give part ownership in the business.

2) What you look for

Deal making. To succeed you must be a wheeler-dealer. Every lender has motivations and expectations, so talk and think in his terms. Unless your loan is backed by solid collateral you will pay a stiff price. Some lenders charge two or three times the interest on safer investments and also demand some of your business as a bonus. Suppliers may give a cash or a credit transfusion because they want your business, with interest secondary. Friends and relatives? You never know what will make them happy.

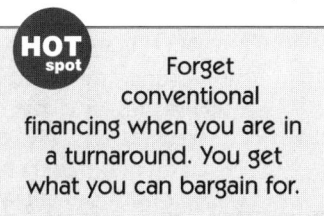

> **HOT spot** Forget conventional financing when you are in a turnaround. You get what you can bargain for.

275

3) Where you can look

HOT spot: Matching your deal to the right financial backer is half the battle. Don't stop with banks, the SBA and other conventional lenders. It usually wastes time to start there.

Start with your present lenders

Tap your present lenders to rewrite your loan, and lend you more, if you can convince them it is the way to salvage their present loan. Lenders will make additional advances if your troubles are behind you, and you won't pester them for more money. The lenders will ask whether the additional loan will insure their loan recovery.

A rescue loan must be relative to the loan at risk. How much more should be risked to protect a $500,000 loan? $25,000? $250,000? The risk/benefit ratio is judgmental and varies between lenders.

> **HINT:** Lenders sometimes cannot pull the plug without endangering their loans.

Find asset-based lenders

Asset-based lenders finance turnaround companies, but want to be solidly collateralized. Asset-based financing can replace existing conventional lenders.

> **note:** Asset-based lenders are well-experienced with troubled companies, and geared to provide specialized audits to monitor assets and control cash flow.

New lenders hesitate to step into the uncomfortable shoes of another lender in jeopardy. Even asset-based financiers want several quarters of good performance to show your company can pay its loan.

Asset-based lenders demand higher interest, tighter controls over the collateral, hair-trigger defaults and strong personal guarantees, or collateral from outside the company. Your personal guarantees or collateral may be inconsequential to the loan, but you then commit to the future of your company and won't walk away easily.

Factoring

If you have substantial accounts receivable, consider factoring.

Many companies routinely factor. But factoring is costly, usually 5- to 10-percent. Larger factors look primarily to the receivables, not the creditworthiness of the company. Accounts-receivable factors are expensive, but a smart temporary measure, until your company gains the financial strength to obtain less costly accounts receivable financing. Some companies permanently factor for fast cash.

Attract venture capitalists

Venture capitalists, disillusioned with the hi-tech startups of the '70s and '80s, now invest in turnaround companies which offer higher returns than do rosy-cheeked startups, who have fewer winners.

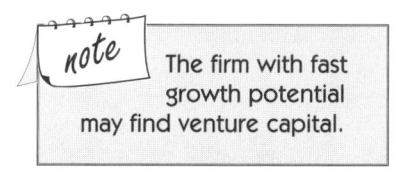

> *note* — The firm with fast growth potential may find venture capital.

Turnaround companies also give venture capitalists greater involvement in management, an intrusion unwelcome by startup entrepreneurs. Some venture capitalists enjoy straightening out corporate cripples. Their management team may stay with the troubled firm for several years, departing when the company is fully stabilized.

> **HOT spot** "Vulture capitalists," as they are sometimes called, will unabashedly bargain for significant ownership in your company and advance their money as a secured loan.

Yet having money does not automatically impart management brilliance. "You probably wouldn't hire the venture capitalist as a management consultant, but for some reason when he shows up with money you hand him the helm." They are also well paid for their management efforts, with options to buy more of your company.

Go public

Several intriguing books have been published that reveal how to invest in financially troubled companies. The near-bankrupt company can be a terrific investment because the selling price can be much lower than the company's actual value. Troubled companies can frequently package a combination of tax benefits, clean balance sheet and a hope for a brighter future into public offering.

One advantage of going public is that you'll give up less ownership than with private placement or venture capital. Some small companies have gone public through Chapter 11 reorganization because you can avoid most SEC registration requirements when you issue stock as part of your reorganization.

Small corporations can now go public with minimum red tape as IPOs or "Initial Public Offerings."

Romance an angel

Perhaps one working (or silent) partner with cash may do the trick. More people are looking for good investments. Silent partners are usually high-income individuals seeking business deals that can earn considerably more than conventional investments. Doctors, lawyers, executors and other professionals are the best candidates.

Candidates experienced in your industry invest faster because their familiarity with the industry bolsters their confidence. Consider those doing business with you, such as present or prospective suppliers.

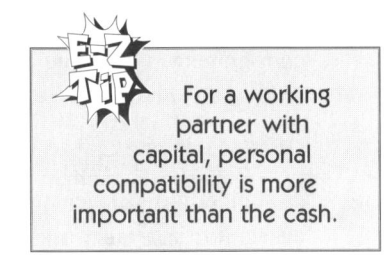

> **E-Z TIP:** For a working partner with capital, personal compatibility is more important than the cash.

> **CAUTION:** Your accountant and lawyer may have clients with investment capital. Avoid close relatives or friends. If you lose their money, you lose a valuable relationship.

Try trade suppliers

Can trade credit provide your refinancing? If low inventories can be bolstered through trade credit, it's as good as cash!

Heavily exposed trade creditors may support you, if more credit improves the odds for collecting what you owe them. You won't convince trade creditors who cling to the axiom that the first loss is the best loss. You should not accept credit when you have no realistic chance to repay. You can personally guarantee future credit, or your banks may issue letters of credit or subordinate their security interest to trade creditors. W.T. Grant's banks guaranteed more than $100 million in new merchandise to restock them.

Many manufacturers are anxious to open new outlets on this basis. Retailers often discover more profitable merchandise lines from consignment sources. A three-store Boston ladies-apparel chain sold, on

> **E-Z TIP:** Consignment agreements remerchandise quite a few retail businesses.

consignment, a new line of artificial furs. They soon discontinued dresses in favor of this new fur line. The revitalized chain now has 20 artificial fur salons.

note Demands for merchandise can forge relationships between supplier and customer into partnerships. The supplier sees the takeover of a troubled distributor or retailer as a potentially profitable way to sell more goods. The inventory-poor business sees the supplier as its lifeline to merchandise.

Money, money everywhere

- How about the SBA? Yes, they make loans, even to stumbling companies—if the loan won't pay unsecured creditors. When your bank says no, try the SBA.

- How about your customers? Do you supply an essential service?

- Can your business be converted into a successful franchise? A franchiser might finance your recovery if your business would make a good franchised outlet.

- Do you deal with the government? Call the Chamber of Commerce for loan programs available for your industry.

- What about your employees? Do they have enough confidence to buy part of your business, or to loan you a few dollars to cover their next paycheck?

Negotiating your best deal

Keep certain realities in mind. Your financier has the negotiating power. More companies are in search of funds than there are capital sources looking to throw money into ailing enterprises. But don't reach for the first financing deal—desperate, anxious companies sometimes give away too much. You

Chapter 16

strike your best deal if you can finance yourself through the turnaround when your company is stabilized, you'll have more bargaining power. But send feelers early so you have financing when you are ready.

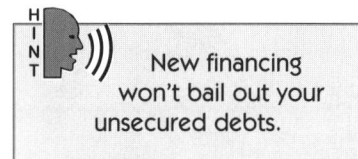

> **HINT:** New financing won't bail out your unsecured debts.

Investors don't save businesses; they want to build businesses. If new financing is to replace existing loans, have your "takeout" agreements ready with your existing lenders.

Understand prospective lenders. Will they support future growth? How a prospective lender responds to opportunities is as important as what it will do in rough weather.

Is the lender flexible or rigid? What relationship has the lender had with its borrowers? Are there signs of overreaching or coercive or slippery practices by the lender?

> **note:** You must investigate the lender's relationship with other borrowers.

Understand the financier's role in the workout. You and your lender must agree on the basic turnaround strategy and future direction for your company. Also review possible contingencies and alternatives, and candidly discuss strategies—if these contingencies materialize. Set performance benchmarks, a timetable to review performance, rewards for success and penalties for poor performance. Also discuss the lender's managerial or financial control.

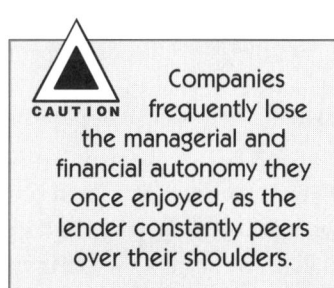

> **CAUTION:** Companies frequently lose the managerial and financial autonomy they once enjoyed, as the lender constantly peers over their shoulders.

How to zero in on the money

Each money source has its own niche—what they will loan, repayment terms and equity participation.

A detailed loan proposal showing six points:

1) the requested loan amount

2) the minimum acceptable loan

3) what you will do with the money

4) who else you will borrow from

5) how you propose to repay

6) the collateral you offer

When you strike out

Striking out can be helpful if it pinpoints a serious weakness in your business or proposal. Find out why you were rejected. Lenders may not be candid, but push for a reason. Your lender may see weaknesses you overlooked or raise unanswered questions other lenders will ask. Listen closely.

You may not get financing because your company's long-term prospects remain poor, or you suffer from obvious mismanagement, prolonged losses or a pattern of fraud or creditor abuse. Lenders will want to see that you first exhausted your internal sources of cash. Tapping your internal resources is important because negotiating outside financing takes time.

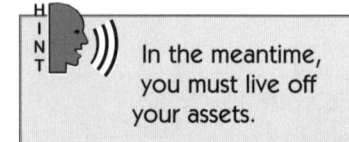

> In the meantime, you must live off your assets.

Chapter 16

Checkpoint

1) How much money do you need for your business?

2) Have you tapped your internal resources to the fullest extent possible?

3) Who are your best loan sources?

4) Have you zipped shut your pocketbook?

5) What are you prepared to give a lender?

6) Have you been turned down for a loan? Why?

How to bail out for a super-soft landing

17

Chapter 17
How to bail out for a super-soft landing

Not every business can be saved. Protect yourself if your business fails.

Answer two key questions:

1) What personal liabilities do you face if your business fails?

2) What personal assets can you lose?

What should you do right now to protect your personal wealth? Don't rationalize that your business can't fail or that you won't end up with creditors chasing you. Don't rationalize that they won't take everything you own.

> **HOT spot** The harsh realities of business surface when you fail. But then it may be too late to avoid personal liability.

It's best to consider these questions before you start your business. Most entrepreneurs don't ask themselves what if: "What if the business fails? What will I lose? What can I do now to protect myself and limit my personal losses if I do fail?'

Corporate shield or Swiss cheese

CAUTION Your corporation will protect you from business debts if it functions as a corporation and you treat it as a corporation. Then creditors must recognize your corporate protection. Forget these rules, and you lose your corporate protection.

285

Troubleshooting Your Business Made E-Z

HINT: Don't commingle assets. Operate your corporation as a separate entity in every respect. Keep corporate funds separate from personal funds. Document transactions between yourself and your corporation, and transactions between different corporations.

Don't incorrectly sign documents. All documents should clearly identify your corporation as the principal and you as its agent. Use your title on checks and other documents. Imprint the name of your corporation on checks, correspondence, contracts, invoices and other documents.

Operate your corporation as a separate entity. Do you operate other corporations? Appoint separate boards of directors. Hold separate corporate meetings and keep separate corporate books. Each corporation must be independent with legal, financial and administrative ties to your other businesses.

Keep adequate corporate records. Creditors can punch holes in your corporate shield when records are inadequate. Document major corporate actions and keep up-to-date, accurate minutes of director and stockholder meetings. *Corporate Record Keeping* from Made E-Z Products, available at most stationery and software outlets, can conveniently handle this.

Don't dissolve your corporation. If your corporation is dissolved by the state, it means you lose corporate protection. Pay all state taxes and corporate franchise fees and keep your corporation in good standing. Put your affairs in order before creditors snoop.

> **HOT spot** Never voluntarily dissolve your corporation if it has outstanding corporate debts, because these debts then become personal obligations.

Creditors who claim that your corporation is only a sham will have an uphill fight if you obey these rules.

Sidestep costly guarantees

Small-business owners frequently guarantee some corporate obligations. Most guarantees are foolish. Avoid future guarantees and sidestep those you have already signed. A guarantee is one bargaining point with prospective suppliers. If a supplier insists on your guarantee, then find a more lenient supplier.

> **E-Z TIP**: Understand your suppliers' concerns and reduce their risks, so they will forego personal guarantees.

Will a supplier who refuses to ship a $20,000 order without your guarantee gamble on $10,000? Can you secure credit through a mortgage on your business rather than a personal guarantee? Or can you limit your guarantee?

Never guarantee an existing debt!

Creditors will push for your personal guarantee once your business is in trouble, so they can chase you and your personal assets if your business goes bust. But why risk personal assets to bail out existing creditors? Don't think your business will pay these debts. Few do.

Don't throw more of your own money into your business or borrow money by pledging personal assets to keep supplies flowing and the rent paid. You will soon run out of resources, and your business will still fail. Bargain for protection. Have your bank mortgage the business to reduce your personal exposure.

> **note**: Banks and other lenders rarely finance a small business without owner guarantees.

Have your partners also sign the guarantees, and share the risk. Creditors chase guarantors with the deepest pockets. Hopefully your partners' pockets are as deep to escape liability on existing guarantees.

1) Verify obligations you guaranteed. You may have signed a guarantee as part of a credit application. Or you may have long-forgotten guarantees.

2) Revoke all guarantees for future credit.

3) Liquidate guaranteed debts before your company folds if you want to walk away clean or set aside funds accumulated as a war chest.

4) Exploit the reality that cooperating with a guaranteed creditor may have great value to your creditor. For instance, a Chicago bank owed $7-million by a failed health clinic agreed my client's willingness to help collect the outstanding receivables was worth considerably more to the bank than his guarantee.

Will lenders need your cooperation to turn your collateral into cash? Exchange cooperation for a guarantee release. But negotiate when your creditors need help. You later may have precious little to negotiate with.

What can you give creditors in return for a canceled guarantee? A mortgage on your business? Returned goods? An immediate part payment?

> Convince creditors that what you offer today is worth more than what they can get chasing you.

Threaten stubborn creditors. Threaten to take even your money out of their pockets! A prolonged Chapter 11 may delay foreclosure and dissipate collateral. Were back bills paid within the 90 days? Threaten bankruptcy to recover those preferential payments! The carrot-and-stick works when you make it a tasty carrot and a big stick!

Don't let the tax collector chase you

As a corporate officer you are responsible for unpaid withholding taxes. Avoid big tax troubles. Pay at least those taxes for which you are personally

Chapter 17

> **HOT spot** — Unpaid state withholding taxes, sales, meals, gas and similar taxes also can be your personal responsibility.

liable. Earmark tax payments to the trust taxes or the IRS will apply them to the non-trust taxes so they can later chase you personally.

Others in your company who share authority and responsibility to pay taxes can also be held liable. Comptrollers and bookkeepers who sign checks should resign once taxes are delinquent because they too can be personally liable. Never make your spouse an officer of the corporation or a signatory on the corporate checking account. Limit tax liabilities to yourself so your spouse can be a safe haven for your personal assets if the IRS goes after you.

Failure to pay collected taxes is a crime, but the IRS seldom prosecutes. Many states prosecute larger cases. If you owe the IRS more than you can repay, don't throw scarce money at the problem. Pay current taxes to show good faith, to avoid criminal liability and to encourage IRS leniency on any future settlement.

> **STRATEGY** — Prioritize taxes that can cause the greatest grief.

You may settle with the IRS for a small fraction of what you owe if you can convince the IRS that is all you can afford. *Solving IRS Problems Made E-Z* reveals how you can join the hundreds of thousands of Americans who "compromise" their tax debts.

Empty your deep pockets

Business owners, oblivious to impending problems, too often don't protect themselves. People in trouble play ostrich.

How can you legally shield your personal assets?

- **Homestead and state exemption laws** that automatically protect some assets from creditors. Convert unprotected stocks and bonds into pension accounts which are protected. Or pay down your home mortgage if your home has full homestead protection.

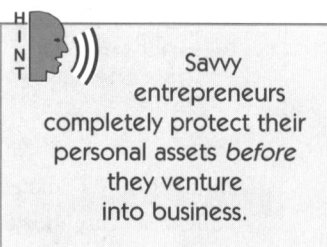

  > **HINT:** Savvy entrepreneurs completely protect their personal assets *before* they venture into business.

- **Gift property to your children or relatives for estate planning.** You can gift $10,000 per year per donee without a gift tax, and you can make a one-time gift of $30,000.

- **Harbor assets in family-limited partnerships, corporations or trusts.** Family-limited partnerships are the safest way to protect your home and other assets from creditors. As the general partner, you completely control the partnership property while the partnership can be owned by other family members, trusts or other entities.

  > **CAUTION:** Irrevocable trusts are effective asset protectors, but you lose control of your assets. A revocable trust will not protect assets.

- **Go offshore.** When you owe creditors and have big money to shelter, set up a trust in an offshore haven to safely shelter money from creditors. It is perfectly legal, effective and not as difficult.

- **Mortgage your assets.** This discourages creditors who no longer have a net worth to chase. The proceeds can buy exempt assets, pay "friendly" creditors, prepay expenses or be deposited offshore. There are hundreds of asset protection strategies in my best selling, *Asset Protection Made E-Z*. Asset protection is part of handling troubled companies. I save businesses, and make certain my clients have a super-soft landing when they bail out.

Chapter 17

HINT: Fraudulent conveyance laws allow creditors to recover last-minute transfers. Transfers made before the liability arose are safer than those incurred subsequently. When you have nothing exposed to your creditors, you have less to worry about. Are you vulnerable? Find yourself a good asset protection lawyer, or give me a call.

How to grab the cash before the crash

Walking away from the business with what you invested in the business is landing on feathers, but how do you do it legally?

1) Repay yourself all loans to your company, but keep your business out of bankruptcy for at least one year. Creditors can recover preferential payments made to you (or any other relative, officer, director or stockholder of your corporation) within the year preceding bankruptcy.

2) Take high wages. Wage payments are less easily challenged than loan repayments, which are recoverable as preferences. Take the maximum wages you can reasonably justify.

3) Stagger withdrawals. Large payments to yourself or family members are easily detected. Small payments to many individuals will be less noticed. A bankruptcy trustee is unlikely to chase numerous individuals to be paid in small amounts. Recouping only what is legitimately due you.

HOT spot: Don't rape your business. Don't skim cash to beat the IRS. Don't do fraudulent scams you'll later regret.

Do you owe money to your business? Did you forget an old $50,000 loan from your business? The bankruptcy trustee will try to collect. To wipe the

291

slate clean legally, deduct from these loans any money the business owes you. You can also transfer personal assets to the business as repayment. If you have personally guaranteed business debts, cancel the loan as payment for your guarantee of the debts.

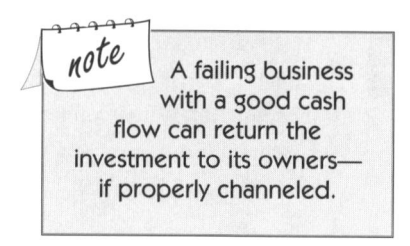

> **note** A failing business with a good cash flow can return the investment to its owners— if properly channeled.

Review these ideas with your accountant and attorney.

Checkpoint

1) Will your corporation shield you from business debts?

2) What business debts have you personally guaranteed? How can you satisfy these guarantees before your business folds?

3) What tax liabilities are outstanding? How can these back taxes be repaid?

4) How deep are your pockets? What personal assets are exposed to creditors? How can they be protected?

5) What does your business owe you? How can you legally recoup this money from the business? How can you cancel what you owe your company so that you have no continuing liability?

Glossary of useful terms

A-C

Adequate Protection

The standard of protection granted a creditor by the trustee or debtor-in-possession in order to avoid the court allowing the creditor to foreclose on its property.

Automatic Stay

An injunction, or court order, that takes effect when a bankruptcy petition is filed. An automatic stay prohibits all collection action against a debtor.

Avoidance Powers

The powers used by a trustee to reserve transfers of the debtor's property.

Bankruptcy Petition

The legal instrument filed with the bankruptcy court that commences a bankruptcy proceeding.

Bar Date

The last date for filing a proof of claim.

Collateral

Property of a debtor in which a creditor has a lien securing its debt.

Conversion

The conversion of a bankruptcy case from one chapter type to another.

Cram-down

The confirmation of a plan to reorganize over the objection of a creditor or class of creditors by the votes of other creditors.

D-Po

Debtor-in-Possession (DIP)

The business debtor in a Chapter 11 reorganization. In a Chapter 11, the debtor retaining possession of the assets involved in the bankruptcy.

Discharge

A discharge in bankruptcy relieves the debtor of the dischargeable debts incurred prior to filing. Discharge is the legal term for the elimination of debt through bankruptcy.

Exemption or Exempt Property

Property of an individual debtor that the law protects from the actions of creditors, such as the debtor's residence or homestead, automobile, and the like.

Foreclosure

A debt-collection procedure whereby property of the debtor is sold on the courthouse steps to satisfy debts. Foreclosure often involves real estate of the debtor.

General, Unsecured Claim

A claim that is neither secured nor granted a priority by the Bankruptcy Code. Most trade debts are general, unsecured claims.

Judicial Lien

A lien created by the order of a court, such as the lien created by taking a judgment against a debtor.

Levy and Execution

A judicial debt-collection procedure in which the court orders the sheriff to seize the debtor's property found in the county to sell in satisfaction of the debtor's debt or debts.

Possessory Security Interest

A security interest or lien on property that requires the creditor to have possession of the property, such as a pawn or pledge.

Pre-T

Preference

A transfer of property of the debtor to a creditor made immediately prior to the debtor's bankruptcy that enables the creditor to receive more than it would have received from the bankruptcy. A preferential transfer must be made while the debtor was insolvent and as payment for a debt that existed prior to the transfer of the property.

Priority

Certain categories of claims are designated as priority claims by the Bankruptcy Code, such as claims for lost wages or taxes. Each classification of claims must be paid in order of priority (the claims in one class must be paid in full before the next class receives any payment).

Redemption

The right of a debtor in a bankruptcy to purchase certain real or personal property from a secured creditor by paying the current value of the property (regardless of the amount owed on the property).

Secured Creditor

A creditor whose debt is secured by a lien on property of the debtor.

Secured Proof of Claim

A proof of claim for a debt that is secured by a lien, a judgment, or other security interest.

Security Interest

A lien on the property in the possession of the debtor that acts as security for the debt owed to the creditor.

Statutory Lien

A lien created by operation of law, such as a mechanic's lien or a tax lien. A statutory lien does not require the consent of the parties or a court order.

Trustee

An officer of the court appointed to take custody of the assets of a bankruptcy estate.

Resources

Where you'll find these Resources:
- Online resources 296
- Related sites 297
- Other resources 298
- State Bar Associations 299

••• Online Resources •••

- American Bankruptcy Institute
  http://www.abiworld.org
- American Consumer Credit Counseling
  http://www.consumercredit.com
- A/R Management Group of Georgia, Inc.
  http://www.armanagement.com/calculators.html
- Center for Debt Management
  http://www.center4debtmanagement.com
- Commercial Law League of America
  http://www.clla.org
- Consumer Counseling Centers of America, Inc.
  http://www.consumercounseling.org/about.html
- Credit Information Exchange
  http://www.rmahq.org/ciex/ciex.html
- Creditworthy, Co.
  http://www.creditworthy.com
- Credit Managers Association of California (CMAC)
  http://www.whatuseek.com/cgi-bin/redirect.go?
  http://www.cmaccom.com
- Council of Better Business Bureaus, Inc.
  http://www.bbb.org
- Debt Counselors of America
  http://www.dca.org/home.htm

Resources

- Dun & Bradstreet, Inc.
  http://www.dnb.com
- Education Index, Business Resources
  http://www.educationindex.com/bus
- Electric Library® Business Edition
  http://www.business.elibrary.com
- Federal Trade Commission-Consumer Protection
  http://www.ftc.gov/bcp/menu-credit.htm
- International Finance & Commodities Institute
  http://finance.wat.ch/IFCI
- Internal Revenue Service Tax Publications
  Bad Debts
  http://www.irs.ustreas.gov/prod/forms_pubs/pubs/p3340801.htm
- Lawdog Center
  http://www.lawdog.com
- Lawlounge
  http://lawlounge.com/topics/corporate/bankruptcy/associations.htm
- LNET-LLC-Limited Liability Companies and
  Partnerships Conference
  http://www.stcl.edu/lnet-llc/lnet-llc.html
- Limited Liability Company Website
  http://www.llcweb.com
- National Small Business Development Center (SBDC)
  Research Network
  http://www.smallbiz.suny.edu
- U.S. Small Business Administration
  http://www.sbaonline.sba.gov/starting
- Small Business Primer
  http://www.ces.ncsu.edu/depts/fcs/business/welcome.html
- Small Office Success
  http://www.smallofficesuccess.com/
- U.S. Business Advisor
  http://www.business.gov

••• Related Sites •••

- 555-1212.com, Inc.
  http://www.555-1212.com
- Equifax, Inc.
  http://www.equifax.com
- Experian Information Solutions, Inc.
  http://www.experian.com
- Institute of Certified Financial Planners
  http://www.icfp.org
- International Association for Financial Planning
  http://www.iafp.org
- Mining Company, The
  Small Business Information
  http://sbinformation.miningco.com/msub2.htm?rf=dp&COB=home

297

Troubleshooting Your Business Made E-Z

- National Association of Personal Financial Advisors
  http://www.napfa.org
- National Foundation for Consumer Credit (NFCC), The
  http://www.nfcc.org
- National Technical Information Service
  Technology Administration
  U.S. Department of Commerce
  http://www.ntis.gov/
- Title 11 - bankruptcy
  Legal Information Institute (LII)
  http://www4.law.cornell.edu/uscode/11
- Trans Union LLC
  http://www.transunion.com
- United States Department of Commerce
  National Technical Information Service
  FedWorld Information
  http://www.fedworld.gov

••• Other Resources •••

U.S. Small Business Administration
Free management assistance publications and business development booklets are available from the U.S. Small Business Administration. Call your nearest SBA office, or write to 409 Third Street S.W., Washington D.C. 20416. Phone: (800) 827-5722.

www.sba.gov

U.S. Department of Commerce
Publishes the *Directory of Federal and State Business Assistance: A Guide for New and Growing Companies*. It includes descriptions of more than 182 federal and state programs and services. Call or write the U.S. Department of Commerce—National Technical Information Service, 5285 Port Royal Rd., Springfield, VA 22161. Phone: (703) 605-6000 or 1-800-553-6847: Order number PB88-101977.

www.doc.gov and *www.ntis.gov*

Dun & Bradstreet
D&B provides a variety of services for the business owner, including collection and credit-rating services. Write for their free brochure: Dun & Bradstreet, Commercial Collection Division, 225 Broadway, New York, NY 10007. 1-800-234-3867

www.dnb.com

The Small Business Service Bureau
A national organization for small-business owners that provides information, management advice and legislative advocacy for its members. Write 544 Main St., Worcester MA 01601.

Garrett Group
Specializes in personal asset protection strategies and turnarounds for small- and mid-sized businesses of all types. 360 S. Military Trail, Deerfield Beach, Fl. 33442. Call (954) 480-8543.

Resources

••• State Bar Associations •••

ALABAMA
Alabama State Bar
415 Dexter Avenue
Montgomery, AL 36104
mailing address:
PO Box 671
Montgomery, AL 36101
(334) 269-1515
http://www.alabar.org

ALASKA
Alaska Bar Association
510 L Street No. 602
Anchorage, AK 99501

mailing address:
PO Box 100279
Anchorage, AK 99510
http://www.alaskabar.org

ARIZONA
State Bar of Arizona
111 West Monroe
Phoenix, AZ 85003-1742
(602) 252-4804
http://www.azbar.org

ARKANSAS
Arkansas Bar Association
400 West Markham
Little Rock, AR 72201
(501) 375-4605
http://www.arkbar.org

CALIFORNIA
State Bar of California
555 Franklin Street
San Francisco, CA 94102
(415) 561-8200
http://www.calbar.org

Alameda County Bar Association
http://www.acbanet.org

COLORADO
Colorado Bar Association
No. 950, 1900 Grant Street
Denver, CO 80203
(303) 860-1115
http://www.cobar.org

CONNECTICUT
Connecticut Bar Association
101 Corporate Place
Rocky Hill, CT 06067-1894
(203) 721-0025
http://www.ctbar.org

DELAWARE
Delaware State Bar Association
1225 King Street, 10th floor
Wilmington, DE 19801
(302) 658-5279
(302) 658-5278 (lawyer referral serv.)
http://www.dsba.org

DISTRICT OF COLUMBIA
District of Columbia Bar
1250 H Street, NW, 6th Floor
Washington, DC 20005
(202) 737-4700

Bar Association of the District of Columbia
1819 H Street, NW, 12th floor
Washington, DC 20006-3690
(202) 223-6600
http://www.badc.org

FLORIDA
The Florida Bar
The Florida Bar Center
650 Apalachee Parkway
Tallahassee, FL 32399-2300
(850) 561-5600
http://www.flabar.org

GEORGIA
State Bar of Georgia
800 The Hurt Building
50 Hurt Plaza
Atlanta, GA 30303
(404) 527-8700
http://www.gabar.org

HAWAII
Hawaii State Bar Association
1136 Union Mall
Penthouse 1
Honolulu, HI 96813
(808) 537-1868
http://www.hsba.org

IDAHO
Idaho State Bar
PO Box 895
Boise, ID 83701
(208) 334-4500
http://www2.state.id.us/isb

ILLINOIS
Illinois State Bar Association
424 South Second Street
Springfield, IL 62701
(217) 525-1760
http://www.illinoisbar.org

INDIANA
Indiana State Bar Association
230 East Ohio Street
Indianapolis, IN 46204
(317) 639-5465
http://www.ai.org/isba

IOWA
Iowa State Bar Association
521 East Locust
Des Moines, IA 50309
(515) 243-3179
http://www.iowabar.org

KANSAS
Kansas Bar Association
1200 Harrison Street
Topeka, KS 66612-1806
(785) 234-5696
http://www.ksbar.org

KENTUCKY
Kentucky Bar Association
514 West Main Street
Frankfort, KY 40601-1883
(502) 564-3795
http://www.kybar.org

LOUISIANA
Louisiana State Bar Association
601 St. Charles Avenue
New Orleans, LA 70130
(504) 566-1600
http://www.lsba.org

MAINE
Maine State Bar Association
124 State Street
PO Box 788
Augusta, ME 04330
(207) 622-7523
http://www.mainebar.org

MARYLAND
Maryland State Bar Association
520 West Fayette Street
Baltimore, MD 21201
(301) 685-7878
http://www.msba.org/msba

MASSACHUSETTS
Massachusetts Bar Association
20 West Street
Boston, MA 02111
(617) 542-3602
(617) 542-9103 (lawyer referral serv)
http://www.massbar.org

MICHIGAN
State Bar of Michigan
306 Townsend Street
Lansing, MI 48933-2083
(517) 372-9030
http://www.michbar.org

MINNESOTA
Minnesota State Bar Association
514 Nicollet Mall
Minneapolis, MN 55402
(612) 333-1183
http://www.mnbar.org

MISSISSIPPI
The Mississippi Bar
643 No. State Street
Jackson, Mississippi 39202
(601) 948-4471
http://www.msbar.org

MISSOURI
The Missouri Bar
P.O. Box 119, 326 Monroe
Jefferson City, Missouri 65102
(314) 635-4128
http://www.mobar.org

MONTANA
State Bar of Montana
46 North Main
PO Box 577
Helena, MT 59624
(406) 442-7660
http://www.montanabar.org

NEBRASKA
Nebraska State Bar Association
635 South 14th Street, 2nd floor
Lincoln, NE 68508
(402) 475-7091
http://www.nebar.com

Troubleshooting Your Business Made E-Z

NEVADA
State Bar of Nevada
201 Las Vegas Blvd.
Las Vegas, NV 89101
(702) 382-2200
http://www.nvbar.org

NEW HAMPSHIRE
New Hampshire Bar Association
112 Pleasant Street
Concord, NH 03301
(603) 224-6942
http://www.nhbar.org

NEW JERSEY
New Jersey State Bar Association
One Constitution Square
New Brunswick, NJ 08901-1500
(908) 249-5000

NEW MEXICO
State Bar of New Mexico
5121 Masthead N.E.
Albuquerque, NM 87125

mailing address:
PO Box 25883
Albuquerque, NM 87125
(505) 843-6132
http://www.nmbar.org

NEW YORK
New York State Bar Association
One Elk Street
Albany, NY 12207
(518) 463-3200
http://www.nysba.org

NORTH CAROLINA
North Carolina State Bar
208 Fayetteville Street Mall
Raleigh, NC 27601

mailing address:
PO Box 25908
Raleigh, NC 27611
(919) 828-4620

North Carolina Bar Association
1312 Annapolis Drive
Raleigh, NC 27608

mailing address:
PO Box 3688
Cary, NC 27519-3688
(919) 677-0561
http://www.ncbar.org

NORTH DAKOTA
State Bar Association of North Dakota
515 1/2 East Broadway, suite 101
Bismarck, ND 58501

mailing address:
PO Box 2136
Bismarck, ND 58502
(701) 255-1404

OHIO
Ohio State Bar Association
1700 Lake Shore Drive
Columbus, OH 43204

mailing address:
PO Box 16562
Columbus, OH 43216-6562
(614) 487-2050
http://www.ohiobar.org

OKLAHOMA
Oklahoma Bar Association
1901 North Lincoln
Oklahoma City, OK 73105
(405) 524-2365
http://www.okbar.org

OREGON
Oregon State Bar
5200 S.W. Meadows Road
PO Box 1689
Lake Oswego, OR 97035-0889
(503) 620-0222
http://www.osbar.org

PENNSYLVANIA
Pennsylvania Bar Association
100 South Street
PO Box 186
Harrisburg, PA 17108
(717) 238-6715
http://www.pabar.org

Pennsylvania Bar Institute
http://www.pbi.org

PUERTO RICO
Puerto Rico Bar Association
PO Box 1900
San Juan, Puerto Rico 00903
(787) 721-3358

RHODE ISLAND
Rhode Island Bar Association
115 Cedar Street
Providence, RI 02903
(401) 421-5740
http://www.ribar.org

SOUTH CAROLINA
South Carolina Bar
950 Taylor Street
PO Box 608
Columbia, SC 29202
(803) 799-6653
http://www.scbar.org

SOUTH DAKOTA
State Bar of South Dakota
222 East Capitol
Pierre, SD 57501
(605) 224-7554
http://www.sdbar.org

TENNESSEE
Tennessee Bar Assn
3622 West End Avenue
Nashville, TN 37205
(615) 383-7421
http://www.tba.org

TEXAS
State Bar of Texas
1414 Colorado
PO Box 12487
Austin, TX 78711
(512) 463-1463
http://www.texasbar.com/start.htm

UTAH
Utah State Bar
645 South 200 East, Suite 3
Salt Lake City, UT 84111
(801) 531-9077
http://www.utahbar.org

VERMONT
Vermont Bar Association
PO Box 100
Montpelier, VT 05601
(802) 223-2020
http://www.vtbar.org

VIRGINIA
Virginia State Bar
707 East Main Street, suite 1
Richmond, VA 23219-0501
(804) 775-0500

Virginia Bar Association
701 East Franklin St., Suite 1
Richmond, VA 23219
(804) 644-0041
http://www.vbar.org

VIRGIN ISLANDS
Virgin Islands Bar Association
P.O. Box 4108
Christiansted, Virgin Islands
(340) 778-7497

WASHINGTON
Washington State Bar Associa
500 Westin Street
2001 Sixth Avenue
Seattle, WA 98121-2599
(206) 727-8200
http://www.wsba.org

WEST VIRGINIA
West Virginia State Bar
2006 Kanawha Blvd. East
Charleston, WV 25311
(304) 558-2456
http://www.wvbar.org

West Virginia Bar Association
904 Security Building
100 Capitol Street
Charleston, WV 25301
(304) 342-1474

WISCONSIN
State Bar of Wisconsin
402 West Wilson Street
Madison, WI 53703
(608) 257-3838
http://www.wisbar.org/home.ht

WYOMING
Wyoming State Bar
500 Randall Avenue
Cheyenne, WY 82001
PO Box 109
Cheyenne, WY 82003
(307) 632-9061
http://www.wyomingbar.or

Save On Legal Fees

with software and books from Made E-Z Products available at your nearest bookstore, or call 1-800-822-4566

Everyday Law Made E-Z
The book that saves legal fees every time it's opened.

Here, in *Everyday Law Made E-Z*, are fast answers to 90% of the legal questions anyone is ever likely to ask, such as:

- How can I control my neighbor's pet?
- Can I change my name?
- What is a common law marriage?
- When should I incorporate my business?
- Is a child responsible for his bills?
- Who owns a husband's gifts to his wife?
- How do I become a naturalized citizen?
- Should I get my divorce in Nevada?
- Can I write my own will?
- Who is responsible when my son drives my car?
- How can my uncle get a Green Card?
- What are the rights of a non-smoker?
- Do I have to let the police search my car?
- What is sexual harassment?
- When is euthanasia legal?
- What repairs must my landlord make?
- What's the difference between fair criticism and slander?
- When can I get my deposit back?
- Can I sue the federal government?
- Am I responsible for a drunken guest's auto accident?
- Is a hotel liable if it does not honor a reservation?
- Does my car fit the lemon law?

Stock No.: BK311
$29.95 8.5" x 11"
500 pages Soft cover
ISBN 1-56382-311-X

Whether for personal or business use, this 500-page information-packed book helps the layman safeguard his property, avoid disputes, comply with legal obligations, and enforce his rights. Hundreds of cases illustrate thousands of points of law, each clearly and completely explained.

MADE E-Z™ PRODUCTS

ss 1999.r2

Whatever you need to know we've made it E-Z!

Informative text and forms you can fill o[ut] on-screen.* From personal to business, le[gal] to leisure—we've made it E-Z!

PERSONAL & FAMILY

For all your family's needs, we have titles that will help keep you organized and guide you through most every aspect of your personal life.

BUSINESS

Whether you're starting from scratch with a home business or you just want to keep your corporate records in shape, we've got the programs for you.

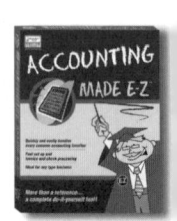

* Not all topics include forms   ss 1999.r2

E-Z to load, E-Z to run, E-Z to use!

For our complete list of titles, call 1-800-822-4566
or visit our web site: www.MadeE-Z.com

LEGAL

Easy to understand text explains how to fill out and file forms to perform all the legal tasks you need to—without all those legal fees!

TRAVEL & LEISURE

Learn health tips or travel all around the world, and then relax with a good crossword puzzle. When your work is done, we've got what you need!

MADE E-Z™
PRODUCTS

Made E-Z Products, 384 S. Military Trail, Deerfield Beach, FL 33442
(800) 822-4566 • fax: (954) 480-8906
web site: http://www.MadeE-Z.com

By the book...

MADE E-Z PRODUCTS

MADE E-Z BOOKS provide all the forms you need to take care of business and save on legal fees – only **$29.95 each!**

Everyday Legal Forms & Agreements Made E-Z ISBN 1-56382-301-2
A do-it-yourself legal library of 301 ready-to-use perforated legal documents for virtually every personal or business need!

Corporate Record Keeping Made E-Z ISBN 1-56382-304-7
Keep your own corporate records current and in compliance... without a lawyer!

Managing Employees Made E-Z ISBN 1-56382-302-0
Over 240 documents to manage your employees more efficiently and legally!

Vital Record Keeping Made E-Z ISBN 1-56382-300-4
201 simple and ready-to-use forms to help you keep organized records for your family, your business and yourself!

Collecting Unpaid Bills Made E-Z ISBN 1-56382-309-8
Essential for anyone who extends credit and needs an efficient way to collect.

Available at:
Super Stores, Office Supply Stores, Drug Stores, Hardware Stores, Bookstores, and other fine retailers.

ss 1999.r2

See an item in this book you would like to order?

	Item#	Qty.	Price Ea.‡
★ **E✦Z Legal Kits**			
Bankruptcy	K100		$23.95
Incorporation	K101		$23.95
Divorce	K102		$29.95
Credit Repair	K103		$21.95
Living Trust	K105		$21.95
Living Will	K106		$23.95
Last Will & Testament	K107		$18.95
Buying/Selling Your Home	K111		$21.95
Employment Law	K112		$21.95
Collecting Child Support	K115		$21.95
Limited Liability Company	K116		$21.95
★ **Made E✦Z Software**			
Accounting Made E-Z	SW1207		$29.95
Asset Protection Made E-Z	SW1157		$29.95
Bankruptcy Made E-Z	SW1154		$29.95
Best Career Oppportunities Made E-Z	SW1216		$29.95
Brain-Buster Crossword Puzzles	SW1223		$29.95
Brain-Buster Jigsaw Puzzles	SW1222		$29.95
Business Startups Made E-Z	SW1192		$29.95
Buying/Selling Your Home Made E-Z	SW1213		$29.95
Car Buying Made E-Z	SW1146		$29.95
Corporate Record Keeping Made E-Z	SW1159		$29.95
Credit Repair Made E-Z	SW1153		$29.95
Divorce Law Made E-Z	SW1182		$29.95
Everyday Law Made E-Z	SW1185		$29.95
Everyday Legal Forms & Agreements	SW1186		$29.95
Incorporation Made E-Z	SW1176		$29.95
Last Wills Made E-Z	SW1177		$29.95
Living Trusts Made E-Z	SW1178		$29.95
Offshore Investing Made E-Z	SW1218		$29.95
Owning a Franchise Made E-Z	SW1202		$29.95
Touring Florence, Italy Made E-Z	SW1220		$29.95
Touring London, England Made E-Z	SW1221		$29.95
Vital Record Keeping Made E-Z	SW1160		$29.95
Website Marketing Made E-Z	SW1203		$29.95
Your Profitable Home Business	SW1204		$29.95
★ **Made E✦Z Guides**			
Bankruptcy Made E-Z	G200		$17.95
Incorporation Made E-Z	G201		$17.95
Divorce Law Made E-Z	G202		$17.95
Credit Repair Made E-Z	G203		$17.95
Living Trusts Made E-Z	G205		$17.95
Living Wills Made E-Z	G206		$17.95
Last Wills Made E-Z	G207		$17.95
Small Claims Court Made E-Z	G209		$17.95
Traffic Court Made E-Z	G210		$17.95
Buying/Selling Your Home Made E-Z	G211		$17.95
Employment Law Made E-Z	G212		$17.95
Collecting Child Support Made E-Z	G215		$17.95
Limited Liability Companies Made E-Z	G216		$17.95
Partnerships Made E-Z	G218		$17.95
Solving IRS Problems Made E-Z	G219		$17.95
Asset Protection Secrets Made E-Z	G220		$17.95
Immigration Made E-Z	G223		$17.95
Buying/Selling a Business Made E-Z	G223		$17.95
★ **Made E✦Z Books**			
Managing Employees Made E-Z	BK308		$29.95
Corporate Record Keeping Made E-Z	BK310		$29.95
Vital Record Keeping Made E-Z	BK312		$29.95
Business Forms Made E-Z	BK313		$29.95
Collecting Unpaid Bills Made E-Z	BK309		$29.95
Everyday Law Made E-Z	BK311		$29.95
Everyday Legal Forms & Agreements	BK307		$29.95
★ **Labor Posters**			
Federal Labor Law Poster	LP001		$11.99
State Labor Law Poster (specify state)			$29.95
★ SHIPPING & HANDLING*			$
★ **TOTAL OF ORDER**:			$

To order :
1. Photocopy this order form.
2. Use the photocopy to complete your order and mail to:

MADE E-Z PRODUCTS

384 S Military Trail, Deerfield Beach, FL 33442
phone: (954) 480-8933 ✦ fax: (954) 480-8906
web site: http://www.e-zlegal.com/

‡Prices current as of 10/99

*Shipping and Handling: Add $3.50 for the first item, $1.50 for each additional item.
**Florida residents add 6% sales tax.

Total payment must accompany all orders.
Make checks payable to: Made E-Z Products, Inc.

NAME _____

COMPANY _____

ORGANIZATION _____

ADDRESS _____

CITY _____ STATE _____ ZIP _____

PHONE ( ) _____

PAYMENT:
❏ CHECK ENCLOSED, PAYABLE TO MADE E-Z PRODUCTS, INC.

❏ PLEASE CHARGE MY ACCOUNT: ❏ MasterCard ❏ VISA   EXP DATE ☐☐☐☐

ACCOUNT NO. ☐☐☐☐☐☐☐☐☐☐☐☐☐☐☐☐

Signature: _____
(required for credit card purchases)

-OR-

For faster service,   Or you can fax
order by phone: your order to us:
(954) 480-8933   **(954) 480-8906**

CHECK OUT THE
MADE E·Z® LIBRARY

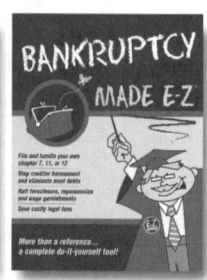

MADE E-Z GUIDES

Each comprehensive guide contains the information you need to learn about (of dozens of topics, plus sample forms applicable).

Most guides also include an appen(of valuable resources, a handy glossa and the valuable 14-page suppleme "How to Save on Attorney Fees."

TITLES

Asset Protection Made E-Z
Shelter your property from financial disaster.
Bankruptcy Made E-Z
Take the confusion out of filing bankruptcy.
Buying/Selling a Business Made E-Z
Position your business and structure the deal for quick results.
Buying/Selling Your Home Made E-Z
Buy or sell your home for the right price right now!
Collecting Child Support Made E-Z
Ensure your kids the support they deserve.
Collecting Unpaid Bills Made E-Z
Get paid–and faster–every time.
Corporate Record Keeping Made E-Z
Minutes, resolutions, notices, and waivers for any corporation.
Credit Repair Made E-Z
All the tools to put you back on track.
Divorce Law Made E-Z
Learn to proceed on your own, without a lawyer.
Employment Law Made E-Z
A handy reference for employers and employees.
Everyday Law Made E-Z
Fast answers to 90% of your legal questions.
Everyday Legal Forms & Agreements Made E-Z
Personal and business protection for virtually any situation.

Incorporation Made E-Z
Information you need to get your company INC'ed.
Last Wills Made E-Z
Write a will the right way, the E-Z way.
Limited Liability Companies Made E-Z
Learn all about the hottest new business entity.
Living Trusts Made E-Z
Trust us to help you provide for your loved ones.
Living Wills Made E-Z
Take steps now to ensure Death with Dignity.
Managing Employees Made E-Z
Your own personnel director in a book.
Partnerships Made E-Z
Get your company started the right way.
Small Claims Court Made E-Z
Prepare for court...or explore other avenues.
Traffic Court Made E-Z
Learn your rights on the road and in court.
Solving IRS Problems Made E-Z
Settle with the IRS for pennies on the dollar.
Trademarks & Copyrights Made E-Z
How to obtain your own copyright or trademark.
Vital Record Keeping Made E-Z
Preserve vital records and important information.

KITS

Each kit includes a clear, concise instruction manual to help you understand your rights and obligations, plus all the information and sample forms you need.

For the busy do-it-yourselfer, it's quick, affordable, and it's E-Z.

ss 1999.r1

Index

A-Co

Accountants 96, 98
Advertising & marketing 157
Asset-based lenders 276
Available resources 107
Avoiding bankruptcy 243
Backup plan 255
Balance sheets 127
Banking & finance charges 155
Bankruptcy 234
Bankruptcy court 98
Business analysis 12
Business consultants 90
Business killers 34
Buying well 149
Cash, raising 140
Cash flow 119
Chapter 11 235
Close-to-the-vest financing 273
Collection agents 195
Commitment 119
Communication 71
Competitiveness 133
Compositions 223
Consultants, turnaround 84
Contracts, burdensome 238
Controls, poor 39
Corporate shield 178
Cost reduction 106

Cr-I

Creditor-proof fortress 177
Creditors 56, 187
Customers 58
Debt settlement checklist 228
Debt shield 183
Debts, reshaping 201
Diversification 38
Dump-buybacks 247
Employees 54
Expense reduction 157
Fact-finding 124
Factoring 277
Fadeouts & walkaways 254
Failure, business 52
Failure to change 34
Family-limited partnerships 290
Financials 61
Goodwill 186
Government red tape 43
Guidelines 91
Homestead laws 290
Hidden assets 144
Idle space 145
Innovation 75
Insolvency attorneys 94
Insurance waste 154
Inventory 142
IRS 236

307

K-Pe

Key assets	182
Key recovery strategies	105
Lawyers	93
Layoffs	162
Lease	184
Legal failure	31
Legal position	134
Loans, problem	199
Loan-shrinking strategies	207
Location	41
Management skills	17, 45
Managerial failure	30
Mortgage	183
Negotiating	74, 225, 280
Objectives	113
Offshore havens	290
Organizational failure	33
Out-of-court settlement	218
Overhead, excess	44
Override payments	191
Partnerships	20
Paycheck	152
Payroll	150
Pennies-on-the-dollar formula	220
Penny-ante management	147
Pension plans	144
Perks	152

Po-V

Politics	166
Prepaid expenses	145
Pricing, unprofitable	42, 171
Professional fees	155
Professional help	81
Profit goals	257
Raising cash	140
Receivables	141
References	87
Refinancing	143
Rent adjustment	153
Reorganization	111
SCORE	87
S.O.B. factor	72
Shrinkage	149
Stabilization	111, 126
Strategies	115
Survival instinct	65
Tax problems	229
Threats	192
Trade suppliers	279
Travel & entertainment costs	156
Turnaround team	80
Turnaround, types	109
Undercapitalization	37
Unsecured creditors	217
Venture capitalists	277